British Literature

Reading Advisory Board for Glencoe/McGraw-Hill

New York, New York   Columbus, Ohio   Chicago, Illinois   Peoria, Illinois   Woodland Hills, California

Acknowledgments

Grateful acknowledgment is given authors, publishers, photographers, museums, and agents for permission to reprint the following copyrighted material. Every effort has been made to determine copyright owners. In case of any omissions, the Publisher will be pleased to make suitable acknowledgments in future editions.

Acknowledgments continued on p. 232

Exclusive Partnerships

To increase students' reading comprehension, media literacy, and test-taking proficiency, **The Glencoe Reader** includes materials developed in association with our exclusive partners.

 A number of selections in this book have been drawn from the pages of *inTIME*, a magazine designed for students by Time Education Program in partnership with Glencoe/McGraw-Hill. The magazine features recent TIME news stories, articles, essays, and reviews.

 With the help of *USA TODAY* editors, certain selections in this book were chosen from recent issues of *USA TODAY*, a nationally distributed daily newspaper noted for its brisk reporting style and engaging graphics.

 The Part 3: Standardized Tests section of this book was developed in association with The Princeton Review, the nation's leader in test preparation. Through its association with Glencoe/McGraw-Hill, The Princeton Review offers the best way for students to excel on standardized tests.

The Princeton Review is not affiliated with Princeton University or Educational Testing Service.

 Three-dimensional interactive graphic organizers, called **Foldables,** have been integrated throughout this book. Created exclusively for Glencoe/McGraw-Hill by teaching specialist Dinah Zike, **Foldables** enhance reading comprehension by helping students develop ways of organizing information that are fun and creative.

Cover art: *Human Achievement* (detail), 1983, Tsing-Fang Chen. Lucia Gallery, NY/SuperStock

Mc Graw Hill Glencoe

The **McGraw·Hill** Companies

Send all inquiries to
Glencoe/McGraw-Hill
8787 Orion Place
Columbus, OH 43240

ISBN 0-07-845933-8
Printed in the United States of America
2 3 4 5 6 7 8 9 10 066 08 07 06 05 04

TABLE OF CONTENTS

PART 1

Fiction, Poetry, and Drama

PART 2 **Nonfiction and Informational Text**

PART 3 Standardized Tests

Reference Section

To Students and Parents

The Glencoe Reader is a special kind of book—one you can actually interact with and make your own. Go ahead. Circle, underline, or highlight parts of a selection that grab your attention or that are hard to understand. Jot down words you want to remember. Fill the margins with your own thoughts and questions. You can mark up this reader in a way that works for you—a way that helps you understand and remember what you read.

The Glencoe Reader will help you work through interesting and challenging reading selections such as

- short stories, poems, dramas, and essays from *Glencoe Literature: The Reader's Choice*
- magazine articles from *inTIME*
- newspaper stories from *USA TODAY*
- textbooks and Internet resources
- everyday reading materials like technical manuals, ads, forms, applications, schedules, and maps
- standardized tests

The Glencoe Reader is interactive and fun. You'll like reading the interesting and varied selections. You'll also discover that the skills and strategies you learn to use in this book will become a natural part of how you read. You'll become a better reader.

The Glencoe Reader is divided into three parts:

Part 1 will help you read all kinds of literature. And you won't just read it, you'll *get* it!

Part 2 will help you learn important strategies to understand nonfiction and informational selections.

Part 3 will help you learn how to read and deal with standardized tests.

In each selection of *The Glencoe Reader,* you'll find a variety of engaging activities to complete on your own or with a partner, a small group, or your entire class. *The Glencoe Reader* will help you become an active, flexible, more powerful reader. So go ahead. Pick up a pencil and go for it!

Note to Parents and Guardians: Ask your students to show you their work as they proceed through this workbook. You might enjoy reading along!

How To Use This Book

The notes and features in *The Glencoe Reader* guide you through the process of reading and making meaning from each selection. As you use these notes and features, you'll be practicing and mastering the skills and strategies that good readers use whenever they read.

Get Set

GET READY TO READ!

Word Power Preview the selection vocabulary words. They're underlined and defined again in the selection.

SHORT STORY

Connect, Did You Know, Reason to Read Before you read, think about your own experience and share your knowledge and opinions. Next, build on what you know about the selection topic. Then set your reason for reading so you can plan how you'll read.

Connect

List and Discuss What makes you decide to help someone? In a small group, list five motives (or reasons) people have for helping others. Then discuss these questions: Is it possible to do a good deed for the wrong reasons? What would you consider to be wrong reasons for doing a favor? Be sure to give support for your answers.

In this short story, you'll read about a wealthy woman named Rosemary who helps a poor girl she meets on the street.

Did You Know?

Building Background This story takes place in England at the beginning of the twentieth century.

* At that time, upper-class people and working-class people didn't mix with one another socially. The main character in this story, Rosemary, is an upper-class woman with a luxurious lifestyle and many servants. One day she meets a poor young woman on the street and decides to take her home for tea.

* Author Katherine Mansfield was interested in the emotions and psychological makeup of her characters. Like many of Mansfield's stories, "A Cup of Tea" contains fascinating, and sometimes surprising, insights into human needs and motivations.

Hot Words Choose words that you think are important, difficult, or interesting. Use your **Hot Words Journal** to build your knowledge of these words.

Reason to Read

Setting a Purpose for Reading Read to find out why Rosemary helps a poor girl—and why she later sends the girl away.

FOLDABLES
Graphic Organizer

As you read, use the following **Foldable** to help you keep track of Rosemary's actions and her reasons for doing what she does.

1. Place a sheet of paper in front of you so that the short side is at the top. Fold the paper in half from side to side.
2. Turn the paper horizontally and fold into thirds.
3. Unfold and cut through the top layer of paper along the fold lines. This will make three tabs.
4. From left to right, label the three tabs *Rosemary's Actions, Rosemary's Reasons,* and *My Opinions.*
5. Under the first tab, record the things Rosemary does. Under the second tab, give reasons for each of her actions. Under the third tab, write adjectives (such as *selfish, shallow, generous, kind,* or *noble*) to describe your opinion of Rosemary's actions.

Foldables These three-dimensional graphic organizers will help you focus on your purpose for reading and keep ideas straight.

Key Goals These are the reading and thinking skills you'll focus on in each lesson. Check out the chart on pages xiv–xvi of this book to see what each skill involves.

word power

Vocabulary Preview

Read the words and definitions below. Use the pronunciation guides to help you say each word aloud. You may already know some of these words, but others might still be unclear. As you read, use context clues to help unlock the meanings and make those words clearer.

quaint (kwānt) *adj.* pleasingly unusual or odd; p. 16

odious (ō′ dē əs) *adj.* causing hate, disgust, or repugnance; p. 16

exotic (ig zot′ ik) *adj.* strangely beautiful or fascinating; p. 16

frail (frāl) *adj.* weak; fragile; p. 22

retort (ri tôrt′) *v.* to reply in a witty, quick, or sharp manner; p. 23

Hot Words Journal

As you read, circle words that you find interesting or that you don't understand. Later you may add them to your **Hot Words Journal** at the back of this book.

What You'll Learn

Key Goals In this lesson, you will learn these key skills, strategies, and concepts.

◀ **Reading Focus:** Respond

◀ **Think It Over:** Draw Conclusions

◀ **Literary Element:** Character

◀ **Reading Coach:** Understanding Author's Style

Read, Respond, Interact

Build Fluency Use these reading aloud opportunities to become a more fluent reader. With practice, your reading will sound smooth and easy.

Reading Coach Let the reading coach help you overcome the trickiest reading task in each selection.

Look for the signal button **A**. It guides you to a side margin activity and back into the reading.

A Cup of Tea

READ ALOUD

Build Fluency Find a quiet place and practice reading aloud the boxed passage. Reread the passage several times until you can get through it without stumbling. **J**

180

Reading Focus

Respond Imagine what the girl must be feeling when she cries out. What is your reaction to her at this point? Write your response on the lines below. **K**

...ounded like "Very good, madam," ...n off.

...your coat, too," said Rosemary. ...and let Rosemary pull. It was quite an effort. The ...helped her at all. She seemed to sta... thought came and we... wanted...

Reading Coach

Understanding Author's Style Do you ever get a new thought mid-sentence? Ever leave a sentence unfinished because you know your listener will understand what you mean? Katherine Mansfield uses dashes (—) and ellipses (. . .) to show changes in thought and to hint at things better left unsaid.

Mark the Text Reread the boxed text and circle the ellipses. What do you think the narrator is hinting at? **A**

Model: Maybe the narrator is suggesting that Rosemary does have some pretty features, but she is not beautiful.

Connotations Words with the same dictionary definitions can have different connotations, or shades of meaning. For example, *quaint* and *bizarre* both mean "odd." But something *quaint* is odd in a pleasing way, while something *bizarre* is odd in a jarring way.

Reading Focus

Respond As you read, take time to think about what you like, dislike, or find interesting about the characters. What do you find interesting about Rosemary? Write your answer below. **B**

A Cup of Tea

Katherine Mansfield

Rosemary Fell was not exactly beautiful. No, you couldn't have called her beautiful. Pretty? Well, if you took her to pieces . . . But why be so cruel as to take anyone to pieces? **A** She was young, brilliant, extremely modern, exquisitely well dressed, amazingly well read in the newest of the new books, and her parties were the most delicious mixture of the really important people and . . . artists—quaint creatures, discoveries of hers, some of them too terrifying for words, but others quite presentable and amusing.

10 Rosemary had been married two years. She had a duck[1] of a boy. No, not Peter—Michael. And her husband absolutely adored her. They were rich, really rich, not just comfortably well off, which is odious and stuffy and sounds like one's grandparents. But if Rosemary wanted to shop she would go to Paris as you and I would go to Bond Street.[2] If she wanted to buy flowers, the car pulled up at that perfect shop in Regent Street, and Rosemary inside the shop just gazed in her dazzled, rather exotic way, and said: "I want those and those and those. Give me four bunches of those. And that jar of roses. Yes, I'll have all the roses in the jar.

20 No, no lilac. I hate lilac. It's got no shape." The attendant bowed and put the lilac out of sight, as though this was only too true; lilac was dreadfully shapeless. "Give me those stumpy little tulips. Those red and white ones." And she was followed to the car by a thin shopgirl staggering under an immense white paper armful that looked like a baby in long clothes. . . . **B**

1. Here, *duck* probably means "a darling" or "a dear," although it could also mean "funny" or "odd but harmless."
2. *Bond Street*—as well as *Regent Street* and *Curzon Street* mentioned later—was, and continues to be, an elegant London street lined with shops that sell expensive, exclusive items.

Vocabulary
quaint (kwānt) *adj.* pleasingly unusual or odd
odious (ō′dē əs) *adj.* causing hate, disgust, or repugnance
exotic (ig zot′ik) *adj.* strangely beautiful or fascinating

Literary Element

Character Rosemary te... the girl "*Do* stop crying. It's so ...exhausting." What does her ...response to the girl's crying tell ...u about Rosemary? **L**

Literary Element These notes will help you understand important features of literature, such as plot, setting, characterization, and imagery.

Word Power Here you'll find some handy tips to help you figure out the vocabulary words as you read them in the selection.

Reading Focus Here you'll learn the best active reading strategies. Models give you an extra boost by showing you how good readers think.

Vocabulary Notes Look at the bottom of selection pages for vocabulary words and definitions and for important footnotes.

Read, Respond, Interact

Your Notes These notepads give you a chance to jot down whatever you want. Make a comment, ask a question, or state an opinion. It's up to you.

A Cup of Tea

Your Notes

Think It Over

Infer When you **infer,** you use your own reason and experience to guess at what the author isn't telling you directly.

Mark the text Underline words and phrases that tell how Philip reacts when he sees the girl. What can you infer about Philip's feelings? Circle any answers that apply. **M**

- Philip is disappointed.
- Philip is surprised.
- Philip is curious.
- Philip is upset.

Think It Over Make your reading more meaningful by thinking about ideas that go beyond the words in the text.

Mark the Text When you see this symbol, you'll make notes in the margin, underline or highlight a bit of text, or circle interesting or difficult words.

A Cup of Tea

Reading Check

Step 1 Ask yourself how well you have understood the story so far. Use these strategies to help you answer any questions you have.

- Reread confusing passages slowly or read them aloud.
- Read on to see if new story information makes the meaning clear.
- Ask a classmate or a teacher, parent, or other adult for help.

Step 2 On the lines below, write a one- or two-sentence summary of what you've read so far.

_____

_____

_____

_____

Think It Over

Draw Conclusions Underline words and phrases that tell how the girl acts in Rosemary's room. Then check the box below that tells what you can conclude from the girl's actions. **I**

- ❏ The girl is frightened and unsure of what to do.
- ❏ The girl wants to leave.
- ❏ The girl has bad manners.

But happily at that moment, for she didn't know how the sentence was going to end, the car stopped. The bell was rung, the door opened, and with a charming, protecting, almost embracing movement, Rosemary drew the other into the hall. Warmth, softness, light, a sweet scent, all those things so familiar to her she never even thought about them, she watched that other receive. It was fascinating. She was like the little rich girl in her nursery with all the cupboards to open, all the boxes to unpack.

Reading Check

"Come, come upstairs," said Rosemary, longing to begin to be generous. "Come up to my room." And, besides, she wanted to spare this poor little thing from being stared at by the servants; she decided as they mounted the stairs she would not even ring for Jeanne, but take off her things by herself. The ——— to be natural!

And "There!" cri——— beautiful big bedroo——— on her wonderful la——— primrose and blue r———

The girl stood just ——— Rosemary didn't min———

"Come and sit dow——— the fire, "in this comf——— dreadfully cold."

"I daren't, madam," said the girl, and she edged backwards.

"Oh, please,"—Rosemary ran forward—"you mustn't be frightened, you mustn't, really. Sit down, and when I've taken off my things we shall go into the next room and have tea and be cosy. Why are you afraid?" And gently she half pushed the thin figure into its deep cradle.

But there was no answer. The girl stayed just as she had been put, with her hands by her sides and her mouth slightly open. To be quite sincere, she looked rather stupid. But Rosemary wouldn't acknowledge it. She leaned over her, saying: "Won't you take off your hat? Your pretty hair is all wet. And one is so much more comfortable without a hat, isn't one?" **I**

Reading Check Here's where you'll think about whether you understand what you've read. Use your understanding to complete a short activity. If you've missed or are unclear about an important point, you'll find tips for reviewing the text.

Show What You Know

Reading WrapUp Here you'll revisit the lesson's key goals in a variety of activities.

READING WRAPUP

Literary Element

Character

A **character** is a person in a literary work. Authors u— characters come alive and seem real. Sometimes au— about the character's qualities:

Literary Element A graphic organizer will help you check your understanding of the lesson's key literary element.

—ary Fell was not exactly beauti—

—ors describe their characters' thou—

—uldn't help noticing how char— —elvet.

—d column of the chart with quot— —mation about each character. In — —als about the character.

Quotation from

READING WRAPUP

A Cup of Tea

Going Solo

→ Understanding Author's Style

Finish the Thought Look back through the story and reread the paragraphs in which the lines below can be found. Think about what the lines mean. If you could finish each sentence —— —— your answers in

Going Solo Express yourself as you complete this activity on your own.

If I'm the more fortunate, you ought to expect . . . (page 19, lines 133–134)

Buddy Up

→ Respond

1. Big Surprise With a partner, review the story and find three moments that surprised you or that gave you a sudden insight. Discuss why these moments surprised you. Then choose one of the moments. On the lines —— —— what happened at that point in the story

TeamWork

→ Draw Conclusions

1. **Generous —**
   wh—
   bad—
   the—
   on t—
   two—
   your—

TeamWork These small group activities are where it really starts to get fun. As you share your thoughts in discussions or work together to puzzle out an answer, your understanding of the selection will grow.

Buddy Up In these activities you'll work with a partner to share ideas about the selection.

2. **Money Isn't Ever—**
   and fashionable, but so—
   Rosemary lack that mor—
   with your group and wri—
   to include reasons and details from the story in your
   answer.

Standardized Test Practice

A Cup of Tea

Choose the best answer for each multiple-choice question. Fill in the circle in the spaces for questions 1 and 2 on the right.

1. Why does Rosemary offer to help the young girl?
   - A. She believes it is her duty.
   - B. She thinks it will be thrilling.
   - C. She was once poor herself.
   - D. She is kind and generous.

2. Which of these words does NOT describe Rosemary?
   - A. thoughtful
   - B. insensitive
   - C. shallow
   - D. needy

Write your answer to open-ended question A in the space provided below.

A. At the end of the story, Rosemary asks Philip two questions: "May I have it?" and "Am I pretty?" What do these questions tell you about —— relationsh—

your answ—

Mult

1. Ⓐ Ⓑ Ⓒ

Op

A. _____

Standardized Test Practice Here you'll find multiple choice items and a short response task in a typical test format. They check your comprehension of the selection and give you practice in reading tests at the same time!

The Glencoe Reader **25**

---

word power

Vocabulary Check

Write the word from the word list that belongs in the blank in each sentence.

quaint *adj.* pleasingly unusual or odd

odious *adj.* causing hate, disgust, or repugnance

exotic *adj.* strangely beautiful or fascinating

frail *v.* weak; fragile

retort *v.* to reply in a witty, quick, or sharp manner

1. In a room full of dull, ordinary people, she was mysterious and _____

2. Once I realized that he had lied to me, I found him _____

3. Drinking milk and exercising will keep your bones from becoming _____

4. "Because I said so!" the mother would often _____ when the little boy asked "Why?"

5. The tiny cottage with its blooming flowers and pretty path was very _____

Word Power This activity gives you a chance to use the vocabulary words you learned in the selection. The word list at the left will help you review.

The Glencoe Reader **xi**

Reading a Variety of Texts

You wouldn't read a bus schedule or a newspaper article the same way you'd read a short story. Your reading purpose and the way you read change with what you read. For that reason, you'll need a special plan for each kind of text. *The Glencoe Reader* will help you develop the skills and strategies that work best for many types of texts.

What Is It? Look at the beginning paragraphs to learn what defines a particular type of text. Then see how that kind of text figures into your life.

Reading Short Stories

Stories are everywhere. They're in newspapers and magazines. They're in television and on film. They're in conversations with family and friends. They're the real and imagined events you hear and talk about every day.

Short stories are brief works of fiction, usually focusing on a single event or on a particular part of a character's life. They examine specific emotions and come to limited conclusions. If life is like a huge patchwork quilt, a short story is one intricate square, studied in detail.

Why Read Short Stories?

Most people read short stories because the stories are interesting or entertaining. Short stories can be hilarious, instructive, tragic, or bizarre. But a good short story does more than simply amuse readers. It offers a unique vision of life, focusing on a part of experience that you

What's the Plan?

The **plot** of a short story is the series of events in which a problem, or **conflict**, is explored. A plot usually includes the following five stages.

• **Exposition** introduces characters, setting, and cor

Why Read? Here's where you'll find the most common reasons for reading a certain kind of text. They'll help you decide your reason for reading.

Exposition   Rising action

Reading Mass Media

Here's a scene that might be familiar: Dad's watching the ball game on TV; Mom's reading the newspaper; your sister is going through a summer sale catalog; and you've logged on to a favorite Web site. Across the street, someone has the stereo on loud. Recognize the common theme here? The answer in two words is *mass media.*

Mass media are the whole extended family of methods (*media*) for communicating with large numbers of people (the *masses*). Some media use print, some use video, some use sound. Mass media take the form of newspapers, magazines, movies, TV and radio, advertisements of all sorts, Web sites, old-fashioned books, and every new-fangled device the recording industry comes up with. Whatever the method, whatever the message, if it reaches lots of people, you can label it part of the mass media.

In the table below, make note of four forms of mass media you used for entertainment during the last twenty-four hours.

Time	Mass Media Used	Purpose

Why Read Mass Media?

This question is a little more complex than it seems. Of course, you read mass media for information or entertainment. But you also read forms of mass media just because they are there! Try sitting in traffic without reading those billboards towering over the highway. Try asking television news producers to stop airing banner headlines during your favorite show. In spite of these occasional nuisances, however, mass media can be a uniting force. Just ask anyone who has ever given money to a charity during a TV telethon. To use a phrase borrowed from one of their many forms, mass media can get people on the same wavelength.

What's the Plan?

Most people don't have the time to read a newspaper or news magazine from beginning to end. For this reason, writers of news stories follow a structure that helps readers find important details quickly and easily. That structure, or form, is known as the inverted pyramid. It is pictured here.

Lead
the main facts of a story

Body
further information on the topic; may include direct

Author's Plan These notes will tell you how authors tend to organize ideas in a particular kind of writing. When you can see the author's plan and know how key ideas are arranged, you'll be better able to follow and understand what the author wants you to know.

Text Features To understand what you read, you have to know what you're looking for. These notes point out the common features of a certain type of text. Look at the sample page to be sure you understand what each feature looks like. Then use the **Find It** prompt to practice finding a text feature.

Reading Tests How you read a test can make the difference between a good score and one that is not so good. Part 3 of *The Glencoe Reader* will help you develop special test-reading skills and strategies so you can improve your performance on standardized tests.

What Do I Look For?

Newspaper and magazine articles often have elements like the **text features** and **text structures** in this article from *inTIME* magazine.

The **headline**, or **title**, catches the eye with large print and often witty wording.

The **deck**, or **subtitle**, includes lively information, inviting readers to continue.

The **lead** of a news story will often provide a concise summary of the entire article.

Quotations from newsmakers or experts support factual information and lighten the style.

Supporting details occur later in the article and may—as here—include **statistics**.

Mark the text **Find It!** Circle a direct quotation in the article. Underline the name of the person who spoke the words.

How Do I Read It?

These **reading strategies** will be especially helpful when yo

Skim: Do you need to read every word on an article or Web site? Glance over a selection before you commit.

Scan: Looking for specific information? Find the information you need by scanning for key facts or phrases.

Summarize: Describing what you've read in a sentence or two is a good way to test your understanding.

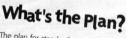 **DO IT!**

Read the mass media selec
- look for **text features** and

Reading Strategies Don't waste your time. To read efficiently, focus your efforts by using the best reading strategies for each type of text. These notes will tell you what strategies will get you where you need to go.

WORLD

PORTRAITS OF PLAGUE

Britain's rampaging foot-and-mouth outbreak raises fears of an epidemic in Europe—and throughout the world

By JAMES O. JACKSON

It is called *fièvre aphteuse* in France, *fiebre aftosa* in Spain, *Maul-und-Klauenseuche* in Germany, and *mundog klovesyge* in Denmark. It is harmless to hu and does not kill most infected animals. Yet foot-and-mouth di has aroused anxiety throughou world in 2001, and the virus th causes the ailment in pigs, she cattle has closed borders, des livelihoods, and brought to a s much of the world's trade in pork, and lamb.

"We are on red alert," Lambert, chief economist at National Cattlemen's Beef A as Department of Agricult inspectors imposed strict c goods and passengers arriv Britain and France. From Seattle, worried officials s European meat imports, c sandwiches, and decontam arriving passengers to pre inadvertent infection by that, like everything els going global.

The worldwide foo alert is a sobering dem how quickly a single is can hop from farm to continent to continent crisis began when a b meat found its way in lunch in Britain's Nor mid-February and th into swill fed to pigs, symptoms appeared danger, the virus wa farms all across the few weeks, it turne Ireland and jumped

animals. The cost: $10 million and rising in compensation to farmers and an estimated $150 million a week in losses to the tourist industry as visitors avoided the countryside.

Death so widespread could bring the virtual collapse of a British cultural economy already near

---

Reading Standardized Tests

Quiet classrooms, number-two pencils, and timed exams. Do you know what this setting suggests? If you said standardized tests, you're right! Pretty soon you and other students across your state will be tested on what you've learned throughout the year. How confident will you be when you sit down to take the test? Mark your level of confidence on the following scale.

This part of *The Glencoe Reader* will teach you reading strategies that will help you feel confident of your ability to succeed on **standardized tests** in **Reading, English/Language Arts**, and **Writing**.

Least Confident ────────────────────── Most Confident

Why Read Standardized Tests?

Read standardized tests to understand various types of test items so you can answer them! Then you'll be able to show how well you've learned your subjects and mastered the skills covered in your state's academic standards.

When you learn how to read the tests in this part of *The Glencoe Reader*, you'll learn strategies that will help you on other standardized tests.

The military, colleges, and even some jobs will require you to take standardized tests. By learning how to read standardized tests now, you'll be better prepared to take other important tests after high school. And scoring well on these standardized tests will help you to take charge of your future!

What's the Plan?

The plan for standardized tests in reading, language arts, and writing depends on the kinds of skills covered.

- Reading tests may have a number of reading selections. The reading selections are followed by multiple-choice questions and possibly a few open-ended questions that you will answer in your own words.

- Language arts tests may consist of multiple-choice questions related to a variety of skills, including spelling, punctuation, grammar, sentence combining, and paragraph organization.

- Writing tests usually provide you with a writing prompt that invites you to think about a familiar topic. You will write your response on blank paper that comes with the test.

The test booklet itself might have the following parts.

An **introduction** that describes the test. It may explain how much time you'll have and how to mark your answers.

Directions that tell you what steps to follow for each part of the test.

Reading passages that are either fiction or nonfiction. These passages may include a visual such as a map, a chart, or an illustration.

Test items that check how well you understand a reading passage or what you know about grammar, punctuation, and spelling. There might also be writing prompts that let you show your writing ability.

The What, Why, and How of Reading

You'll need to use the skills and strategies in the following chart to respond to questions and prompts in the selections. As you begin a new lesson, look carefully at the **Key Goals** on the **Get Ready To Read** page. Then find those skills in this chart and read about what they are and how to use them. Don't forget to read about why each skill or strategy is important. The more you refer to the chart, the more these active reading strategies will become a natural part of the way you read. For more about these skills and strategies, see the **Reading Handbook.**

Skill/Strategy

What Is It?	Why It's Important	How To Do It
Preview Previewing is looking over a selection before you read.	Previewing lets you begin to see what you already know and what you'll need to know. It helps you set a purpose for reading.	Look at the title, illustrations, headings, captions, and graphics. Look at how ideas are organized. Ask questions about the text.
Skim Skimming is looking over an entire selection quickly to get a general idea of what the piece is about.	Skimming will tell you what a selection is about. If the selection you skim isn't what you're looking for, you won't need to read the entire piece.	Read the title of the selection and quickly look over the entire piece. Read headings and captions and maybe part of the first paragraph to get a general idea of the selection's content.
Scan Scanning is glancing quickly over a selection in order to find specific information.	Scanning helps you pinpoint information quickly. It saves you time when you have a number of selections to look at.	As you move your eyes quickly over the lines of text, look for key words or phrases that will help you locate the information you're looking for.
Predict Predicting is taking an educated guess about what will happen in a selection.	Predicting gives you a reason to read. You want to find out if your prediction and the selection events match, don't you? As you read, adjust or change your prediction if it doesn't fit what you learn.	Combine what you already know about an author or subject with what you learned in your preview to guess at what will be included in the text.
Summarize Summarizing is stating the main ideas of a selection in your own words and in a logical sequence.	Summarizing shows whether you've understood something. It teaches you to rethink what you've read and to separate main ideas from supporting information.	Ask yourself: What is this selection about? Answer *who, what, where, when, why,* and *how?* Put that information in a logical order.

What Is It?	Why It's Important	How To Do It
Clarify Clarifying is looking at difficult sections of text in order to clear up what is confusing.	Authors will often build ideas one on another. If you don't clear up a confusing passage, you may not understand main ideas or information that comes later.	Go back and reread a confusing section more slowly. Look up words you don't know. Ask questions about what you don't understand. Sometimes you may want to read on to see if further information helps you.
Question Questioning is asking yourself whether information in a selection is important. Questioning is also regularly asking yourself whether you've understood what you've read.	When you ask questions as you read, you're reading strategically. As you answer your questions, you're making sure that you'll get the gist of a text.	Have a running conversation with yourself as you read. Keep asking: Is this idea important? Why? Do I understand what this is about? Might this information be on a test later?
Visualize Visualizing is picturing a writer's ideas or descriptions in your mind's eye.	Visualizing is one of the best ways to understand and remember information in fiction, nonfiction, and informational text.	Carefully read how a writer describes a person, place, or thing. Then ask yourself: What would this look like? Can I see how the steps in this process would work?
Monitor Comprehension Monitoring your comprehension means thinking about whether you're understanding what you're reading.	The whole point of reading is to understand a piece of text. When you don't understand a selection, you're not really reading it.	Keep asking yourself questions about main ideas, characters, and events. When you can't answer a question, review, read more slowly, or ask someone to help you.
Identify Sequence Identifying sequence is finding the logical order of ideas or events.	In a work of fiction, events usually happen in chronological (time) order. With nonfiction, understanding the logical sequence of ideas in a piece helps you follow a writer's train of thought. You'll remember ideas better when you know the logical order a writer uses.	Think about what the author is trying to do. Tell a story? Explain how something works? Present information? Look for clues or signal words that might point to time order, steps in a process, or order of importance.
Determine Main Idea Determining an author's main idea is finding the most important thought in a paragraph or in a selection.	Finding main ideas gets you ready to summarize. You also discover an author's purpose for writing when you find the main ideas in a selection.	Think about what you know about the author and the topic. Look for how the author organizes ideas. Then look for the one idea that all of the sentences in a paragraph or all the paragraphs in a selection are about.
Respond Responding is telling what you like, dislike, find surprising or interesting in a selection.	When you react in a personal way to what you read, you'll enjoy a selection more and remember it better.	As you read, think about how you feel about story elements or ideas in a selection. What's your reaction to the characters in a story? What grabs your attention as you read?

What Is It?	Why It's Important	How To Do It
Connect Connecting means linking what you read to events in your own life or to other selections you've read.	You'll "get into" your reading and recall information and ideas better by connecting events, emotions, and characters to your own life.	Ask yourself: Do I know someone like this? Have I ever felt this way? What else have I read that is like this selection?
Review Reviewing is going back over what you've read to remember what's important and to organize ideas so you'll recall them later.	Reviewing is especially important when you have new ideas and a lot of information to remember.	Filling in a graphic organizer, such as a chart or diagram, as you read helps you organize information. These study aids will help you review later.
Interpret Interpreting is when you use your own understanding of the world to decide what the events or ideas in a selection mean.	Every reader constructs meaning on the basis of what he or she understands about the world. Finding meaning as you read is all about you interacting with the text.	Think about what you already know about yourself and the world. Ask yourself: What is the author really trying to say here? What larger idea might these events be about?
Infer Inferring is when you use your reason and experience to guess at what an author does not come right out and say.	Making inferences is a large part of finding meaning in a selection. Inferring helps you look more deeply at characters and points you toward the theme or message in a selection.	Look for clues the author provides. Notice descriptions, dialogue, events, and relationships that might tell you something the author wants you to know.
Draw Conclusions Drawing a conclusion is using a number of pieces of information to make a general statement about people, places, events, and ideas.	Drawing conclusions helps you find connections between ideas and events. It's another tool to help you see the larger picture.	Notice details about characters, ideas, and events. Then make a general statement on the basis of these details. For example, a character's actions might lead you to conclude that he is kind.
Analyze Analyzing is looking at separate parts of a selection in order to understand the entire selection.	Analyzing helps you look critically at a piece of writing. When you analyze a selection, you'll discover its theme or message, and you'll learn the author's purpose for writing.	To analyze a story, think about what the author is saying through the characters, setting, and plot. To analyze nonfiction, look at the organization and main ideas. What do they suggest?
Synthesize Synthesizing is combining ideas to create something new. You may synthesize to reach a new understanding, or you may actually create a new ending to a story.	Synthesizing helps you move to a higher level of thinking. Creating something new of your own goes beyond remembering what you learned from someone else.	Think about the ideas or information you've learned in a selection. Ask yourself: Do I understand something more than the main ideas here? Can I create something else from what I now know?
Evaluate Evaluating is making a judgment or forming an opinion about something you read. You can evaluate a character, an author's craft, or the value of the information in a text.	Evaluating helps you become a wise reader. For example, when you judge whether an author is qualified to speak about a topic or whether the author's points make sense, you can avoid being misled by what you read.	As you read, ask yourself questions such as: Is this character realistic and believable? Is this author qualified to write on this subject? Is this author biased? Does this author present opinions as facts?

Fiction, Poetry, and Drama

Reading Short Stories

Stories are everywhere. They're in newspapers and magazines. They're in television and on film. They're in conversations with family and friends. They're the real and imagined events you hear and talk about every day.

Short stories are brief works of fiction, usually focusing on a single event or on a particular part of a character's life. They examine specific emotions and come to limited conclusions. If life is like a huge patchwork quilt, a short story is one intricate square, studied in detail.

> **Mark the text** ▸ **In the list below, check each kind of story that you have read. On the lines, tell which kind of story you enjoy the most and why.**
>
> _____ ghost story   _____ mystery
>
> _____ science fiction   _____ romance
>
> _____ tragedy   _____ adventure
>
> _____ tall tale   _____ legend
>
> _____
>
> _____

Why Read Short Stories?

Most people read short stories because the stories are interesting or entertaining. Short stories can be hilarious, instructive, tragic, or bizarre. But a good short story does more than simply amuse readers. It offers a unique vision of life, focusing on a part of experience that you may not have noticed or presenting a new viewpoint. For the brief time it takes to read, a good short story lets you see through another person's eyes and perhaps understand the world in a new way.

What's the Plan?

The **plot** of a short story is the series of events in which a problem, or **conflict,** is explored. A plot usually includes the following five stages.

- **Exposition** introduces characters, setting, and conflict.

- **Rising action** develops the conflict.

- **Climax** is a point of high excitement, often a turning point.

- **Falling action** shows the results of the climax.

- **Resolution** reveals the final outcome.

This diagram shows the five stages of plot development.

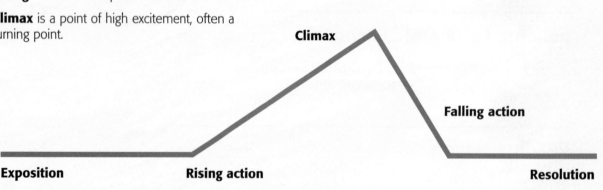

Climax

Falling action

Exposition   Rising action   Resolution

What Do I Lk For?

The opening of Graham Greene's "A Shocking Accident" includes **literary elements** that appear in many short stories.

> The **protagonist** is the story's main character.

> **Setting** is the time and place in which the events of a short story occur. Setting also includes characters' values and beliefs.

> **Point of view** is the perspective from which the narrator tells the story. In **third-person limited** point of view, the narrator is outside the story and tells only what one character could know.

> **Dialogue**—conversation between characters—helps develop the plot and show what the characters are like.

> **Tone** reflects an author's attitude towards his or her subject matter. The tone of a short story might be humorous, bitter, sad, or sympathetic.

 **Mark the text** **Find it!** Circle a passage that tells how Jerome feels about his father.

A Shocking Accident

Graham Greene

Jerome was called into his housemaster's room in the break between the second and the third class on a Thursday morning. He had no fear of trouble, for he was a warden—the name that the proprietor and headmaster of a rather expensive preparatory school had chosen to give to approved, reliable boys in the lower forms (from a warden one became a guardian and finally before leaving, it was hoped for Marlborough or Rugby, a crusader). The housemaster, Mr. Wordsworth, sat behind his desk with an appearance of perplexity and apprehension. Jerome had the odd impression when he entered that he was a cause of fear.

"Sit down, Jerome," Mr. Wordsworth said. "All going well with the trigonometry?"

"Yes, sir."

"I've had a telephone call, Jerome. From your aunt. I'm afraid I have bad news for you."

"Yes, sir?"

"Your father has had an accident."

"Oh."

Mr. Wordsworth looked at him with some surprise. "A serious accident."

"Yes, sir?"

Jerome worshipped his father: the verb is exact. As man re-creates God, so Jerome re-created his father—from a restless widowed author into a mysterious adventurer who traveled in far places—Nice, Beirut, Majorca, even the Canaries. The time had arrived about his eighth birthday when Jerome believed that his father either "ran guns" or was a member of the British Secret Service. Now it occurred to him that his father might have been wounded in "a hail of machine-gun bullets."

How Do I Read It?

These **reading strategies** will help you get the most out of short stories.

Predict: Every so often, try guessing what's going to happen next. Then read on to see if your prediction matches what happens.

Connect: Look for things in the story that are like something or someone you know. Making connections between your life and the lives of the fictional characters will help make your reading experience richer.

Monitor Comprehension: Make sure you understand what you read. Ask yourself questions about your reading. If you can't answer them, read a little slower or ask for help.

Respond: "Don't be ridiculous." "How could she do that?" "Watch out!" If you find yourself responding like this, you're probably getting a lot out your reading!

For more information on **reading strategies,** see pages 216–222 in the **Reading Handbook.**

DO IT!

Read the short stories that follow. Be sure to

• analyze **literary elements** and the **author's plan**

• use **reading strategies** to help you get the most from your reading

GET READY TO READ!

Connect

Journal Think about an event that you really looked forward to before it happened. How did the reality compare to what you had imagined? In your journal, describe your expectations and the reality. Then tell how you felt afterward. In a group, share your thoughts about setting high expectations.

In this short story, you'll read about a boy from Dublin who looks forward to performing a romantic errand for a girl he has a crush on.

Did You Know?

Building Background This story, "Araby," comes from *Dubliners,* a collection of autobiographical fiction stories by James Joyce.

- Like the narrator of "Araby," the young Joyce and his family lived for a while on North Richmond Street in Dublin, Ireland.
- Joyce was educated in Catholic schools in Dublin, but he eventually left the city and its strict religious and social conventions.
- The word *Araby* refers to the poetic name Europeans gave Arabia. In the 1800s, Europeans viewed the Middle East and the Far East (which were then known as the Orient) as mysterious and exciting.
- In May 1894, Dublin hosted "Araby in Dublin," a fair described as a "Grand Oriental Fete."

Reason to Read

Setting a Purpose for Reading Read to find out how the main character's expectations of an event match the reality.

word power

Vocabulary Preview
Read the definitions of these words from "Araby." Use the pronunciation guides to help you say each word aloud. You may already know some of these words, but others might still be unclear. As you read, use context clues to help unlock their meanings.

imperturbable (im´ pər tur´ bə bəl) *adj.* not easily excited or disturbed; calm; p. 5

diverge (də vurj´) *v.* to move in different directions from a common point; branch out; p. 6

converge (con vurj´) *v.* to come together in a common interest or conclusion; center; p. 7

impinge (im pinj´) *v.* to strike or dash; collide; p. 7

annihilate (ə nī´ ə lāt´) *v.* to reduce to nothing; obliterate; p. 8

amiability (ā´ mē ə bil´ ə tē) *n.* kindness, friendliness; p. 8

garrulous (gar´ ə ləs) *adj.* given to too much talking, especially about unimportant matters; p. 9

Hot Words Journal

As you read, circle any words that you find interesting or that you don't understand. Later you may add them to your **Hot Words Journal** at the back of this book and complete one of the activities there.

What You'll Learn

Key Goals In this lesson, you will learn these key skills, strategies, and concepts.

- **Reading Focus:** Visualize
- **Think It Over:** Infer
- **Literary Element:** Setting
- **Reading Coach:** Understanding Words Used in Unfamiliar Ways

Araby

James Joyce

North Richmond Street, being blind,[1] was a quiet street except at the hour when the Christian Brothers' School set the boys free. An uninhabited house of two stories stood at the blind end, detached from its neighbors in a square ground. The other houses of the street, conscious of decent lives within them, gazed at one another with brown imperturbable faces. **A** The former tenant of our house, a priest, had died in the back drawing room. Air, musty from having been long enclosed, hung in all the rooms, and the waste room behind the kitchen was littered with old useless papers. Among these I found a few paper-covered books, the pages of which were curled and damp: *The Abbot,* by Walter Scott, *The Devout Communicant* and *The Memoirs of Vidocq.*[2] I liked the last best because its leaves were yellow. The wild garden behind the house contained a central apple tree and a few straggling bushes under one of which I found the late tenant's rusty bicycle pump. He had been a very charitable priest; in his will he had left all his money to institutions and the furniture of his house to his sister.

When the short days of winter came dusk fell before we had well eaten our dinners. When we met in the street the houses had grown somber. The space of sky above us was the color of ever-changing violet and towards it the lamps of the street lifted their feeble lanterns. The cold air stung us and we played till our bodies glowed. Our shouts echoed in the silent street. The career of our play brought us through the dark muddy lanes behind the

10

20

---

1. Here, *blind* means "dead-end."
2. *The Abbot* is a historical novel; *The Devout Communicant* is a religious manual; *The Memoirs of Vidocq* is the story of a French soldier.

Vocabulary

imperturbable (im´ per tur´ bə bəl) *adj.* not easily excited or disturbed; calm

---

Reading Focus

→ **Visualize** As you read, use your mind like a camera. Zoom in on the descriptive details that the author uses and take mental pictures, or **visualize,** the setting, characters, and events. These mental pictures can help you get into the story.

Use the descriptive details in this passage to take a mental picture of North Richmond Street. On the lines below, describe your picture. **A**

_____

_____

_____

_____

_____

_____

_____

---

word power

Using Word Parts If you're unfamiliar with an underlined word, try this strategy. Break the word up into its parts. First examine the base, or root, of the word. Is it familiar? Next, focus on the letters added to the beginning or end of the root. Do they affect its meaning? Try to come up with a definition of the word. Then check your definition by reading the definition for the underlined word at the bottom of the page.

Hot Words

Mark the text **Choose your own words.**
As you continue reading this story, circle any words that you find interesting or that you don't understand. You'll come back to these words later.

Reading Coach

⚷ Understanding Words Used in Unfamiliar Ways
Joyce sometimes uses familiar words in unfamiliar ways. If a sentence doesn't seem clear to you, check to see whether an unusual use of a common word is causing the confusion. Then use context clues to figure out how the word is being used.

In this paragraph, the word *defined* is used in an unfamiliar way. **B**

Mark the text Find and underline the word *defined.* What does it mean in this context? Check the box next to your answer.

❏ explained

❏ made clear or distinct

❏ identified the essential qualities of

Keep This in Mind

Use these symbols to record your reactions as you read.

? I have a question about something here.

! This really caught my attention.

★ This information is important.

houses where we ran the gantlet³ of the rough tribes from the cottages, to the back doors of the dark dripping gardens where odors arose from the ashpits, to the dark odorous stables where a
30 coachman smoothed and combed the horse or shook music from the buckled harness. When we returned to the street, light from the kitchen windows had filled the areas. If my uncle was seen turning the corner we hid in the shadow until we had seen him safely housed. Or if Mangan's sister came out on the doorstep to call her brother in to his tea we watched her from our shadow peer up and down the street. We waited to see whether she would remain or go in and, if she remained, we left our shadow and walked up to Mangan's steps resignedly. She was waiting for us, her figure defined by the light from the half-opened door. Her
40 brother always teased her before he obeyed and I stood by the railings looking at her. Her dress swung as she moved her body and the soft rope of her hair tossed from side to side. **B**

Every morning I lay on the floor in the front parlor watching her door. The blind was pulled down to within an inch of the sash so that I could not be seen. When she came out on the doorstep my heart leaped. I ran to the hall, seized my books and followed her. I kept her brown figure always in my eye and, when we came near the point at which our ways <u>diverged</u>, I quickened my pace and passed her. This happened morning after morning.
50 I had never spoken to her, except for a few casual words, and yet her name was like a summons to all my foolish blood.

Her image accompanied me even in places the most hostile to romance. On Saturday evenings when my aunt went marketing I had to go to carry some of the parcels. We walked through the flaring streets, jostled by drunken men and bargaining women, amid the curses of laborers, the shrill litanies⁴ of shopboys who stood on guard by the barrels of pigs' cheeks, the nasal chanting

---

3. *Gantlet* [or *gauntlet*] refers to an outdated punishment in which the offender was made to run between two rows of men who struck at him with switches or weapons as he passed. Here, it means a series of challenges.

4. As it is used here, *litany* is a repetitive announcement to attract customers.

Vocabulary

diverge (di vurj´) *v.* to move in different directions from a common point; branch out

of street singers, who sang a *come-you-all* about O'Donovan Rossa,[5] or a ballad about the troubles in our native land. These noises converged in a single sensation of life for me: I imagined that I bore my chalice safely through a throng of foes. Her name sprang to my lips at moments in strange prayers and praises which I myself did not understand. My eyes were often full of tears (I could not tell why) and at times a flood from my heart seemed to pour itself out into my bosom. I thought little of the future. I did not know whether I would ever speak to her or not or, if I spoke to her, how I could tell her of my confused adoration. But my body was like a harp and her words and gestures were like fingers running upon the wires. **C**

60

One evening I went into the back drawing room in which the priest had died. It was a dark rainy evening and there was no sound in the house. Through one of the broken panes I heard the rain impinge upon the earth, the fine incessant needles of water playing in the sodden beds. Some distant lamp or lighted window gleamed below me. I was thankful that I could see so little. All my senses seemed to desire to veil themselves and, feeling that I was about to slip from them, I pressed the palms of my hands together until they trembled, murmuring: *O love! O love!* many times. **D**

70

At last she spoke to me. When she addressed the first words to me I was so confused that I did not know what to answer. She asked me was I going to *Araby.*[6] I forget whether I answered yes or no. It would be a splendid bazaar, she said; she would love to go.

80

—And why can't you? I asked.

While she spoke she turned a silver bracelet round and round her wrist. She could not go, she said, because there would be a retreat[7] that week in her convent.[8] Her brother and two other boys were fighting for their caps and I was alone at the railings. She

---

5. A *come-you-all* is a ballad; *O'Donovan Rossa* was a nineteenth-century Irish nationalist.
6. *Araby* was a bazaar held in 1894 in Dublin.
7. A *retreat* is a time of group withdrawal for prayer and meditation.
8. Here, a *convent* is a school run by an order of Catholic nuns.

Vocabulary

converge (kən vurj´) *v.* to come together in a common interest or conclusion; center

impinge (im pinj´) *v.* to strike or dash; collide

Infer Writers don't always tell you everything about a character. Sometimes you have to use clues from the story to **infer,** or make guesses, about how a character feels or why a character acts in a certain way. In this passage, you can infer the boy's feelings for Mangan's sister. **C**

Model: *The boy has a wild crush on Mangan's sister. I can infer that by the way he says "my heart leaped" and "her name was like a summons to all my foolish blood." He also uses words with religious overtones, such as* litanies, chanting, chalice, prayers, *and* adoration. *This makes me think that he views his love for her as holy and pure.*

Reading Focus

Visualize Underline the details in the boxed passage that help you picture where the boy is and what he's doing. *Mark the text* On the lines below, write three or four adjectives that describe what you see. **D**

_____

_____

Think It Over

← **Infer** Think about how well the boy knows Mangan's sister and about what the word *Araby* means. Why does the sound of the word *Araby* "cast an Eastern enchantment" over the boy? **E**

_____

_____

_____

_____

📖 Reading Check

Step 1 Ask yourself how well you understand the story so far. Have you put question marks next to anything? If so, these strategies can help you answer your questions.

• Reread confusing passages slowly or read them aloud.

• Think about connections between the story and your own life.

• Ask a classmate or a teacher, parent, or other adult for help.

Step 2 Would you say the boy's feelings for Mangan's sister have had a positive or a negative effect on him so far? Give reasons for your opinion on the lines below.

_____

_____

_____

_____

_____

90 held one of the spikes, bowing her head towards me. The light from the lamp opposite our door caught the white curve of her neck, lit up her hair that rested there and, falling, lit up the hand upon the railing. It fell over one side of her dress and caught the white border of a petticoat, just visible as she stood at ease.

—It's well for you, she said.

—If I go, I said, I will bring you something.

What innumerable follies laid waste my waking and sleeping thoughts after that evening! I wished to <u>annihilate</u> the tedious intervening days. I chafed against the work of school. At night in my bedroom and by day in the classroom her image came

100 between me and the page I strove to read. The syllables of the word *Araby* were called to me through the silence in which my soul luxuriated and cast an Eastern enchantment over me. I asked for leave to go to the bazaar on Saturday night. **E** My aunt was surprised and hoped it was not some Freemason[9] affair. I answered few questions in class. I watched my master's face pass from <u>amiability</u> to sternness; he hoped I was not beginning to idle. I could not call my wandering thoughts together. I had hardly any patience with the serious work of life which, now that it stood between me and my desire, seemed to me child's play,

110 ugly monotonous child's play.

········· **📖 Reading Check** ·········

On Saturday morning I reminded my uncle that I wished to go to the bazaar in the evening. He was fussing at the hall stand, looking for the hat brush, and answered me curtly:

—Yes, boy, I know.

As he was in the hall I could not go into the front parlor and lie at the window. I left the house in bad humor and walked slowly towards the school. The air was pitilessly raw and already my heart misgave me.

---

9. The *Freemasons* are part of a secret fraternity who were known to be anti-Catholic.

Vocabulary
annihilate (ə nīʹ ə lātʹ) *v.* to reduce to nothing; obliterate
amiability (āʹ mē ə bilʹ ə tē) *n.* kindliness; friendliness

When I came home to dinner my uncle had not yet been home. Still it was early. I sat staring at the clock for some time and, when 120 its ticking began to irritate me, I left the room. I mounted the staircase and gained the upper part of the house. The high cold empty gloomy rooms liberated me and I went from room to room singing. From the front window I saw my companions playing below in the street. Their cries reached me weakened and indistinct and, leaning my forehead against the cool glass, I looked over at the dark house where she lived. I may have stood there for an hour, seeing nothing but the brown-clad figure cast by my imagination, touched discreetly by the lamplight at the curved neck, at the hand upon the railings and at the border below the dress. 130

When I came downstairs again I found Mrs. Mercer sitting at the fire. She was an old garrulous woman, a pawnbroker's widow, who collected used stamps for some pious purpose. I had to endure the gossip of the tea table. The meal was prolonged beyond an hour and still my uncle did not come. Mrs. Mercer stood up to go: she was sorry she couldn't wait any longer, but it was after eight o'clock and she did not like to be out late, as the night air was bad for her. When she had gone I began to walk up and down the room, clenching my fists. My aunt said:

—I'm afraid you may put off your bazaar for this night of Our 140 Lord.

At nine o'clock I heard my uncle's latchkey in the hall door. I heard him talking to himself and heard the hall stand rocking when it had received the weight of his overcoat. I could interpret these signs. When he was midway through his dinner I asked him to give me the money to go to the bazaar. He had forgotten.

—The people are in bed and after their first sleep now, he said. I did not smile. My aunt said to him energetically:

—Can't you give him the money and let him go? You've kept him late enough as it is. **F** 150

My uncle said he was very sorry he had forgotten. He said he believed in the old saying: *All work and no play makes Jack a dull boy.* He asked me where I was going and, when I had told him a second time he asked me did I know *The Arab's Farewell to His*

Vocabulary

garrulous (gar′ ə ləs) *adj.* given to too much talking, especially about unimportant matters

---

Literary Element

➤ **Setting** The **setting** of a literary work is the time and place in which the events occur. Setting also includes the ideas, customs, values, and beliefs of the people who live in that time and place. What do you learn about the customs and beliefs of this community from the scene described on this page? Put a check by all the statements below that apply. **F**

❏ Religion is important.

❏ Women's independence is valued.

❏ Children are treated as equals.

❏ Men control the money.

❏ People are encouraged to strive for great things.

Your Notes

Reading Focus

Connect Put yourself in the boy's place. Would you want to arrive at the bazaar so late? Jot down your thoughts on the lines below. **G**

_____

_____

_____

_____

Think It Over

→ Infer After looking forward so eagerly to buying something for Mangan's sister, why does the boy have difficulty remembering his reason for coming to Araby? **Mark the text** Underline clues that help you infer the reason. Then explain your inference below. **H**

_____

_____

_____

_____

Steed.[10] When I left the kitchen he was about to recite the opening lines of the piece to my aunt.

I held a florin[11] tightly in my hand as I strode down Buckingham Street towards the station. The sight of the streets thronged with buyers and glaring with gas recalled to me the purpose of my
160 journey. I took my seat in a third-class carriage of a deserted train. After an intolerable delay the train moved out of the station slowly. It crept onward among ruinous houses and over the twinkling river. At Westland Row Station a crowd of people pressed to the carriage doors; but the porters moved them back, saying that it was a special train for the bazaar. I remained alone in the bare carriage. In a few minutes the train drew up beside an improvised wooden platform. I passed out on to the road and saw by the lighted dial of a clock that it was ten minutes to ten. In front of me was a large building which displayed the magical name. **G**

170 I could not find any sixpenny entrance and, fearing that the bazaar would be closed, I passed in quickly through a turnstile, handing a shilling to a weary-looking man. I found myself in a big hall girdled at half its height by a gallery. Nearly all the stalls were closed and the greater part of the hall was in darkness. I recognized a silence like that which pervades a church after a service. I walked into the center of the bazaar timidly. A few people were gathered about the stalls which were still open. Before a curtain, over which the words *Café Chantant*[12] were written in colored lamps, two men were counting money on a
180 salver.[13] I listened to the fall of the coins.

Remembering with difficulty why I had come I went over to one of the stalls and examined porcelain vases and flowered tea sets. At the door of the stall a young lady was talking and laughing with two young gentlemen. I remarked their English accents and listened vaguely to their conversation. **H**

—O, I never said such a thing!

—O, but you did!

—O, but I didn't!

---

10. *[The . . . Steed]* is a sentimental poem by Caroline Norton.
11. A *florin* was a coin worth two shillings, which, at the time, equaled about fifty cents.
12. *Café Chantant* was a popular cafe that provided musical entertainment.
13. A *salver* is a tray commonly used to serve food and drinks.

—Didn't she say that?

—Yes. I heard her.

—O, there's a . . . fib!

Observing me the young lady came over and asked me did I wish to buy anything. The tone of her voice was not encouraging; she seemed to have spoken to me out of a sense of duty. I looked humbly at the great jars that stood like eastern guards at either side of the dark entrance to the stall and murmured:

—No, thank you.

The young lady changed the position of one of the vases and went back to the two young men. They began to talk of the same subject. Once or twice the young lady glanced at me over her shoulder.

I lingered before her stall, though I knew my stay was useless, to make my interest in her wares seem the more real. Then I turned away slowly and walked down the middle of the bazaar. I allowed the two pennies to fall against the sixpence in my pocket. I heard a voice call from one end of the gallery that the light was out. The upper part of the hall was now completely dark.

Gazing up into the darkness I saw myself as a creature driven and derided by vanity; and my eyes burned with anguish and anger.

190

200

210

Reading Check

Reading Check

Step 1 Review the notes you wrote and the passages you marked as you read. Did Araby live up to the boy's expectations? Explain why or why not.

_____

_____

_____

_____

_____

Step 2 Now put yourself in the boy's position. Explain how you would have felt or acted when you reached the bazaar.

_____

_____

_____

_____

Choose three words, either from the underlined vocabulary in the story or from the words you circled as you read. Record them in your **Hot Words Journal** at the back of this book and complete an activity listed there.

READING WRAPUP

Going Solo

🔑 Understanding Words Used in Unfamiliar Ways

Making It Clear While reading the story, you practiced using context clues to help you find the meaning of a familiar word used in an unfamiliar way. The following words, all found on page 8, are also used in unfamiliar ways. Find the words on the page and look at the context to discover how Joyce is using them. If you like, refer to a dictionary for additional help. Then, on the line next to the word, write a definition of the word as it is used in the story.

well (line 94) _____

Eastern (line 102) _____

humor (line 116) _____

Buddy Up

🔑 Visualize

1. At the Bazaar With a partner, turn to page 10 and reread lines 170 to 180. Afterward, take turns describing the mental pictures you formed of the bazaar. Discuss the similarities and differences in your descriptions. Then write a description that you both agree describes the bazaar.

_____

_____

2. At Home The mental pictures you create early in a story can help you understand action that occurs later. Review the description of North Richmond Street you wrote for the Visualize note on page 5 and compare it to what your partner wrote. Then read together the paragraph that starts at the bottom of page 7, beginning "While she spoke." Using your descriptions as a starting place, decide where on North Richmond street the boy and the girl are standing and give any additional details about the street that the paragraph provides.

_____

_____

_____

TeamWork

🔑 Infer

1. What did you say? What did you mean? With your group, discuss the conversation between the two young gentlemen and the young lady at the bazaar that takes place on pages 10 and 11. Decide together on answers to the following questions and write your responses on the lines.

What connection does the boy make between this flirtatious conversation and his own experience?

_____

_____

What "fib" suddenly becomes clear to him?

_____

2. Passages Reread the last sentence in the story. With your group, discuss what inferences you can make about why the boy feels that he's been "driven and derided by vanity" and why he's angry. Use clues from the story to help you understand the boy's feelings. Write two inferences that can be made from this sentence.

_____

_____

_____

_____

Literary Element

← Setting

Setting is the time and place in which the events of a literary work occur. The setting includes not only physical surroundings but also the ideas, customs, values, and beliefs of the people who live there. The setting in James Joyce's "Araby" plays an important part in the story. Fill in the details of the setting in the space provided.

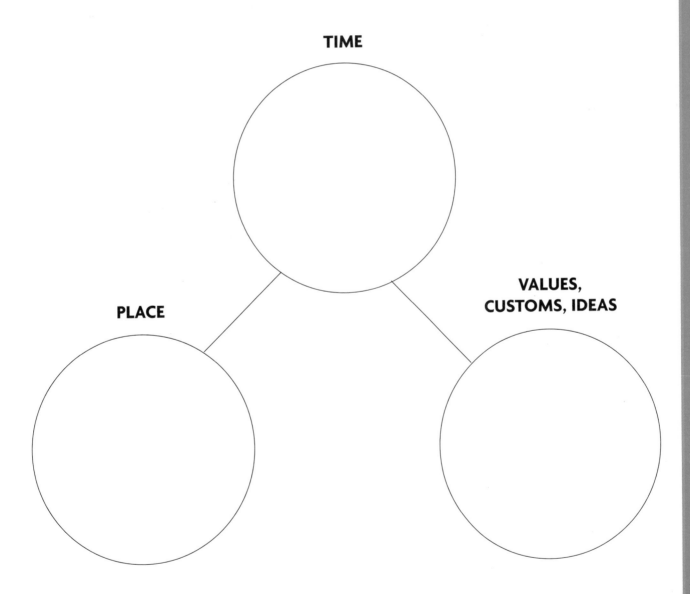

TIME

PLACE

VALUES, CUSTOMS, IDEAS

READING WRAPUP

continued

Standardized Test Practice

Choose the best answer for each multiple-choice question. Fill in the circle in the spaces for questions 1 and 2 on the right.

1. Why does the narrator go to Araby?

   A. He wants to buy Mangan's sister a gift.

   B. He has always dreamed of going to a bazaar.

   C. Mangan's sister asks him to go in her place.

   D. He does not want to go on a retreat with the rest of the neighborhood children.

2. What does the narrator realize when he gets to the bazaar?

   A. It is too late to buy anything.

   B. He should have listened to his uncle.

   C. His romantic illusions are simply fantasy.

   D. He has sacrificed his childhood for nothing.

Write your answer to open-ended question A in the space provided below.

A. Why do you think Araby becomes so important to the narrator? Use details from the story to support your answer.

Multiple-Choice Questions

1. Ⓐ Ⓑ Ⓒ Ⓓ   2. Ⓐ Ⓑ Ⓒ Ⓓ

Open-Ended Question

A. _____

_____

_____

_____

word power

Vocabulary Check

From the word list, write the word that belongs in the blank in each sentence.

imperturbable *adj.* not easily excited or disturbed; calm

diverge *v.* to move in different directions from a common point; to branch out

converge *v.* to come together in a common interest or conclusion; to center

impinge *v.* to strike or dash; to collide

annihilate *v.* to reduce to nothing; to obliterate

amiability *n.* kindliness; friendliness

garrulous *adj.* given to too much talking, especially about unimportant matters

1. Throughout the crisis, Aunt Amelia remained collected and _____.

2. This medicine is so powerful that it will _____ the virus.

3. Evan always had a story, but sometimes his _____ manner was annoying.

4. We wanted to work together since our views on the issue seemed to _____.

5. Dessie's warmth and _____ put me at ease.

6. Bear to the left when you get to the spot where the roads _____.

7. Hailstones make a dreadful racket when they _____ on our roof.

GET READY TO READ!

Connect

List and Discuss What makes you decide to help someone? In a small group, list five motives (or reasons) people have for helping others. Then discuss these questions: Is it possible to do a good deed for the wrong reasons? What would you consider to be wrong reasons for doing a favor? Be sure to give support for your answers.

In this short story, you'll read about a wealthy woman named Rosemary who helps a poor girl she meets on the street.

Did You Know?

Building Background This story takes place in England at the beginning of the twentieth century.

- At that time, upper-class people and working-class people didn't mix with one another socially. The main character in this story, Rosemary, is an upper-class woman with a luxurious lifestyle and many servants. One day she meets a poor young woman on the street and decides to take her home for tea.

- Author Katherine Mansfield was interested in the emotions and psychological makeup of her characters. Like many of Mansfield's stories, "A Cup of Tea" contains fascinating, and sometimes surprising, insights into human needs and motivations.

Reason to Read

Setting a Purpose for Reading Read to find out why Rosemary helps a poor girl—and why she later sends the girl away.

As you read, use the following **Foldable** to help you keep track of Rosemary's actions and her reasons for doing what she does.

1. Place a sheet of paper in front of you so that the short side is at the top. Fold the paper in half from side to side.
2. Turn the paper horizontally and fold into thirds.
3. Unfold and cut through the top layer of paper along the fold lines. This will make three tabs.

4. From left to right, label the three tabs ***Rosemary's Actions, Rosemary's Reasons,*** and ***My Opinions.***
5. Under the first tab, record the things Rosemary does. Under the second tab, give reasons for each of her actions. Under the third tab, write adjectives (such as *selfish, shallow, generous, kind,* or *noble*) to describe your opinion of Rosemary's actions.

word power

Vocabulary Preview

Read the words and definitions below. Use the pronunciation guides to help you say each word aloud. You may already know some of these words, but others might still be unclear. As you read, use context clues to help unlock the meanings and make those words clearer.

quaint (kwānt) *adj.* pleasingly unusual or odd; p. 16

odious (ō′dē əs) *adj.* causing hate, disgust, or repugnance; p. 16

exotic (ig zot′ik) *adj.* strangely beautiful or fascinating; p. 16

frail (frāl) *adj.* weak; fragile; p. 22

retort (ri tôrt′) *v.* to reply in a witty, quick, or sharp manner; p. 23

Hot Words Journal

As you read, circle words that you find interesting or that you don't understand. Later you may add them to your **Hot Words Journal** at the back of this book.

What You'll Learn

Key Goals In this lesson, you will learn these key skills, strategies, and concepts.

- **Reading Focus:** Respond

- **Think It Over:** Draw Conclusions

- **Literary Element:** Character

- **Reading Coach:** Understanding Author's Style

A Cup of Tea

Katherine Mansfield

Rosemary Fell was not exactly beautiful. No, you couldn't have called her beautiful. Pretty? Well, if you took her to pieces . . . But why be so cruel as to take anyone to pieces? **A** She was young, brilliant, extremely modern, exquisitely well dressed, amazingly well read in the newest of the new books, and her parties were the most delicious mixture of the really important people and . . . artists—<u>quaint</u> creatures, discoveries of hers, some of them too terrifying for words, but others quite presentable and amusing.

10   Rosemary had been married two years. She had a duck[1] of a boy. No, not Peter—Michael. And her husband absolutely adored her. They were rich, really rich, not just comfortably well off, which is <u>odious</u> and stuffy and sounds like one's grandparents. But if Rosemary wanted to shop she would go to Paris as you and I would go to Bond Street.[2] If she wanted to buy flowers, the car pulled up at that perfect shop in Regent Street, and Rosemary inside the shop just gazed in her dazzled, rather <u>exotic</u> way, and said: "I want those and those and those. Give me four bunches of those. And that jar of roses. Yes, I'll have all the roses in the jar.

20   No, no lilac. I hate lilac. It's got no shape." The attendant bowed and put the lilac out of sight, as though this was only too true; lilac was dreadfully shapeless. "Give me those stumpy little tulips. Those red and white ones." And she was followed to the car by a thin shopgirl staggering under an immense white paper armful that looked like a baby in long clothes. . . . **B**

---

1. Here, *duck* probably means "a darling" or "a dear," although it could also mean "funny" or "odd but harmless."
2. *Bond Street*—as well as *Regent Street* and *Curzon Street* mentioned later—was, and continues to be, an elegant London street lined with shops that sell expensive, exclusive items.

Vocabulary

quaint (kwānt) *adj.* pleasingly unusual or odd
odious (ō′dē əs) *adj.* causing hate, disgust, or repugnance
exotic (ig zot′ik) *adj.* strangely beautiful or fascinating

One winter afternoon she had been buying something in a little antique shop in Curzon Street. It was a shop she liked. For one thing, one usually had it to oneself. And then the man who kept it was ridiculously fond of serving her. He beamed whenever she came in. He clasped his hands; he was so gratified he could 30 scarcely speak. Flattery, of course. All the same, there was something . . .

"You see, madam," he would explain in his low respectful tones, "I love my things. I would rather not part with them than sell them to someone who does not appreciate them, who has not that fine feeling which is so rare. . . ." And, breathing deeply, he unrolled a tiny square of blue velvet and pressed it on the glass counter with his pale fingertips. **C**

Today it was a little box. He had been keeping it for her. He had shown it to nobody as yet. An exquisite little enamel box with 40 a glaze so fine it looked as though it had been baked in cream. On the lid a minute[3] creature stood under a flowery tree, and a more minute creature still had her arms around his neck. Her hat, really no bigger than a geranium petal, hung from a branch; it had green ribbons. And there was a pink cloud like a watchful cherub floating above their heads. Rosemary took her hands out of her long gloves. She always took off her gloves to examine such things. Yes, she liked it very much. She loved it; it was a great duck. She must have it. And, turning the creamy box, opening and shutting it, she couldn't help noticing how 50 charming her hands were against the blue velvet. The shopman, in some dim cavern of his mind, may have dared to think so too. For he took a pencil, leaned over the counter, and his pale bloodless fingers crept timidly towards those rosy, flashing ones, as he murmured gently: "If I may venture to point out to madam, the flowers on the little lady's bodice."[4] **D**

"Charming!" Rosemary admired the flowers. But what was the price? For a moment the shopman did not seem to hear. Then a murmur reached her. "Twenty-eight guineas,[5] madame."

"Twenty-eight guineas." Rosemary gave no sign. She laid the 60 little box down; she buttoned her gloves again. Twenty-eight

---

3. *Minute* means "tiny."
4. A *bodice* is the fitted part of a dress from the waist to the shoulder.
5. A *guinea* was a British gold coin worth about one pound and five pence.

Think It Over

Draw Conclusions To **draw a conclusion,** think about how details in a story work together to tell you something about a character or an event. For example, think about Rosemary's wealth, her hunger for fine things, and her shopping habits. Why do you think the shopkeeper beams at Rosemary and compliments her taste? Check the best answer. **C**

❑ He likes Rosemary.

❑ He wants Rosemary to buy something.

❑ He thinks Rosemary is beautiful.

Literary Element

Character A person in a story or a play is called a **character.** You can learn about Rosemary, the main character in this story, from how she acts and what she says and thinks. You can also notice how other characters react to her.

Mark the text▷ Underline a detail in the boxed passage that tells what Rosemary does or what she thinks. What does this detail say about her character? Write your answer below. **D**

_____

_____

Draw Conclusions What is Rosemary's mood when she leaves the shop? Underline or highlight the words in this paragraph that give clues about Rosemary's mood. Then describe her mood on the lines below. **E**

Visualize Take a moment to picture the rich, well-dressed Rosemary talking to the poor, shivering young girl. Quickly sketch what you see in your mind's eye in the frame below. **F**

Your Sketch

guineas. Even if one is rich . . . She looked vague.[6] She stared at a plump teakettle like a plump hen above the shopman's head, and her voice was dreamy as she answered: "Well, keep it for me—will you? I'll . . ."

But the shopman had already bowed as though keeping it for her was all any human being could ask. He would be willing, of course, to keep it for her forever.

The discreet door shut with a click. She was outside on the
70 step, gazing at the winter afternoon. Rain was falling, and with the rain it seemed the dark came too, spinning down like ashes. There was a cold bitter taste in the air, and the new-lighted lamps looked sad. Sad were the lights in the houses opposite. Dimly they burned as if regretting something. And people hurried by, hidden under their hateful umbrellas. Rosemary felt a strange pang. She pressed her muff to her breast; she wished she had the little box, too, to cling to. Of course, the car was there. She'd only to cross the pavement. But still she waited. There are moments, horrible moments in life, when one emerges from
80 shelter and looks out, and it's awful. One oughtn't to give way to them. One ought to go home and have an extra-special tea. But at the very instant of thinking that, a young girl, thin, dark, shadowy—where had she come from?—was standing at Rosemary's elbow and a voice like a sigh, almost like a sob, breathed: "Madam, may I speak to you a moment?" **E**

"Speak to me?" Rosemary turned. She saw a little battered creature with enormous eyes, someone quite young, no older than herself, who clutched at her coat collar with reddened hands, and shivered as though she had just come out of the
90 water.

"M-madam," stammered the voice. "Would you let me have the price of a cup of tea?"

"A cup of tea?" There was something simple, sincere in that voice; it wasn't in the least the voice of a beggar. "Then have you no money at all?" asked Rosemary.

"None, madam," came the answer.

"How extraordinary!" Rosemary peered through the dusk, and the girl gazed back at her. **F** How more than extraordinary! And suddenly it seemed to Rosemary such an adventure. It was like

---
6. Here, *vague* means "uncertain."

something out of a novel by Dostoevsky,[7] this meeting in the   100
dusk. Supposing she took the girl home? Supposing she did do
one of those things she was always reading about or seeing on the
stage, what would happen? It would be thrilling. And she heard
herself saying afterwards to the amazement of her friends: "I
simply took her home with me," as she stepped forward and said
to that dim person beside her: "Come home to tea with me." **G**

The girl drew back startled. She even stopped shivering for a
moment. Rosemary put out a hand and touched her arm. "I
mean it," she said, smiling. And she felt how simple and kind her
smile was. "Why won't you? Do. Come home with me now in my   110
car and have tea."

"You—you don't mean it, madam," said the girl, and there was
pain in her voice.

"But I do," cried Rosemary. "I want you to. To please me. Come
along."

The girl put her fingers to her lips and her eyes devoured
Rosemary. "You're—you're not taking me to the police station?"
she stammered. **H**

"The police station!" Rosemary laughed out. "Why should I be
so cruel? No, I only want to make you warm and to hear—   120
anything you care to tell me."

Hungry people are easily led. The footman held the door of
the car open, and a moment later they were skimming through
the dusk.

"There!" said Rosemary. She had a feeling of triumph as she
slipped her hand through the velvet strap. She could have said,
"Now I've got you," as she gazed at the little captive she had
netted. But of course she meant it kindly. Oh, more than kindly.
She was going to prove to this girl that—wonderful things did
happen in life, that—fairy godmothers were real, that—rich   130
people had hearts, and that women *were* sisters. She turned
impulsively, saying: "Don't be frightened. After all, why shouldn't
you come back with me? We're both women. If I'm the more
fortunate, you ought to expect . . ."

---

7. Fyodor *Dostoevsky,* a Russian writer who is considered one of the
   world's greatest novelists, often dramatized moral and psychological
   issues and wrote of the poor.

Hot Words

Mark the text **Choose your own words**
As you continue reading this story,
circle any words that you find
interesting or that you don't
understand. You'll come back to
these words later.

Literary Element

Character Reread the
boxed text. Pay special attention
to what Rosemary thinks to
herself before inviting the girl
to tea. What do her thoughts
tell you about Rosemary? Write
your answer on the lines
below. You may want to add
to your **Foldable** at this time
too. **G**

_____

_____

_____

_____

_____

Reading Focus

Respond Reread lines
107–118. Does the girl's
reaction to Rosemary's
invitation surprise you? Circle *Yes*
or *No.* **H**

Yes   **No**

Explain your response here.

_____

_____

_____

_____

_____

📖 Reading Check

Step 1 Ask yourself how well you have understood the story so far. Use these strategies to help you answer any questions you have.

- Reread confusing passages slowly or read them aloud.
- Read on to see if new story information makes the meaning clear.
- Ask a classmate or a teacher, parent, or other adult for help.

Step 2 On the lines below, write a one- or two-sentence summary of what you've read so far.

_____

_____

_____

_____

_____

Think It Over

🔑 **Draw Conclusions**

Mark the text Underline words and phrases that tell how the girl acts in Rosemary's room. Then check the box below that tells what you can conclude from the girl's actions. **1**

❑ The girl is frightened and unsure of what to do.

❑ The girl wants to leave.

❑ The girl has bad manners.

But happily at that moment, for she didn't know how the sentence was going to end, the car stopped. The bell was rung, the door opened, and with a charming, protecting, almost embracing movement, Rosemary drew the other into the hall. Warmth, softness, light, a sweet scent, all those things so familiar to her she never even thought about them, she watched that other receive. It was fascinating. She was like the little rich girl in her nursery with all the cupboards to open, all the boxes to unpack.

📖 Reading Check

"Come, come upstairs," said Rosemary, longing to begin to be generous. "Come up to my room." And, besides, she wanted to spare this poor little thing from being stared at by the servants; she decided as they mounted the stairs she would not even ring for Jeanne, but take off her things by herself. The great thing was to be natural!

And "There!" cried Rosemary again, as they reached her beautiful big bedroom with the curtains drawn, the fire leaping on her wonderful lacquer furniture, her gold cushions and the primrose and blue rugs.

The girl stood just inside the door; she seemed dazed. But Rosemary didn't mind that.

"Come and sit down," she cried, dragging her big chair up to the fire, "in this comfy chair. Come and get warm. You look so dreadfully cold."

"I daren't, madam," said the girl, and she edged backwards.

"Oh, please,"—Rosemary ran forward—"you mustn't be frightened, you mustn't, really. Sit down, and when I've taken off my things we shall go into the next room and have tea and be cosy. Why are you afraid?" And gently she half pushed the thin figure into its deep cradle.

But there was no answer. The girl stayed just as she had been put, with her hands by her sides and her mouth slightly open. To be quite sincere, she looked rather stupid. But Rosemary wouldn't acknowledge it. She leaned over her, saying: "Won't you take off your hat? Your pretty hair is all wet. And one is so much more comfortable without a hat, isn't one?" **1**

There was a whisper that sounded like "Very good, madam," and the crushed hat was taken off.

"Let me help you off with your coat, too," said Rosemary.

The girl stood up. But she held on to the chair with one hand and let Rosemary pull. It was quite an effort. The other scarcely helped her at all. She seemed to stagger like a child, and the thought came and went through Rosemary's mind, that if people wanted helping they must respond a little, just a little, otherwise it became very difficult indeed. And what was she to do with the coat now? She left it on the floor, and the hat too. She was just going to take a cigarette off the mantelpiece when the girl said quickly, but so lightly and strangely: "I'm very sorry, madam, but I'm going to faint. I shall go off, madam, if I don't have something." **J**

"Good heavens, how thoughtless I am!" Rosemary rushed to the bell.

"Tea! Tea at once! And some brandy immediately!"

The maid was gone again, but the girl almost cried out. "No, I don't want no brandy. I never drink brandy. It's a cup of tea I want, madam." And she burst into tears.

It was a terrible and fascinating moment. Rosemary knelt beside her chair.

"Don't cry, poor little thing," she said. "Don't cry." And she gave the other her lace handkerchief. She really was touched beyond words. She put her arm round those thin, birdlike shoulders.

Now at last the other forgot to be shy, forgot everything except that they were both women, and gasped out: "I can't go on no longer like this. I can't bear it. I shall do away with myself. I can't bear no more." **K**

"You shan't have to. I'll look after you. Don't cry any more. Don't you see what a good thing it was that you met me? We'll have tea and you'll tell me everything. And I shall arrange something. I promise. *Do* stop crying. It's so exhausting. Please!" **L**

The other did stop just in time for Rosemary to get up before the tea came. She had the table placed between them. She plied the poor little creature with everything, all the sandwiches, all the bread and butter, and every time her cup was empty she filled it with tea, cream and sugar. People always said sugar was so

180

190

200

Build Fluency Find a quiet place and practice reading aloud the boxed passage. Reread the passage several times until you can get through it without stumbling. **J**

Reading Focus

↞ **Respond** Imagine what the girl must be feeling when she cries out. What is your reaction to her at this point? Write your response on the lines below. **K**

_____

_____

_____

_____

Literary Element

↞ **Character** Rosemary tells the girl "*Do* stop crying. It's so exhausting." What does her response to the girl's crying tell you about Rosemary? **L**

_____

_____

_____

_____

Your Notes

---

210   nourishing. As for herself she didn't eat; she smoked and looked away tactfully so that the other should not be shy.

    And really the effect of that slight meal was marvelous. When the tea table was carried away a new being, a light, <u>frail</u> creature with tangled hair, dark lips, deep, lighted eyes, lay back in the big chair in a kind of sweet languor,[8] looking at the blaze. Rosemary lit a fresh cigarette; it was time to begin.

    "And when did you have your last meal?" she asked softly.

    But at that moment the door handle turned.

    "Rosemary, may I come in?" It was Philip.

220   "Of course."

    He came in. "Oh, I'm so sorry," he said, and stopped and stared.

    "It's quite all right," said Rosemary smiling. "This is my friend, Miss—"

    "Smith, madam," said the languid[9] figure, who was strangely still and unafraid.

    "Smith," said Rosemary. "We are going to have a little talk."

    "Oh, yes," said Philip. "Quite," and his eye caught sight of the coat and hat on the floor. He came over to the fire and turned

230 his back to it. "It's a beastly afternoon," he said curiously, still looking at that listless figure, looking at its hands and boots, and then at Rosemary again.

    "Yes, isn't it?" said Rosemary enthusiastically. "Vile."

    Philip smiled his charming smile. "As a matter of fact," said he, "I wanted you to come into the library for a moment. Would you? Will Miss Smith excuse us?"

    The big eyes were raised to him, but Rosemary answered for her. "Of course she will." And they went out of the room together.

240   "I say," said Philip, when they were alone. "Explain. Who is she? What does it all mean?" **M**

    Rosemary, laughing, leaned against the door and said: "I picked her up in Curzon Street. Really. She's a real pick-up. She

---

8. *Languor* means "a dreamy, lazy mood or quality."
9. *Languid* means "lacking energy or vitality."

Vocabulary
frail (frāl) *adj.* weak; fragile

Infer When you **infer,** you use your own reason and experience to guess at what the author isn't telling you directly.

Mark the text Underline words and phrases that tell how Philip reacts when he sees the girl. What can you infer about Philip's feelings? Circle any answers that apply. **M**

- Philip is disappointed.
- Philip is surprised.
- Philip is curious.
- Philip is upset.

asked me for the price of a cup of tea, and I brought her home with me."

"But what on earth are you going to do with her?" cried Philip.

"Be nice to her," said Rosemary quickly. "Be frightfully nice to her. Look after her. I don't know how. We haven't talked yet. But show her—treat her—make her feel—"

"My darling girl," said Philip, "you're quite mad, you know. It simply can't be done."

"I knew you'd say that," retorted Rosemary. "Why not? I want to. Isn't that a reason? And besides, one's always reading about these things. I decided—"

"But," said Philip slowly, and he cut the end of a cigar, "she's so astonishingly pretty."

"Pretty?" Rosemary was so surprised that she blushed. "Do you think so? I—I hadn't thought about it."

"Good Lord!" Philip struck a match. "She's absolutely lovely. Look again, my child. I was bowled over when I came into your room just now. However . . . I think you're making a ghastly mistake. Sorry, darling, if I'm crude and all that. But let me know if Miss Smith is going to dine with us in time for me to look up *The Milliner's Gazette.*"[10] **O**

> "You absurd creature!" said Rosemary, and she went out of the library, but not back to her bedroom. She went to her writing room and sat down at her desk. Pretty! Absolutely lovely! Bowled over! Her heart beat like a heavy bell. Pretty! Lovely! She drew her check book towards her. But no, checks would be no use, of course. She opened a drawer and took out five pound notes, looked at them, put two back, and holding the three squeezed in her hand, she went back to her bedroom. **P**

Half an hour later Philip was still in the library, when Rosemary came in.

"I only wanted to tell you," said she, and she leaned against the door again and looked at him with her dazzled exotic gaze, "Miss Smith won't dine with us tonight."

250

260

270

----

10. A *milliner* is one who makes or sells women's hats. A *gazette* is a newspaper.

Vocabulary

retort (ri tôrt´) *v.* to reply in a witty, quick, or sharp manner

---

Reading Coach

➡ **Understanding Author's Style** Reread the highlighted text. Underline the sentence that contains dashes. What do these dashes suggest about Rosemary's plan to help the girl? Write your answer below. **N**

_____

_____

_____

_____

Reading Focus

Predict What do you think will happen next? Write a prediction here. **O**

_____

_____

_____

Think It Over

➡ **Draw Conclusions** Reread the boxed text. Why does Rosemary's heart beat like a heavy bell? **P**

_____

_____

Why does she go back to the bedroom with money in her hand?

_____

_____

_____

Infer Rosemary puts on makeup and jewelry before going in to see Philip. What does this tell you about how Rosemary is feeling? **Q**

_____

_____

_____

Reading Check

Step 1 Take a moment to think about the story and review your **Foldable.** In the end, what happened to Rosemary's promise to help look after the girl? Why? Write your answer below.

_____

_____

_____

Step 2 In your own life, have you ever done someone a favor for the wrong reasons? What happened?

_____

_____

_____

_____

Choose three words to record in your **Hot Words Journal** at the back of this book. Then complete one of the activities listed there.

Philip put down the paper. "Oh, what's happened? Previous engagement?"

280 Rosemary came over and sat down on his knee. "She insisted on going," said she, "so I gave the poor little thing a present of money. I couldn't keep her against her will, could I?" she added softly.

Rosemary had just done her hair, darkened her eyes a little, and put on her pearls. She put up her hands and touched Philip's cheeks. **Q**

"Do you like me?" said she, and her tone, sweet, husky, troubled him.

"I like you awfully," he said, and he held her tighter. "Kiss me."

290 There was a pause.

Then Rosemary said dreamily, "I saw a fascinating little box today. It cost twenty-eight guineas. May I have it?"

Philip jumped her on his knee. "You may, little wasteful one," said he.

But that was not really what Rosemary wanted to say.

"Philip," she whispered, and she pressed his head against her bosom, "am I _pretty_?"

Reading Check

Going Solo

Understanding Author's Style

Finish the Thought Look back through the story and reread the paragraphs in which the lines below can be found. Think about what the lines mean. If you could finish each sentence, what would you say? Write your answers in the spaces provided.

> **Well, keep it for me—will you? I'll . . .**
> (page 18, lines 64–65)

_____

_____

> **If I'm the more fortunate, you ought to expect . . .** (page 19, lines 133–134)

_____

Buddy Up

Respond

1. Big Surprise With a partner, review the story and find three moments that surprised you or that gave you a sudden insight. Discuss why these moments surprised you. Then choose one of the moments. On the lines below, describe what happened at that point in the story and summarize why you were surprised.

_____

_____

_____

2. Talk Back! With your partner, role-play a conversation in which you tell Rosemary what you think of her actions and give her some advice. Your partner can respond as Rosemary might. Summarize your conversation on the lines below.

_____

_____

_____

_____

TeamWork

Draw Conclusions

1. Generous or Stingy? With your group, decide whether you think Rosemary is generous or stingy. Look back to the story to find out how much money she gives the girl. Then see how much money she wants to spend on the enamel box. Use footnote 5 to figure out how the two sums compare. What conclusions can you draw? Write your conclusions and your reasons below.

_____

_____

_____

_____

2. Money Isn't Everything! Rosemary is young, rich, and fashionable, but something's missing. What does Rosemary lack that money can't buy? Discuss this question with your group and write your conclusion below. Be sure to include reasons and details from the story in your answer.

_____

_____

_____

_____

_____

READING WRAPUP

continued

Literary Element

← Character

A **character** is a person in a literary work. Authors use various methods to make their characters come alive and seem real. Sometimes authors make a direct statement about the character's qualities:

> **Rosemary Fell was not exactly beautiful.**

Sometimes authors describe their characters' thoughts, actions, words, or appearance:

> **She couldn't help noticing how charming her hands were against the blue velvet.**

Fill in the second column of the chart with quotations from the story that reveal important information about each character. In the third column, tell what each quotation reveals about the character.

Character	Quotation from story	What it reveals about character
Rosemary		
Miss Smith (the girl)		
Philip		

Standardized Test Practice

Choose the best answer for each multiple-choice question. Fill in the circle in the spaces for questions 1 and 2 on the right.

1. Why does Rosemary offer to help the young girl?
   A. She believes it is her duty.
   B. She thinks it will be thrilling.
   C. She was once poor herself.
   D. She is kind and generous.

2. Which of these words does NOT describe Rosemary?
   A. thoughtful
   B. insensitive
   C. shallow
   D. needy

Write your answer to open-ended question A in the space provided below.

A. At the end of the story, Rosemary asks Philip two questions: "May I have it?" and "Am I pretty?" What do these questions tell you about their relationship? Use details from the story to support your answer.

Multiple-Choice Questions

1. Ⓐ Ⓑ Ⓒ Ⓓ   2. Ⓐ Ⓑ Ⓒ Ⓓ

Open-Ended Question

A. _____

_____

_____

_____

word power

Vocabulary Check

Write the word from the word list that belongs in the blank in each sentence.

quaint *adj.* pleasingly unusual or odd

odious *adj.* causing hate, disgust, or repugnance

exotic *adj.* strangely beautiful or fascinating

frail *adj.* weak; fragile

retort *v.* to reply in a witty, quick, or sharp manner

1. In a room full of dull, ordinary people, she was mysterious and _____.

2. Once I realized that he had lied to me, I found him _____.

3. Drinking milk and exercising will keep your bones from becoming _____.

4. "Because I said so!" the mother would often _____ when the little boy asked "Why?"

5. The tiny cottage with its blooming flowers and pretty path was very _____.

GET READY TO READ!

Connect

Small Group Discussion Think about a scary story that you've read, heard, or seen on screen. In a small group, take turns giving brief descriptions of scary stories. What makes each story scary? Work together to make a list of characteristics that the scary stories have in common. Then share your list with the class.

In this short story, you'll read about Mrs. Drover, an English woman who finds a mysterious letter in her abandoned London home.

Did You Know?

Building Background This story takes place during World War II when Germany was bombing London.

- On fifty-seven nights in a row, the German air force bombed London in an effort to wipe out the city and destroy the fighting spirit of England's people.

- Many families moved to the English countryside to escape. Those who could not afford to move had to take shelter where they could find it during those long nights of horror.

- For some people, the stresses of World War II reminded them of World War I, which they had lived through about twenty-five years earlier.

Reason to Read

Setting a Purpose for Reading Read to find out how the writer creates an air of suspense.

As you read, use the following **Foldable** to keep track of the spooky things in the story and Mrs. Drover's reactions to them.

1. Place a sheet of paper in front of you so that the short side is at the top. Fold the paper in half from the left side to the right side.

2. Fold the top down about 1 inch as shown.

3. Open the paper and label the left column **Spooky Things** and the right column **Mrs. Drover's Reactions.**

4. In the left column, jot down strange things about the setting and the events of the story. In the right column, jot down the things Mrs. Drover does that let you know she is scared.

word power

Vocabulary Preview

Read the definitions of these words from "The Demon Lover." Use the pronunciation guides to help you say each word aloud. As you read the story, use context clues to help unlock the meaning of these words and any others you don't know.

prosaic (prō zā′ ik) *adj.* commonplace; ordinary; p. 29

intermittent (in′ tər mit′ ənt) *adj.* alternately starting and stopping; p. 31

precipitately (pri sip′ ə tət lē) *adv.* without deliberation; hastily; abruptly; p. 31

emanate (em′ ə nāt) *v.* to come forth from a source; issue; p. 35

impassively (im pas′ iv lē) *adv.* in an emotionless manner; p. 36

Hot Words Journal

As you read, circle any words that you find interesting or that you don't understand. Later you may add them to your **Hot Words Journal** at the back of this book.

What You'll Learn

Key Goals In this lesson, you will learn these key skills, strategies, and concepts.

- **Reading Focus:** Predict

- **Think It Over:** Infer

- **Literary Element:** Suspense

- **Reading Coach:** Understanding Complicated Sentences

The Demon Lover

Elizabeth Bowen

Towards the end of her day in London Mrs. Drover went round to her shut-up house to look for several things she wanted to take away. Some belonged to herself, some to her family, who were by now used to their country life. It was late August; it had been a steamy, showery day: at the moment the trees down the pavement glittered in an escape of humid yellow afternoon sun. Against the next batch of clouds, already piling up ink-dark, broken chimneys and parapets[1] stood out. In her once familiar street, as in any unused channel, an unfamiliar queerness had silted up;[2] a cat wove itself in and out of railings, but no human eye watched Mrs. Drover's return.

Shifting some parcels under her arm, she slowly forced round her latchkey in an unwilling lock, then gave the door, which had warped, a push with her knee. **A** Dead air came out to meet her as she went in.

The staircase window having been boarded up, no light came down into the hall. But one door, she could just see, stood ajar, so she went quickly through into the room and unshuttered the big window in there. Now the <u>prosaic</u> woman, looking about her, was more perplexed[3] than she knew by everything that she saw, by traces of her long former habit of life—the yellow smoke stain up the white marble mantelpiece, the ring left by a vase on the top of the escritoire; the bruise in the wallpaper where, on the door being thrown open widely, the china handle had always hit the wall. The piano, having gone away to be stored,

Did You Know?

An *escritoire* is a writing table or desk.

1. A *parapet* is a low, protective railing or wall along the edge of a roof or balcony.
2. Here, *silted up* means "built up."
3. *Perplexed* means "bewildered" or "puzzled."

Vocabulary

prosaic (prō zā´ ik) *adj.* commonplace; ordinary

Reading Coach

➡ **Understanding Complicated Sentences**
Bowen's sentences are long and packed with vivid details. If you find yourself getting lost in a long sentence, try finding the **subject** and the **main action.** The subject tells whom or what the sentence is about. The main action tells what the subject does or has. Some sentences have more than one subject or main action. Other sentences have two or more subjects *and* main actions. To understand the boxed sentence, you might have a conversation with yourself like the one in the model. **A**

Model: The sentence is about Mrs. Drover, so "she" must be the subject of the sentence. I can ask myself, What does Mrs. Drover do? She forces her key around in the lock and gives the door a push with her knee. The rest of the sentence contains details.

READ ALOUD

word power

Read Aloud When you come to an underlined vocabulary word, try this strategy: First read aloud the sentence in which the word appears. Then reread the sentence, substituting the definition at the bottom of the page for the underlined word.

Hot Words

Mark the text **Choose your own words**
As you continue reading this story, circle any words that you find interesting or that you don't understand. You'll come back to these words later.

Literary Element

Suspense When you feel **suspense,** you can't wait to find out what happens—even though you're scared that it might not be something good. Writers produce suspense by creating a threat to the main character and including mysterious events. Here, the writer builds suspense by describing Mrs. Drover's thoughts as she tries to figure out how the letter could have ended up on the hall table. **B**

Mark the text Review the boxed passage. Underline the reasons why it is strange that Mrs. Drover found the letter on the hall table. What makes the letter so mysterious? Write your thoughts on the lines below.

_____

_____

_____

_____

30 had left what looked like claw marks on its part of the parquet.[4] Though not much dust had seeped in, each object wore a film of another kind; and, the only ventilation being the chimney, the whole drawing room smelled of the cold hearth. Mrs. Drover put down her parcels on the escritoire and left the room to proceed upstairs; the things she wanted were in a bedroom chest.

She had been anxious to see how the house was—the part-time caretaker she shared with some neighbors was away this week on his holiday, known to be not yet back. At the best of times he did not look in often, and she was never sure that she trusted him.

40 There were some cracks in the structure, left by the last bombing,[5] on which she was anxious to keep an eye. Not that one could do anything—

A shaft of refracted[6] daylight now lay across the hall. She stopped dead and stared at the hall table—on this lay a letter addressed to her.

She thought first—then the caretaker _must_ be back. All the same, who, seeing the house shuttered, would have dropped a letter in at the box? It was not a circular,[7] it was not a bill. And the post office redirected, to the address in the country,
50 everything for her that came through the post. The caretaker (even if he _were_ back) did not know she was due in London today—her call here had been planned to be a surprise—so his negligence in the manner of this letter, leaving it to wait in the dusk and the dust, annoyed her. Annoyed, she picked up the letter, which bore no stamp. But it cannot be important, or they would know . . . **B** She took the letter rapidly upstairs with her, without a stop to look at the writing till she reached what had been her bedroom, where she let in light. The room looked over the garden and other gardens: the sun had gone in; as the clouds
60 sharpened and lowered, the trees and rank[8] lawns seemed already to smoke with dark. Her reluctance to look again at the letter came from the fact that she felt intruded upon—and by

_____

4. _Parquet_ is inlaid wood, often of different colors, that is worked into geometric patterns or mosaic and is used especially for flooring.

5. _The last bombing_ indicates that the story takes place during World War II.

6. _Refracted_ means "coming in at an angle."

7. Here, a _circular_ is a printed advertisement.

8. As it is used here, _rank_ means "overgrown with weeds."

someone contemptuous[9] of her ways. However, in the tenseness preceding the fall of rain she read it: it was a few lines.

Dear Kathleen: You will not have forgotten that today is our anniversary, and the day we said. The years have gone by at once slowly and fast. In view of the fact that nothing has changed, I shall rely upon you to keep your promise. I was sorry to see you leave London, but was satisfied that you would be back in time. You may expect me, therefore, at the hour arranged. Until then . . .   K. **C**

70

Mrs. Drover looked for the date: it was today's. She dropped the letter on to the bedsprings, then picked it up to see the writing again—her lips, beneath the remains of lipstick, beginning to go white. She felt so much the change in her own face that she went to the mirror, polished a clear patch in it and looked at once urgently and stealthily[10] in. She was confronted by a woman of forty-four, with eyes starting out under a hat brim that had been rather carelessly pulled down. She had not put on any more powder since she left the shop where she ate her solitary tea. The pearls her husband had given her on their marriage hung loose round her now rather thinner throat, slipping in the V of the pink wool jumper her sister knitted last autumn as they sat round the fire. Mrs. Drover's most normal expression was one of controlled worry, but of assent.[11] Since the birth of the third of her little boys, attended by a quite serious illness, she had had an <u>intermittent</u> muscular flicker to the left of her mouth, but in spite of this she could always sustain a manner that was at once energetic and calm. **D**

80

Turning from her own face as <u>precipitately</u> as she had gone to meet it, she went to the chest where the things were, unlocked it, threw up the lid and knelt to search. But as rain began to come crashing down she could not keep from looking over her shoulder at the stripped bed on which the letter lay. Behind the

90

---

9. *Contemptuous* means "scornful."
10. *Stealthily* means "secretly."
11. Here, *assent* means "resignation."

Vocabulary

intermittent (in′tər mit′ənt) *adj.* alternately starting and stopping
precipitately (pri sip′ə tət lē) *adv.* without deliberation; hastily; abruptly

---

Keep This in Mind

Use these symbols to record your reactions as you read.

? I have a question about something here.

! This really caught my attention.

★ This information is important.

Think It Over

Infer Writers don't always tell you everything directly. Sometimes they give you clues, and you have to **infer,** or guess, what those clues mean. Reread the letter to Mrs. Drover. What can you infer about the person who sent it? Check all statements below that apply. **C**

❏ The person disapproves of the war.

❏ The person knows Mrs. Drover from a long time ago.

❏ The person has been keeping track of Mrs. Dover for some time.

Predict Use story clues and your own experiences to **predict,** or guess, what will happen in the story. What do you think Mrs. Drover will do next? Write your prediction on the lines below. **D**

_____

_____

_____

Literary Element

🗝 **Suspense** The suspense is building because Mrs. Drover feels threatened by the mysterious letter. Take another look at this paragraph. How does the church clock's striking the hour contribute to the suspense? Write your thoughts here. **E**

_____

_____

_____

Reading Focus **Monitor Comprehension** Take time to think about whether you understand what you're reading. Skim back over this paragraph. Who are the young girl and the soldier? When does this scene take place? Write your answers below. **F**

_____

_____

_____

_____

🗝 **Infer** Reread the boxed dialogue. What is the young girl supposed to wait for? Why? Write your answer below. **G**

_____

_____

blanket of rain the clock of the church that still stood struck six—with rapidly heightening apprehension she counted each of the slow strokes. "The hour arranged . . . My God," she said, "*what* hour? How should I . . . ? After twenty-five years . . ." **E**

The young girl talking to the soldier in the garden had not 100 ever completely seen his face. It was dark; they were saying good-bye under a tree. Now and then—for it felt, from not seeing him at this intense moment, as though she had never seen him at all—she verified his presence for these few moments longer by putting out a hand, which he each time pressed, without very much kindness, and painfully, on to one of the breast buttons of his uniform. That cut of the button on the palm of her hand was, principally, what she was to carry away. This was so near the end of a leave from France that she could only wish him already gone. It was August 1916.[12] Being not 110 kissed, being drawn away from and looked at intimidated Kathleen till she imagined spectral[13] glitters in the place of his eyes. Turning away and looking back up the lawn she saw, through branches of trees, the drawing-room window alight: she caught a breath for the moment when she could go running back there into the safe arms of her mother and sister, and cry: "What shall I do, what shall I do? He has gone." **F**

Hearing her catch her breath, her fiancé said, without feeling: "Cold?"

"You're going away such a long way."

120 "Not so far as you think."

"I don't understand?"

"You don't have to," he said. "You will. You know what we said."

"But that was—suppose you—I mean, suppose."

"I shall be with you," he said, "sooner or later. You won't forget that. You need do nothing but wait." **G**

Only a little more than a minute later she was free to run up the silent lawn. Looking in through the window at her mother and sister, who did not for the moment perceive her, she already felt that unnatural promise drive down between her and the rest 130 of all human kind. No other way of having given herself could

---

12. *August 1916* indicates that this flashback takes place during the First World War.

13. *Spectral* means "ghostly."

have made her feel so apart, lost and foresworn.[14] She could not have plighted a more sinister troth.[15]

Kathleen behaved well when, some months later, her fiancé was reported missing, presumed killed. Her family not only supported her but were able to praise her courage without stint[16] because they could not regret, as a husband for her, the man they knew almost nothing about. They hoped she would, in a year or two, console herself—and had it been only a question of consolation things might have gone much straighter ahead. But her trouble, behind just a little grief, was a complete dislocation from everything. She did not reject other lovers, for these failed to appear: for years she failed to attract men—and with the approach of her thirties she became natural enough to share her family's anxiousness on this score. She began to put herself out, to wonder; and at thirty-two she was very greatly relieved to find herself being courted by William Drover. She married him, and the two of them settled down in this quiet, arboreal[17] part of Kensington:[18] in this house the years piled up, her children were born and they all lived till they were driven out by the bombs of the next war. Her movements as Mrs. Drover were circumscribed,[19] and she dismissed any idea that they were still watched. **H**

Infer What can you infer from the highlighted sentence? Put a check mark next to the correct answer below. **H**

❑ Mrs. Drover hasn't thought about her old fiancé since he was reported missing.

❑ Mrs. Drover wishes she could have married the man she was once engaged to.

❑ Mrs. Drover may never have felt completely separated from her old fiancé.

📖 Reading Check

As things were—dead or living the letter writer sent her only a threat. Unable, for some minutes, to go on kneeling with her back exposed to the empty room, Mrs. Drover rose from the chest to sit on an upright chair whose back was firmly against the wall. The desuetude[20] of her former bedroom, her married London home's whole air of being a cracked cup from which memory, with its reassuring power, had either evaporated or

📖 Reading Check

Step 1 Ask yourself, Have I understood what I've read so far? Did you put a question mark next to anything? If so, choose one or more of these strategies to help answer your questions.

• Reread confusing passages or read them aloud.

• Read on to see whether new story information helps make a passage clear.

• Ask a classmate or a teacher, parent, or other adult for help.

Step 2 When you understand what you've read so far, explain what Mrs. Drover thinks of the man who wrote the letter.

_____

_____

_____

---

14. Here, *foresworn* means "abandoned."
15. *[She . . . troth.]* She could not have pledged herself to a more evil promise.
16. To praise without *stint* is to praise generously and without reservation.
17. *Arboreal* indicates that there were many trees where they lived.
18. *Kensington* is a wealthy district in London.
19. *Circumscribed* means "restricted."
20. *Desuetude* (des′wə to̅o̅d′) means "in a state of disuse."

Understanding Complicated Sentences

Mark the text ⟩ Circle two subjects and underline two main actions in the boxed sentence. (Hint: The colon divides the sentence into two sections.) Then summarize the sentence on the lines below. **I**

_____

_____

_____

_____

Think It Over

Infer What are the circumstances that Mrs. Drover doesn't care to consider? Why doesn't she want to consider them? Write your answer on the lines below. **J**

_____

_____

_____

_____

READ ALOUD

Build Fluency Practice reading aloud the boxed passage until you can read it smoothly, without stumbling over any words. **K**

160 leaked away, made a crisis—and at just this crisis the letter writer had, knowledgeably, struck. The hollowness of the house this evening canceled years on years of voices, habits, and steps. Through the shut windows she only heard rain fall on the roofs around. To rally[21] herself, she said she was in a mood—and for two or three seconds shutting her eyes, told herself that she had imagined the letter. But she opened them—there it lay on the bed.

On the supernatural side of the letter's entrance she was not permitting her mind to dwell. Who, in London, knew she meant to call at the house today? Evidently, however, this had been known.

170 The caretaker, _had_ he come back, had had no cause to expect her: he would have taken the letter in his pocket, to forward it, at his own time, through the post. **I** There was no other sign that the caretaker had been in—but, if not? Letters dropped in at doors of deserted houses do not fly or walk to tables in halls. They do not sit on the dust of empty tables with the air of certainty that they will be found. There is needed some human hand—but nobody but the caretaker had a key. Under circumstances she did not care to consider, a house can be entered without a key. **J** It was possible that she was not alone now. She might be being

180 waited for, downstairs. Waited for—until when? Until "the hour arranged." At least that was not six o'clock: six has struck.

She rose from the chair and went over and locked the door.

The thing was, to get out. To fly? No, not that: she had to catch her train. As a woman whose utter dependability was the keystone of her family life she was not willing to return to the country, to her husband, her little boys and her sister, without the objects she had come up to fetch. Resuming work at the chest she set about making up a number of parcels in a rapid, fumbling-decisive way.

These, with her shopping parcels, would be too much to carry;

190 these meant a taxi—at the thought of the taxi her heart went up and her normal breathing resumed. I will ring up the taxi now; the taxi cannot come too soon: I shall hear the taxi out there running its engine, till I walk calmly down to it through the hall. **K**

I'll ring up—But no: the telephone is cut off . . . She tugged at a knot she had tied wrong.

The idea of flight . . . He was never kind to me, not really. I don't remember him kind at all. Mother said he never

---

21. Here, _rally_ means "to calm and encourage."

considered me. He was set on me, that was what it was—not love. Not love, not meaning a person well. What did he do, to make me promise like that? I can't remember—But she found that she could.

She remembered with such dreadful acuteness that the twenty-five years since then dissolved like smoke and she instinctively looked for the weal[22] left by the button on the palm of her hand. She remembered not only all that he said and did but the complete suspension of *her* existence during that August week. I was not myself—they all told me so at the time. She remembered—but with one white burning blank as where acid has dropped on a photograph: *under no conditions* could she remember his face.

So, wherever he may be waiting, I shall not know him. You have no time to run from a face you do not expect.

The thing was to get to the taxi before any clock struck what could be the hour. She would slip down the street and round the side of the square to where the square gave on the main road. She would return in the taxi, safe, to her own door, and bring the solid driver into the house with her to pick up the parcels from room to room. The idea of the taxi driver made her decisive, bold: she unlocked her door, went to the top of the staircase and listened down. **L**

She heard nothing—but while she was hearing nothing the *passé*[23] air of the staircase was disturbed by a draft that traveled up to her face. It <u>emanated</u> from the basement: down there a door or window was being opened by someone who chose this moment to leave the house. **M**

The rain had stopped; the pavements steamily shone as Mrs. Drover let herself out by inches from her own front door into the empty street. The unoccupied houses opposite continued to meet her look with their damaged stare. Making towards the thoroughfare and the taxi, she tried not to keep looking behind. Indeed, the silence was so intense—one of those creeks of

200

210

220

230

---

22. A *weal* is a bruise or mark on the skin; a welt.
23. As it is used here, *passé* means "stale."

Vocabulary
emanate (em´ə nāt) *v.* to come forth from a source; issue

Reading Focus

👉 **Predict** Do your predictions from page 35 match what happens at the end of the story? If not, that's okay. Surprising twists make reading fun!

📖 Reading Check

Step 1 After reading, take a few minutes to think about the story. Review your **Foldable** and the passages you marked as you read. Look at the list of characteristics of scary stories that you made in the Connect activity. Then answer this question: How is this story like other scary stories you know? Write your answer below.

_____

_____

_____

_____

Step 2 Do you think the events in this story could really happen? Explain your answer on the lines below.

_____

_____

_____

Hot Words

Mark the text **Choose three words,** either from the underlined vocabulary in the story or from the words you circled as you read. Record them in your **Hot Words Journal** at the back of this book and complete an activity listed there.

London silence exaggerated this summer by the damage of war—that no tread could have gained on hers unheard. Where her street debouched[24] on the square where people went on living, she grew conscious of, and checked, her unnatural pace. Across the open end of the square two buses <u>impassively</u> passed
240 each other: women, a perambulator, cyclists, a man wheeling a barrow signalized, once again, the ordinary flow of life. At the square's most populous corner should be—and was—the short taxi rank. This evening, only one taxi—but this, although it presented its blank rump, appeared already to be alertly waiting for her. Indeed, without looking round the driver started his engine as she panted up from behind and put her hand on the door. As she did so, the clock struck seven. The taxi faced the main road: to make the trip back to her house it would have to turn—she had settled
250 back on the seat and the taxi *had* turned before she, surprised by its knowing movement, recollected that she had not "said where." She leaned forward to scratch at the glass panel that divided the driver's head from her own.

The driver braked to what was almost a stop, turned round and slid the glass panel back: the jolt of this flung Mrs. Drover forward till her face was almost into the glass. Through the aperture[25] driver and passenger, not six inches between them, remained for an eternity eye to eye. Mrs. Drover's mouth hung open for some seconds before she could issue her first scream. After that she
260 continued to scream freely and to beat with her gloved hands on the glass all round as the taxi, accelerating without mercy, made off with her into the hinterland[26] of deserted streets.

Did You Know?
A *perambulator* is a baby carriage.

📖 Reading Check

24. *Debouched* (di boōshd′) means "emerged."
25. An *aperture* (ap′ər chər) is an opening.
26. Here, *hinterland* means "remoteness."

Vocabulary
impassively (im pas′iv lē) *adv.* in an emotionless manner

Going Solo

☞ Predict

Taxi! Taxi! What do you predict will happen to Mrs. Drover after the story ends? Try to come up with three scenarios. Then use your predictions to complete the sentences below in different ways.

1. Mrs. Drover will _____

_____

2. Mrs. Drover will _____

_____

3. Mrs. Drover will _____

_____

Buddy Up

☞ Understanding Complicated Sentences

Making Sense While reading, you practiced finding the subjects and main actions of some long, complicated sentences. Now work with a partner to find the three subjects and three main actions of the sentence in lines 9–11. Write your answers on the lines below.

Subject: _____

Main action: _____

Subject: _____

Main action: _____

Subject: _____

Main action: _____

TeamWork

☞ Infer

1. **What Do You Think?** Review the information you wrote in your **Foldable** as you read the story. With your group, discuss the following questions. Then jot down your answers on the lines below.

Imagine that Mrs. Drover gets back to her family safely. Do you think she'll tell them what happened? Why or why not?

_____

_____

Imagine that the taxi driver won't let Mrs. Drover out of the car. What will she do?

_____

_____

2. **You Look Like You've Seen a Ghost!** With your group, discuss whether the taxi driver is Mrs Drover's former fiancé alive after twenty-five years, her former fiancé come back from the dead, or just a normal taxi driver. Take turns sharing your ideas and be sure to support your ideas with specific details from the story. Summarize your conclusions on the lines below.

_____

_____

_____

_____

Literary Element

← Suspense

When a story is **suspenseful,** you feel nervous about what's going to happen next, especially to a character that you care about. Often the characters in suspenseful stories feel nervous, too, because they know their lives might be about to change in some dramatic way—often for the worse.

Writers produce suspense by creating a threat to the main character and by including mysterious events. Writers usually build suspense throughout a story, saving the most suspenseful moment for just before the climax.

Answer the following questions about the suspenseful characteristics of "The Demon Lover."

1. What is the first thing that makes Mrs. Drover nervous? What increases her nervousness?
2. Who or what threatens Mrs. Drover?
3. What is the most suspenseful moment in the story? When does it occur?
4. Were you nervous for Mrs. Drover as you read the story? Why or why not?

Standardized Test Practice

Choose the best answer for each multiple-choice question. Fill in the circle in the spaces for questions 1 and 2 on the right.

1. Which word best describes the feeling that the setting creates at the beginning of the story?

   A. threatening

   B. wonderful

   C. sorrowful

   D. exciting

2. How does Mrs. Drover act and feel as she leaves her house in search of a taxi?

   A. sad to leave her house

   B. as if she is being pursued

   C. excited to see her former fiancé

   D. as if she has nothing to worry about

Write your answer to open-ended question A in the space provided below.

A. What does Mrs. Drover's reaction to finding the letter suggest about her personality and her way of life? Use details from the story to support your answer.

Multiple-Choice Questions

1. Ⓐ Ⓑ Ⓒ Ⓓ   2. Ⓐ Ⓑ Ⓒ Ⓓ

Open-Ended Question

A. _____

_____

_____

_____

_____

word power

Vocabulary Check

Write the word from the word list that belongs in the blank in each sentence.

prosaic *adj.* commonplace; ordinary

intermittent *adj.* alternately starting and stopping

precipitately *adv.* without deliberation; hastily; abruptly

emanate *v.* to come forth from a source; issue

impassively *adv.* in an emotionless manner

1. When the teacher asked the question, Jill answered _____ because she wanted to show off how much she had studied.

2. The homeless man asked for change, but people passed by _____.

3. I want something interesting for dinner, not _____ meat loaf.

4. As darkness fell, a greenish light began to _____ from the cave.

5. The squeak was hard to find, since it was _____.

GET READY TO READ!

Connect

Ideas Web Have you ever seen people trying to cope with a natural disaster? Think about TV news reports you've watched on weather disasters like hurricanes, tornadoes, snowstorms, or floods. Maybe you've seen movies showing other destructive forces of nature like an invasion of insects or a herd of stampeding animals. How might you cope if you were faced with a natural disaster? Fill out the web below with some ideas.

coping with natural disasters

In this short story, you'll read about a farm family—Margaret, her husband Richard, and her father-in-law Stephen—who face an invasion of locusts.

Did You Know?

Building Background Locusts are flying and hopping insects that belong to the grasshopper family. Locusts terribly damage crops wherever they swarm in search of food. "A Mild Attack of Locusts" takes place on a farm in Africa where maize, or corn, is the main crop.

- In Africa, hungry swarms of locusts have eaten as much as 20,000 tons of grain in just one day—all the grain in fields for miles around.
- Certain kinds of locusts appear in cycles—every seven, thirteen, or seventeen years.
- Locusts pose a huge threat to farmers in many places around the world.

Reason to Read

Setting a Purpose for Reading Read to find out how Margaret and her family face the threat of locusts on their African farm.

word power

Vocabulary Preview

Read the definitions of these words from "A Mild Attack of Locusts." Use the pronunciation guides to help you say each word aloud. As you read the story, use context clues to help unlock the meaning of these words and any others you don't know.

acrid (ak′ rid) *adj.* burning or biting to the taste or smell; p. 42

emphatically (em fat′ ik ə lē) *adv.* strongly or forcefully; p. 45

irremediable (ir′ i mē′ dē ə bəl) *adj.* not able to be fixed or cured; p. 45

imminent (im′ ə nənt) *adj.* about to happen; p. 49

Hot Words Journal

As you read, circle words that you find interesting or that you don't understand. Later you may add them to your **Hot Words Journal** at the back of this book.

What You'll Learn

Key Goals In this lesson, you will learn these key skills, strategies, and concepts.

- **Reading Focus:** Visualize
- **Think It Over:** Draw Conclusions
- **Literary Element:** Imagery
- **Reading Coach:** Reading Dialogue

A Mild Attack of Locusts

Doris Lessing

The rains that year were good; they were coming nicely just as the crops needed them—or so Margaret gathered[1] when the men said they were not too bad. She never had an opinion of her own on matters like the weather, because even to know about what seems a simple thing like the weather needs experience. Which Margaret had not got. The men were Richard her husband, and old Stephen, Richard's father, a farmer from way back; and these two might argue for hours whether the rains were ruinous or just ordinarily exasperating. Margaret had been on the farm three years. She still did not understand how they did not go bankrupt altogether, when the men never had a good word for the weather, or the soil, or the government. But she was getting to learn the language. Farmers' language. And they neither went bankrupt nor got very rich. They jogged along doing comfortably.

10

Their crop was maize. Their farm was three thousand acres on the ridges that rise up toward the Zambesi escarpment[2]—high, dry windswept country, cold and dusty in winter, but now, in the wet season, steamy with the heat rising in wet soft waves off miles of green foliage. Beautiful it was, with the sky blue and brilliant halls of air, and the bright green folds and hollows of country beneath, and the mountains lying sharp and bare twenty miles off across the rivers. The sky made her eyes ache; she was not used to it. **A** One does not look so much at the sky in the city she came from. So that evening when Richard said: "The government is sending out warnings that locusts are expected, coming down from the breeding grounds up North," **B** her instinct was to look about her at the trees. Insects—swarms of them—horrible! But Richard and the old man had raised their eyes and were looking up over the mountain. "We haven't had locusts in seven years," they said. "They go in cycles, locusts do." And then: "There goes our crop for this season!"

20

30

---

1. As it is used here, *gathered* means "concluded."
2. The *Zambesi escarpment* is a series of steep cliffs along the Zambesi River in southern Africa.

Reading Focus

← **Visualize** You'll get much more out of a short story if you picture the people, places, and events as you read.

Mark the text → Underline the words and phrases in the boxed text that help you visualize the farm. Then describe the farm in your own words. **A**

Model: *The huge farm looks really beautiful. The sky is so blue, and the plants are so green.*

Reading Coach

← **Reading Dialogue** The conversation, or spoken words, in a story is called **dialogue.** Quotation marks show the exact words that the characters say. To tell who's speaking, see if a character's name appears either before or after the words enclosed in quotation marks. Look at the highlighted lines. Which character is speaking? **B**

_____

What important event does the character describe?

_____

Literary Element

➜ **Imagery** As you read, notice words and phrases that appeal to the sense of sight, hearing, taste, smell, or touch. Such descriptive language is called **imagery.** Underline  the description that helps you clearly see that the locusts have arrived. What phrase do you think is most vivid? **C**

Think It Over

➜ **Draw Conclusions** When you draw a conclusion, you put details together to make a general statement about something. From the actions described in this paragraph, what conclusion can you draw about the situation now facing the people on the farm? **D**

Keep This in Mind

Use these symbols to record your reactions as you read.

? I have a question about something here.

! This really caught my attention.

★ This information is important.

But they went on with the work of the farm just as usual until one day they were coming up the road to the homestead for the midday break, when old Stephen stopped, raised his finger and pointed: "Look, look, there they are!"

Out ran Margaret to join them, looking at the hills. Out came the servants from the kitchen. They all stood and gazed. Over the rocky levels of the mountain was a streak of rust-colored air.
40 Locusts. There they came. **C**

At once Richard shouted at the cookboy. Old Stephen yelled at the houseboy. The cookboy ran to beat the old ploughshare[3] hanging from a tree branch, which was used to summon the laborers at moments of crisis. The houseboy ran off to the store to collect tin cans, any old bit of metal. The farm was ringing with the clamor of the gong; and they could see the laborers come pouring out of the compound, pointing at the hills and shouting excitedly. Soon they had all come up to the house, and Richard and old Stephen were giving them orders—Hurry, hurry, hurry. **D**

50 And off they ran again, the two white men with them, and in a few minutes Margaret could see the smoke of fires rising from all around the farmlands. Piles of wood and grass had been prepared there. There were seven patches of bared soil, yellow and oxblood color and pink, where the new mealies[4] were just showing, making a film of bright green; and around each drifted up thick clouds of smoke. They were throwing wet leaves on to the fires now, to make it <u>acrid</u> and black. Margaret was watching the hills. Now there was a long, low cloud advancing, rust-color still, swelling forward and out as she looked. The telephone was
60 ringing. Neighbors—quick, quick, there come the locusts. Old Smith had had his crop eaten to the ground. Quick, get your fires started. For of course, while every farmer hoped the locusts would overlook his farm and go on to the next, it was only fair to warn each other; one must play fair. Everywhere, fifty miles over the countryside, the smoke was rising from myriads[5] of fires.

---

3. A *ploughshare* is the cutting blade of a plow.
4. A *mealie* is a corn plant.
5. *Myriads* means "a great or countless number."

Vocabulary
acrid (ak´rid) *adj.* burning or biting to the taste or smell

Margaret answered the telephone calls, and between calls she stood watching the locusts. The air was darkening. A strange darkness, for the sun was blazing—it was like the darkness of a veldt[6] fire, when the air gets thick with smoke. The sunlight comes down distorted,[7] a thick, hot orange. Oppressive it was, too, with the heaviness of a storm. The locusts were coming fast. Now half the sky was darkened. Behind the reddish veils in front, which were the advance guards of the swarm, the main swarm showed in dense black cloud, reaching almost to the sun itself. **E**

Margaret was wondering what she could do to help. She did not know. Then up came old Stephen from the lands. "We're finished, Margaret, finished! Those beggars can eat every leaf and blade off the farm in half an hour! And it is only early afternoon—if we can make enough smoke, make enough noise till the sun goes down, they'll settle somewhere else perhaps. . . ." And then: "Get the kettle going. It's thirsty work, this."

So Margaret went to the kitchen, and stoked up the fire, and boiled the water. Now, on the tin roof of the kitchen she could hear the thuds and bangs of falling locusts, or a scratching slither as one skidded down. Here were the first of them. From down on the lands came the beating and banging and clanging of a hundred gasoline cans and bits of metal. Stephen impatiently waited while one gasoline can was filled with tea, hot, sweet and orange-colored, and the other with water. **F** In the meantime, he told Margaret about how twenty years back he was eaten out, made bankrupt, by the locust armies. And then, still talking, he hoisted up the gasoline cans, one in each hand, by the wood pieces set cornerwise across each, and jogged off down to the road to the thirsty laborers. By now the locusts were falling like hail on to the roof of the kitchen. It sounded like a heavy storm. Margaret looked out and saw the air dark with a crisscross of the insects, and she set her teeth and ran out into it—what the men could do, she could. Overhead the air was thick, locusts everywhere. The locusts were flopping against her, and she brushed them off, heavy red-brown creatures, looking at her with their beady old-men's eyes while they

70

80

90

100

---

6. The *veldt* (**velt, felt**) is a rolling grassland region in southern Africa that has scattered bushes and trees.

7. Here, *distorted* means "unnatural in appearance."

Reading Focus

← **Visualize** Picture the scene described here. Think about what the sky looks like and where the locusts are located. In the frame below, quickly sketch what you see in your mind's eye. **E**

Your Sketch

Literary Element

← **Imagery** In the boxed text, *Mark the text* circle the sound imagery— the words that describe noises. What things are making all this noise? Write your answer below. **F**

_____

_____

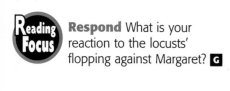

Respond What is your reaction to the locusts' flopping against Margaret? **G**

📖 Reading Check

Step 1 Ask yourself how well you understand what you have read so far. These strategies can help you answer questions you still have.

- Reread confusing passages or read them aloud.
- Think about connections between the story and your own life.
- Ask a classmate or a teacher, parent, or other adult for help.

Step 2 When you understand what you have read, write a one-sentence summary of the story to this point on the lines below.

READ ALOUD

Build Fluency Find a quiet place and practice reading the boxed passage aloud. Reread the passage several times until you can read it smoothly. **H**

---

clung with hard, serrated[8] legs. She held her breath with disgust and ran through into the house. **G** There it was even more like being in a heavy storm. The iron roof was reverberating,[9] and the clamor of iron from the lands was like thunder. Looking out, all the trees were queer and still, clotted with insects, their boughs weighed to the ground. The earth seemed to be moving, locusts crawling everywhere, she could not see the lands at all, so thick was the swarm. Toward the mountains it was like looking into driving rain—even as she watched, the sun was blotted out with a 110 fresh onrush of them. It was a half-night, a perverted blackness. Then came a sharp crack from the bush—a branch had snapped off. Then another. A tree down the slope leaned over and settled heavily to the ground. Through the hail of insects a man came running. More tea, more water was needed. She supplied them. She kept the fires stoked and filled cans with liquid, and then it was four in the afternoon, and the locusts had been pouring across overhead for a couple of hours. Up came old Stephen again, crunching locusts underfoot with every step, locusts clinging all over him; he was cursing and swearing, banging with his old hat at 120 the air. At the doorway he stopped briefly, hastily pulling at the clinging insects and throwing them off, then he plunged into the locust-free living room.

"All the crops finished. Nothing left," he said.

📖 Reading Check

But the gongs were still beating, the men still shouting, and Margaret asked: "Why do you go on with it, then?"

"The main swarm isn't settling. They are heavy with eggs. They are looking for a place to settle and lay. If we can stop the main body settling on our farm, that's everything. If they get a chance to lay their eggs, we are going to have everything eaten flat with 130 hoppers[10] later on." He picked a stray locust off his shirt and split it down with his thumbnail—it was clotted inside with eggs. "Imagine that multiplied by millions. You ever seen a hopper swarm on the march? Well, you're lucky." **H**

---

8. *Serrated* means "jagged" or "saw-toothed."
9. *Reverberating* means "echoing."
10. *Hoppers* are baby locusts.

Margaret thought an adult swarm was bad enough. Outside now the light on the earth was a pale, thin yellow, clotted with moving shadows; the clouds of moving insects thickened and lightened like driving rain. Old Stephen said, "They've got the wind behind them, that's something."

"Is it very bad?" asked Margaret fearfully, and the old man said emphatically: "We're finished. This swarm may pass over, but once they've started, they'll be coming down from the North now one after another. And then there are the hoppers—it might go on for two or three years."   140

Margaret sat down helplessly, and thought: Well, if it's the end, it's the end. What now? We'll all three have to go back to town. . . . But at this, she took a quick look at Stephen, the old man who had farmed forty years in this country, been bankrupt twice, and she knew nothing would make him go and become a clerk in the city. Yet her heart ached for him, he looked so tired, the worry lines deep from nose to mouth. Poor old   150 man. . . . He had lifted up a locust that had got itself somehow into his pocket, holding it in the air by one leg. "You've got the strength of a steel-spring in those legs of yours," he was telling the locust, good-humoredly. Then, although he had been fighting locusts, squashing locusts, yelling at locusts, sweeping them in great mounds into the fires to burn for the last three hours, nevertheless he took this one to the door and carefully threw it out to join its fellows, as if he would rather not harm a hair of its head. This comforted Margaret; all at once she felt irrationally cheered. ■ She remembered it was not the first time   160 in the last three years the man had announced their final and irremediable ruin.

"Get me a drink, lass," he then said, and she set the bottle of whisky by him.

In the meantime, out in the pelting storm of insects, her husband was banging the gong, feeding the fires with leaves, the insects clinging to him all over—she shuddered. "How can you bear to let them touch you?" she asked. He looked at her, disapproving. She felt suitably humble—just as she had when he

---

Vocabulary

emphatically (em fat′ ik ə lē) *adv.* strongly or forcefully
irremediable (ir′ i mē′ dē ə bəl) *adj.* not able to be fixed or cured

Word Power

Using Reference Books
Reference books can help you learn the meaning of underlined vocabulary words and other words from the story that you might not know.

- Look in a **dictionary** for definitions and sample sentences.

- Look in a **thesaurus** for synonyms. Seeing words with similar meanings may help you to understand the unfamiliar word.

Think It Over

Draw Conclusions
Mark the text Underline details in the boxed text that explain how Stephen treats the locust that he takes out of his pocket. What conclusion can you draw from these details? Check the best answer. ■

❑ Stephen is kind and respects the locust's strength.

❑ Stephen holds a grudge against this locust for being his lifelong enemy.

❑ Stephen is glad to get rid of this locust and watch it fly away.

Reading Focus

Monitor Comprehension
Do you understand why Margaret is crying? Reread the highlighted text. Then list four farming problems that make Margaret feel so sad. **J**

Reading Focus

🔑 **Visualize** Skim back over this paragraph. What descriptive phrases create the clearest pictures in your mind? Write two of these phrases on the lines below. **K**

Reading Coach

🔑 **Reading Dialogue** When two or more people are speaking, an indented line and quotation marks help you see when the speaker changes. Place a check next to each indented line in the boxed text to show the change of speakers. **L**

Mark the text

170 had first taken a good look at her city self, hair waved and golden, nails red and pointed. Now she was a proper farmer's wife, in sensible shoes and a solid skirt. She might even get to letting locusts settle on her—in time.

Having tossed back a whisky or two, old Stephen went back into the battle, wading now through glistening brown waves of locusts.

Five o'clock. The sun would set in an hour. Then the swarm would settle. It was as thick overhead as ever. The trees were ragged mounds of glistening brown.

180 Margaret began to cry. It was all so hopeless—if it wasn't a bad season, it was locusts; if it wasn't locusts, it was army-worm[11] or veldt fires. Always something. **J** The rustling of the locust armies was like a big forest in the storm; their settling on the roof was like the beating of the rain; the ground was invisible in a sleek, brown, surging tide—it was like being drowned in locusts, submerged by the loathsome brown flood. It seemed as if the roof might sink in under the weight of them, as if the door might give in under their pressure and these rooms fill with them—and it was getting so dark . . . she looked up. The air was thinner;

190 gaps of blue showed in the dark, moving clouds. The blue spaces were cold and thin—the sun must be setting. Through the fog of insects she saw figures approaching. First old Stephen, marching bravely along, then her husband, drawn and haggard with weariness. Behind them the servants. All were crawling all over with insects. The sound of the gongs had stopped. She could hear nothing but the ceaseless rustle of a myriad wings. **K** The two men slapped off the insects and came in.

"Well," said Richard, kissing her on the cheek, "the main swarm has gone over."

200 "For the Lord's sake," said Margaret angrily, still half-crying, "what's here is bad enough, isn't it?" For although the evening air was no longer black and thick, but a clear blue, with a pattern of insects whizzing this way and that across it, everything else—trees, buildings, bushes, earth, was gone under the moving brown masses. **L**

---

11. An *army-worm* is any of various insect larvae that travel in groups and destroy vegetation.

"If it doesn't rain in the night and keep them here—if it doesn't rain and weight them down with water, they'll be off in the morning at sunrise."

"We're bound to have some hoppers. But not the main swarm—that's something."

Margaret roused herself, wiped her eyes, pretended she had not been crying, and fetched them some supper, for the servants were too exhausted to move. She sent them down to the compound to rest.

She served the supper and sat listening. There is not one maize plant left, she heard. Not one. The men would get the planters out the moment the locusts had gone. They must start all over again.

But what's the use of that, Margaret wondered, if the whole farm was going to be crawling with hoppers? But she listened while they discussed the new government pamphlet that said how to defeat the hoppers. You must have men out all the time, moving over the farm to watch for movement in the grass. When you find a patch of hoppers, small lively black things, like crickets, then you dig trenches around the patch or spray them with poison from pumps supplied by the government. The government wanted them to cooperate in a world plan for eliminating this plague forever. You should attack locusts at the source. Hoppers, in short. The men were talking as if they were planning a war, and Margaret listened, amazed. **M**

In the night it was quiet; no sign of the settled armies outside, except sometimes a branch snapped, or a tree could be heard crashing down.

Margaret slept badly in the bed beside Richard, who was sleeping like the dead, exhausted with the afternoon's fight. In the morning she woke to yellow sunshine lying across the bed—clear sunshine, with an occasional blotch of shadow moving over it. She went to the window. Old Stephen was ahead of her. There he stood outside, gazing down over the bush. And she gazed, astounded—and entranced, much against her will. For it looked as if every tree, every bush, all the earth, were lit with pale flames. The locusts were fanning their wings to free them of the night dews. There was a shimmer of red-tinged gold light everywhere.

Visualize Richard and Stephen discuss the government pamphlet's ideas for battling locusts "as if they were planning a war." Circle the phrases in this paragraph that help you picture a war against the locusts. **M**

Your Notes

Think It Over

Draw Conclusions Use the details in the boxed text to draw conclusions about Margaret's coping skills. How does she manage to deal with the attack of the locusts? Check each answer that applies. **N**

❑ She relies on her family to comfort her.

❑ She accepts her terrible losses.

❑ She appreciates nature's beauty even in disaster.

Reading Focus

Connect Do you know anyone like old Stephen? Explain. **O**

She went out to join the old man, stepping carefully among the insects. They stood and watched. Overhead the sky was blue, blue and clear.

"Pretty," said old Stephen, with satisfaction.

Well, thought Margaret, we may be ruined, we may be bankrupt, but not everyone has seen an army of locusts fanning

250 their wings at dawn. **N**

Over the slopes, in the distance, a faint red smear showed in the sky, thickened and spread. "There they go," said old Stephen. "There goes the main army, off south."

And now from the trees, from the earth all round them, the locusts were taking wing. They were like small aircraft, maneuvering for the take-off, trying their wings to see if they were dry enough. Off they went. A reddish brown steam was rising off the miles of bush, off the lands, the earth. Again the sunlight darkened.

260 And as the clotted branches lifted, the weight on them lightening, there was nothing but the black spines of branches, trees. No green left, nothing. All morning they watched, the three of them, as the brown crust thinned and broke and dissolved, flying up to mass with the main army, now a brownish-red smear in the southern sky. The lands which had been filmed with green, the new tender mealie plants, were stark and bare. All the trees stripped. A devastated landscape. No green, no green anywhere.

By midday the reddish cloud had gone. Only an occasional

270 locust flopped down. On the ground were the corpses and the wounded. The African laborers were sweeping these up with branches and collecting them in tins.

"Ever eaten sun-dried locust?" asked old Stephen. "That time twenty years ago, when I went broke, I lived on mealie meal and dried locusts for three months. They aren't bad at all—rather like smoked fish, if you come to think of it." **O**

But Margaret preferred not even to think of it.

After the midday meal the men went off to the lands. Everything was to be replanted. With a bit of luck another swarm

280 would not come traveling down just this way. But they hoped it would rain very soon, to spring some new grass, because the cattle would die otherwise—there was not a blade of grass left on

the farm. As for Margaret, she was trying to get used to the idea of three or four years of locusts. Locusts were going to be like bad weather, from now on, always <u>imminent</u>. She felt like a survivor after war—if this devastated and mangled countryside was not ruin, well, what then was ruin?

But the men ate their supper with good appetites.

"It could have been worse," was what they said. "It could be much worse."

290

Reading Check

Reading Check

Step 1 Take a few moments to think about the story. Review your notes and any passages you marked. Think about what Margaret's husband and father-in-law say at the end of the story about the invasion of locusts: "It could be much worse." How have the two farmers faced this disaster of nature?

_____

_____

_____

_____

_____

Step 2 Now think about your own life. How would you cope if a natural disaster struck your community?

_____

_____

_____

_____

Hot Words

Choose three words, either from the underlined vocabulary in the story or from the words you circled as you read. Record them in your **Hot Words Journal** at the back of this book and complete an activity listed there.

Vocabulary
imminent (im′ ə nənt) *adj.* about to happen

Reading WrapUp

Going Solo

← Reading Dialogue

Imagine That The story ends with Richard and Stephen's short dialogue sizing up the damage of the locust attack. What do you think Margaret would say if she were to add her own remarks to the conversation? Write three or four lines of her dialogue from a conversation you imagine. Remember to use quotation marks to show Margaret's exact spoken words.

_____

_____

_____

_____

Buddy Up

← Visualize

1. Painting with Words Colorful details in the story help you picture the locusts' movements. With a partner, find at least three details that make you clearly see the locusts in action. Write those details on the lines below.

_____

_____

_____

2. Picture Perfect Imagine that you and a partner are photographers who work for a newspaper in Africa. Your job is to take three snapshots of the locust attack described in the story. With a partner, choose three vivid moments from the story that you both can picture as interesting photos. Describe the subjects of your photos on the lines below.

_____

_____

_____

_____

TeamWork

← Draw Conclusions

1. Clue Hunt By the end of the story, you might draw the conclusion that Margaret has adjusted to farm life. With a small group, search for clues throughout the story that show she has taken steps to make this adjustment. Summarize your group's clues on the lines below.

_____

_____

_____

_____

_____

_____

2. Survival Tips In a small group, take turns telling one conclusion each of you has drawn about how to survive a locust attack. Remember to form a general statement based on details from the story. Then work together to write your conclusions down as part of a survival guide.

_____

_____

_____

_____

_____

_____

Standardized Test Practice

Choose the best answer for each multiple-choice question. Fill in the circle in the spaces for questions 1 and 2 on the right.

1. How do the farmers first become aware that the locusts are coming?
    A. They notice the sky darken above the mountains.
    B. They smell smoke from the fires of nearby farms.
    C. They hear the warnings sent out by the government.
    D. They listen to the alarm of a cookboy beating a gong.

2. What jobs does Margaret do to help the farmers during the invasion of locusts?
    A. She collects cans and finds bits of metal.
    B. She stokes the fire and fills cans with water and tea.
    C. She gathers piles of wood and looks for wet leaves.
    D. She digs trenches and sprays insect poison.

Write your answer to open-ended question A in the space provided below.

A. Why is Margaret more upset than the farmers over the destruction caused by the locusts? Use details from the story to support your answer.

Multiple-Choice Questions

1. Ⓐ Ⓑ Ⓒ Ⓓ   2. Ⓐ Ⓑ Ⓒ Ⓓ

Open-Ended Question

A. _____

_____

_____

_____

_____

 **Vocabulary Check**

From the word list, write the word that belongs in the blank in each sentence.

acrid *adj.* burning or biting to the taste or smell

emphatically *adv.* strongly or forcefully

irremediable *adj.* not able to be fixed or cured

imminent *adj.* about to happen

1. The smoky oak logs created a sharp, _____ odor.

2. After the stream became polluted, the damaging effects on wildlife were _____.

3. From the dark skies and high winds, we knew a storm was _____.

4. During her speech, the mayor spoke _____ about her plans to improve the schools.

Reading *Poetry*

It would be hard to think of an experience or an event that poetry can't describe. First love? Lost love? The death of a president? The death of a pet mouse? The beauty of a sunset? The hard life of a city slum? The horror of war? The fragrance of homemade bread? You name it; poetry will have the right words for it.

Poetry is unlike the **prose** you normally read and speak because it is written in lines. You can identify a poem in print just by looking at the shape it makes on the page.

Mark the text Poets choose words carefully to fit meaning, rhythm, and rhyme. Circle the words in parentheses that you think Alexander Pope might have used in these lines from "An Essay on Criticism."

True ease in writing comes from (*hard work / art / practice*), not chance,

As those move easiest who have learned to (*dance / fence / glance*).

'Tis not enough no harshness gives (*insult / disrespect / offense*),

The (*meaning / sound / thought*) must seem an echo to the sense.

Why Read Poetry?

Poems can be surprising and delightful, so you can read them to have fun. Poems can create new experiences, so you can read them to learn about the world. Poems can show new ways to look at something, so you can read them to gain insight.

Poems can create interesting sounds, so you can read them to enjoy their music. Poems can talk about things that are hard to express in words, so you can read them to stir thought. Poetry can have a power that ordinary language simply doesn't have.

What's the Plan?

Poetry is different from **prose** in several ways.

- Poetry looks different. It can have short **lines** or long lines—it doesn't keep going all the way to the margin. It can have groupings of lines called **stanzas.** Stanzas group ideas together, something like paragraphs do in prose.

- Poetry uses sound more than prose does. Many poems have **rhythm**—a pattern of beats, or stressed syllables. Some poems have **rhyme**—repeated sounds at the ends of words.

- Poetry uses more imagery than most prose does. **Imagery** is language that helps readers see, hear, feel, smell, and taste the things a poem describes.

Poetry and prose are also alike in some ways. Both often have a **theme,** or main message, such as an idea about life or a way of seeing something.

What Do I Look For?

Many poems share the features shown here in Aphra Behn's "On Her Loving Two Equally."

The **speaker** is the voice that tells the poem. This may or may not be the poet.

Stanzas divide many poems into groups of lines, much the way paragraphs divide prose.

Inversion is a reversal of the word order you would normally expect. "Is" would normally come before "present." Poets use inversion to maintain a pattern of rhyme or rhythm.

A **rhyme scheme** is a regular pattern of end rhymes within a poem. Here each stanza concludes with two consecutive lines that rhyme, known as a **rhyming couplet.**

Mark the text **Find it!** Circle three rhyming couplets in the poem. You can include couplets that almost rhyme.

On Her Loving Two Equally

Aphra Behn

How strong does my passion flow,
Divided equally twixt two?
Damon had ne'er subdued my heart
Had not Alexis took his part;
5 Nor could Alexis powerful prove,
Without my Damon's aid, to gain my love.

When my Alexis present is,
Then I for Damon sigh and mourn;
But when Alexis I do miss,
10 Damon gains nothing but my scorn.
But if it chance they both are by,
For both alike I languish, sigh, and die.

Cure then, thou mighty wingéd god,
This restless fever in my blood;
15 One golden-pointed dart take back:
But which, O Cupid, wilt thou take?
If Damon's, all my hopes are crossed;
Or that of my Alexis, I am lost.

How Do I Read It?

These **reading strategies** will be especially useful when you read poetry.

Visualize: Many poems contain rich visual images. Use your imagination to create pictures in your mind as you read.

Clarify: Some poems are like puzzles. Part of the fun comes from working out difficult passages. If you get stuck, see if a friend or a teacher can help.

Evaluate: Did you enjoy the poem? What did you think of the poet's language, images, and ideas? Poems should make you think. Don't be afraid to form opinions about what you read.

Reread: Good poems should be savored. With every reading you can find something new and interesting.

For more information on **reading strategies,** see pages 216–222 in the **Reading Handbook.**

Read the poems that follow. Be sure to

- learn to appreciate the **literary elements** and the **author's plan**
- use **reading strategies** to help you get the most from your reading

Connect

Anticipation Guide Sometimes people want more money than they could ever use and will do anything to get still more. Wanting money this strongly is called greed. Read the following statements about money and greed. Put a check mark in front of the statements you agree with.

❏ Greed makes people act mean and selfish.

❏ If someone you don't know well says, "Trust me with your money," you should do so.

❏ Having a lot of money is always a good thing.

❏ If you have a lot of money, you should help out your friends.

With a small group, discuss the reasons why you either do or do not agree with each statement.

In this poem, you'll find out how money and greed influence the actions of three men.

Did You Know?

Building Background In *The Canterbury Tales*, twenty-nine people meet by chance and decide to travel together. It is the 1300s, and they are all traveling to a town called Canterbury to visit a holy shrine. They first run into one another at a tavern. At that time, a tavern was part of an inn, or hotel, where people stopped for food and drink and to spend the night.

The innkeeper suggests that it would be a good idea to have a storytelling contest. He says that each traveler should tell a good story to pass the time while traveling. He will later judge who tells the best tale.

On the following pages, you will be reading "The Pardoner's Tale." You've probably never heard of a pardoner. In those days a pardoner was a church representative who could forgive people their sins in exchange for a donation to charity. Some pardoners (like this one) were corrupt and greedy and kept the donated money for themselves. They would even "sell" pardons in order to make money! That makes this pardoner's tale seem pretty hypocritical. His story is a sermon teaching that it's wrong to love money too much. He tells his listeners that his tale gives a lesson on how "Greed is the root of all evil."

As "The Pardoner's Tale" begins, three evil men (called rioters) are in a tavern talking to a serving boy. Someone has just died, and the men want to know who it was. The people in the tavern speak of Death as if death were a real person. They call Death a "thief" because he has stolen the lives of so many people.

word power

Vocabulary Preview

Read the definitions of these words from "The Pardoner's Tale." Use the pronunciation guides to help you say each word aloud. As you read the poem, use context clues to help unlock the meaning of these words and any others you don't know.

spry (sprī) *adj.* lively; agile; p. 56

adversary (ad′vər ser′ē) *n.* opponent; enemy; p. 56

prudent (pro͞od′ənt) *adj.* cautious; careful; p. 62

gratify (grat′ə fī′) *v.* to satisfy; give in to; p. 64

tarry (tar′ē) *v.* to delay in doing something, especially in coming or going; p. 66

deftly (deft′lē) *adv.* quickly and skillfully; nimbly; p. 66

saunter (sôn′tər) *v.* to walk at a leisurely pace; stroll; p. 68

transcend (tran send′) *v.* to go beyond; exceed; p. 68

Hot Words Journal

As you read, circle words that you find interesting or that you don't understand. Later, you may add them to your **Hot Words Journal** at the back of this book.

Reason to Read

Setting a Purpose for Reading Read to find out what happens when three men who are out looking for Death discover a pile of gold instead—and become greedy for more.

 Use the following **Foldable** to track what happens in the tale.

1. Place a sheet of paper in front of you so that the short side is at the top. Fold the paper into thirds from top to bottom.

2. Turn the paper horizontally. Then unfold the paper and draw lines along the folds.

3. Label the first column **Introduction (lines 1–50).** Label the second column **Plot: Main Events (lines 51–211).** Label the third column **Conclusion (lines 212–238).**

4. Jot down notes in your **Foldable** as you read. In the **Introduction** column, write notes about the setting and about the characters. In the **Plot** column, note what happens as the three men search for Death. In the **Conclusion** column, record what happens to the three men after they find the money.

What You'll Learn

Key Goals In this lesson, you will learn these key skills, strategies, and concepts.

- **Reading Focus:** Question
- **Think It Over:** Evaluate
- **Reading Coach:** Reading Side Notes

🗝 Reading Side Notes

Notice that sometimes a tiny circle is placed at the end of a word or a line. The circle tells you there's a side note on the right-hand page. That note explains a word's meaning, translates a phrase into modern English, or gives helpful background information. The boldface number before the side note matches the number of the line in which the word or phrase appears.

Read lines 1–5 and use the side notes to help you understand what is happening. Now write answers in your own words to the questions below. **A**

What time is it when the tale begins?

_____

_____

Where are the rioters?

_____

_____

What does the sound of the bell announce?

_____

_____

_____

from The Canterbury Tales
from The Pardoner's Tale

Geoffrey Chaucer

It's of three rioters I have to tell
Who, long before the morning service bell,°
Were sitting in a tavern for a drink.
And as they sat, they heard the hand-bell clink
5 Before a coffin going to the grave;° **A**
One of them called the little tavern-knave°
And said "Go and find out at once—look spry!—
Whose corpse is in that coffin passing by;
And see you get the name correctly too."
10 "Sir," said the boy, "no need, I promise you;
Two hours before you came here I was told.
He was a friend of yours in days of old,
And suddenly, last night, the man was slain,°
Upon his bench, face up, dead drunk again.
15 There came a privy° thief, they call him Death,
Who kills us all round here, and in a breath
He speared him through the heart, he never stirred.
And then Death went his way without a word.
He's killed a thousand in the present plague,°
20 And, sir, it doesn't do to be too vague
If you should meet him; you had best be wary.
Be on your guard with such an adversary,
Be primed to meet him everywhere you go,
That's what my mother said. It's all I know." **B**
25   The publican° joined in with, "By St. Mary,
What the child says is right; you'd best be wary,
This very year he killed, in a large village
A mile away, man, woman, serf at tillage,°
Page in the household, children—all there were.
30 Yes, I imagine that he lives round there.
It's well to be prepared in these alarms,
He might do you dishonor." "Huh, God's arms!"
The rioter said, "Is he so fierce to meet?

Vocabulary

spry (sprī) *adj.* lively; agile
adversary (ad′vər ser′ē) *n.* opponent; enemy

2 long before . . . bell: long before 9 A.M.

4–5 hand-bell . . . grave: During this time, a bell was rung next to the coffin in a funeral procession.

6 tavern-knave: serving boy.

13 slain: killed.

15 privy: secretive.

19 killed . . . plague: In 1348 and 1349, at least a third of the population of England died from the plague called the Black Death.

25 publican: tavernkeeper or innkeeper.

28 tillage: plowing.

Reading Focus

🔑 **Question** Questioning is asking about what you've read. To help you know what's going on in the poem, have a conversation with yourself as you read. Ask yourself questions like these: Is this idea important? Why is this character behaving this way? What could happen because of the way this character is behaving? Answering your questions will make the poem's action and ideas clearer. **B**

Model: *After reading this section, I can ask myself, What's the boy warning the three rioters about? He says that Death has killed a thousand people. He also says that you can meet Death "everywhere you go," so be careful.*

word power

Using Context Clues Try using these strategies to figure out the meaning of new words.

• Look for a synonym or antonym in the nearby text as a clue.

• Look to see if other words or phrases clarify the meaning.

• Check for a description of an action associated with the word.

Think It Over

→ **Evaluate** When you **evaluate** the actions of characters in your reading, you make judgments about them.

Mark the text Underline or highlight the lines in the boxed text that describe the vow the rioters make. Why might this vow not be a good idea? On the lines below, explain your answer. **C**

_____

_____

_____

_____

Keep This in Mind

Write these symbols on the pages to record your reactions as you read.

? I have a question about something here.

! This really caught my attention.

★ This information is important.

I'll search for him, by Jesus, street by street.
35 God's blessed bones! I'll register a vow!
Here, chaps! The three of us together now,
Hold up your hands, like me, and we'll be brothers
In this affair, and each defend the others,
And we will kill this traitor Death, I say!
40 Away with him as he has made away
With all our friends. God's dignity! Tonight!" **C**

    They made their bargain, swore with appetite,
These three, to live and die for one another
As brother-born might swear to his born brother.
45 And up they started in their drunken rage
And made towards this village which the page
And publican had spoken of before.
Many and grisly° were the oaths they swore,
Tearing Christ's blessed body to a shred;°
50 "If we can only catch him, Death is dead!" **D**

    When they had gone not fully half a mile,
Just as they were about to cross a stile,°
They came upon a very poor old man
Who humbly greeted them and thus began,
55 "God look to you, my lords, and give you quiet!"
To which the proudest of these men of riot
Gave back the answer, "What, old fool? Give place!
Why are you all wrapped up except your face?
Why live so long? Isn't it time to die?" **E**

60   The old, old fellow looked him in the eye
And said, "Because I never yet have found,
Though I have walked to India, searching round
Village and city on my pilgrimage,
One who would change his youth to have my age.
65 And so my age is mine and must be still
Upon me, for such time as God may will.

    "Not even Death, alas, will take my life;
So, like a wretched prisoner at strife°
Within himself, I walk alone and wait
70 About the earth, which is my mother's gate,°
Knock-knocking with my staff from night to noon

FOLDABLES
Graphic Organizer

Don't forget about your **Foldable!** You've just finished the introduction (lines 1–50), so now is a good time to jot down notes about the characters, what they're doing, and where the action is taking place. Record these notes in the *Introduction* column of your **Foldable.** **D**

48 grisly: gruesome.

49 Tearing . . . shred: Their swearing included such expressions as "God's arms" (line 32) and "God's blessed bones" (line 35).

52 stile: a stairway used to climb over a wall or fence.

It Over Think

Draw Conclusions Chaucer uses dialogue to help you get to know the characters. Read lines 51–59 and answer this question: What does the conversation between the old man and the three rioters tell you about their personalities? Write your conclusions on the lines below. **E**

Old man:

_____

_____

Three rioters:

_____

_____

68 strife: conflict

70 mother's gate: entrance to the grave.

Hot Words

Mark the text **Choose your own words**
As you read, circle words you find interesting or difficult. You'll come back to these words later.

Reading Focus **Question** Reread the old man's prayer in the boxed text. Whom do you think the old man is addressing? Place a check mark next to the correct answer below. **F**

❏ his mother, who has died

❏ God

❏ the earth

❏ Death

And crying, 'Mother, open to me soon!
Look at me, mother, won't you let me in?
See how I wither, flesh and blood and skin!
75 Alas! When will these bones be laid to rest?
Mother, I would exchange—for that were best—
The wardrobe in my chamber, standing there
So long, for yours! Aye, for a shirt of hair°
To wrap me in!' She has refused her grace,
80 Whence comes the pallor of my withered face. **F**
    "But it dishonored you when you began
To speak so roughly, sir, to an old man,
Unless he had injured you in word or deed.
It says in holy writ, as you may read,
85 'Thou shalt rise up before the hoary° head
And honor it.' **G** And therefore be it said
'Do no more harm to an old man than you,
Being now young, would have another do
When you are old'—if you should live till then.
90 And so may God be with you, gentlemen,
For I must go whither I have to go."
    "By God," the gambler said, "you shan't do so,
You don't get off so easy, by St. John!
I heard you mention, just a moment gone,
95 A certain traitor Death who singles out
And kills the fine young fellows hereabout.
And you're his spy, by God! You wait a bit.
Say where he is or you shall pay for it,
By God and by the Holy Sacrament!
100 I say you've joined together by consent
To kill us younger folk, you thieving swine!"
    "Well, sirs," he said, "if it be your design
To find out Death, turn up this crooked way
Towards that grove, I left him there today
105 Under a tree, and there you'll find him waiting.
He isn't one to hide for all your prating.°
You see that oak? He won't be far to find.
And God protect you that redeemed mankind,
Aye, and amend° you!" Thus that ancient man.

Reading Coach

Reading Side Notes
Read from line 84 to the period in line 86. Use the side note to help you understand the point the old man is trying to get across to the three rioters. Check the box below that best summarizes the old man's message. **G**

❑ Respect your elders.

❑ Grow old with dignity.

78 shirt of hair: usually a rough shirt worn as self-punishment; here, a burial cloth.

85 hoary: whitened with age.

Your Notes

106 prating: chattering; babbling; talking.

109 amend: improve.

Reading Check

Step 1 How well have you understood the poem so far? Have you put question marks next to anything? If so, here are some strategies to help you answer your questions.

• Reread confusing lines or read them aloud.

• Think about connections between the poem and your own life.

• Ask a classmate or a teacher, parent, or other adult for help.

Step 2 Summarize what has happened so far by completing this statement:
Three drunken rioters are warned to be wary of Death. But . . .

_____

_____

_____

_____

_____

_____

Reading Check

110　At once the three young rioters began
　　To run, and reached the tree, and there they found
　　A pile of golden florins° on the ground,
　　New-coined, eight bushels of them as they thought.
　　No longer was it Death those fellows sought,
115　For they were all so thrilled to see the sight,
　　The florins were so beautiful and bright,
　　That down they sat beside the precious pile.
　　The wickedest spoke first after a while.
　　"Brothers," he said, "you listen to what I say.
120　I'm pretty sharp although I joke away.
　　It's clear that Fortune° has bestowed this treasure
　　To let us live in jollity and pleasure.
　　Light come, light go! We'll spend it as we ought.
　　God's precious dignity! Who would have thought
125　This morning was to be our lucky day?
　　　"If one could only get the gold away,
　　Back to my house, or else to yours, perhaps—
　　For as you know, the gold is ours, chaps—
　　We'd all be at the top of fortune, hey?
130　But certainly it can't be done by day.
　　People would call us robbers—a strong gang,
　　So our own property would make us hang.
　　No, we must bring this treasure back by night
　　Some <u>prudent</u> way, and keep it out of sight. **H**
135　And so as a solution I propose
　　We draw for lots and see the way it goes;
　　The one who draws the longest, lucky man,
　　Shall run to town as quickly as he can
　　To fetch us bread and wine—but keep things dark°—
140　While two remain in hiding here to mark
　　Our heap of treasure. If there's no delay,
　　When night comes down we'll carry it away,
　　All three of us, wherever we have planned." **I**

Vocabulary
prudent (pro͞od′ ənt) *adj.* cautious; careful

112 **florins:** coins of the thirteenth century.

121 **Fortune:** fate.

139 **keep things dark:** act in secret; don't give us away.

Think It Over

◆━ **Evaluate** Reread lines 121–134. Review the rioter's statements about having a right to the gold. What kind of person do you think he is? Check the box below that best summarizes his character. **H**

❑ He's realistic and practical.

❑ He's selfish and dishonest.

❑ He's thankful for his good fortune.

Think It Over

Analyze Think about the rioter's plan. Underline the passage that tells how they will decide which "lucky" man gets to go to town. Do you think the one who has to go into town is the lucky one? Write your answer on the lines below. **I**

_____

_____

_____

_____

Reading Focus

Visualize Can you picture what's happening here? Where is the youngest of the three men going? What are the other two men doing? In the frame below, quickly sketch what the characters are doing. **J**

Your Sketch

Reading Focus

Respond What was the first thought that came to you when you read the highlighted lines? **K**

He gathered lots and hid them in his hand
145 Bidding them draw for where the luck should fall.
It fell upon the youngest of them all,
And off he ran at once towards the town.

As soon as he had gone the first sat down
And thus began a parley° with the other:
150 "You know that you can trust me as a brother;
Now let me tell you where your profit lies;
You know our friend has gone to get supplies
And here's a lot of gold that is to be
Divided equally amongst us three.
155 Nevertheless, if I could shape things thus
So that we shared it out—the two of us—
Wouldn't you take it as a friendly act?" **J**

"But how?" the other said. "He knows the fact
That all the gold was left with me and you;
160 What can we tell him? What are we to do?"

"Is it a bargain," said the first, "or no?
For I can tell you in a word or so
What's to be done to bring the thing about."
"Trust me," the other said, "you needn't doubt
165 My word. I won't betray you, I'll be true." **K**

"Well," said his friend, "you see that we are two,
And two are twice as powerful as one.
Now look; when he comes back, get up in fun
To have a wrestle; then, as you attack,
170 I'll up and put my dagger through his back
While you and he are struggling, as in game;
Then draw your dagger too and do the same.
Then all this money will be ours to spend,
Divided equally of course, dear friend.
175 Then we can gratify our lusts and fill
The day with dicing° at our own sweet will."
Thus these two miscreants° agreed to slay
The third and youngest, as you heard me say. **L**

The youngest, as he ran towards the town,
180 Kept turning over, rolling up and down

Vocabulary
gratify (grat′ ə fī′) v. to satisfy; give in to

149 parley (pär′lē): a discussion, especially with an enemy.

Reading Focus

Clarify When you **clarify,** you look at difficult sections of text to clear up what's confusing. Do you understand the plan proposed by the wickedest rioter? To clarify your understanding, fill in the blanks below to outline his plan step-by-step. **L**

1. When the youngest rioter returns from town, one of the other rioters will

_____

_____

2. Then the wickedest rioter will

_____

3. After that, the other rioter will

_____

4. Finally the two will _____

_____

176 dicing: gambling with dice.

177 miscreants (mis′krē ənts): evildoers; villains.

Think It Over

← **Evaluate** At any point in the tale, did you feel sorry for the youngest rioter? What do you think about him now? Complete the sentences below by jotting down your opinions about the youngest rioter. **M**

Earlier in the story, I thought the youngest rioter was

_____

_____

_____

Now, I think the youngest rioter is

_____

_____

_____

_____

Reading Focus

← **Question** What question might you ask the youngest rioter now? **N**

_____

_____

_____

_____

Within his heart the beauty of those bright
New florins, saying, "Lord, to think I might
Have all that treasure to myself alone!
Could there be anyone beneath the throne
185 Of God so happy as I then should be?"
      And so the Fiend,° our common enemy,
Was given power to put it in his thought
That there was always poison to be bought,
And that with poison he could kill his friends.
190 To men in such a state the Devil sends
Thoughts of this kind, and has a full permission
To lure them on to sorrow and perdition;°
For this young man was utterly content
To kill them both and never to repent. **M**
195   And on he ran, he had no thought to <u>tarry</u>,
Came to the town, found an apothecary°
And said, "Sell me some poison if you will,
I have a lot of rats I want to kill
And there's a polecat too about my yard
200 That takes my chickens and it hits me hard;
But I'll get even, as is only right,
With vermin that destroy a man by night."
      The chemist answered, "I've a preparation
Which you shall have, and by my soul's salvation
205 If any living creature eat or drink
A mouthful, ere he has the time to think,
Though he took less than makes a grain of wheat,
You'll see him fall down dying at your feet;
Yes, die he must, and in so short a while
210 You'd hardly have the time to walk a mile,
The poison is so strong, you understand." **N** **O**
      This cursed fellow grabbed into his hand
The box of poison and away he ran
Into a neighboring street, and found a man
215 Who lent him three large bottles. He withdrew
And <u>deftly</u> poured the poison into two.

Vocabulary

tarry (tar′ē) *v.* to delay in doing something, especially in coming or going
deftly (deft′lē) *adv.* quickly and skillfully; nimbly

FOLDABLES
Graphic Organizer

Don't forget about your **Foldable!** Be sure you've added notes to the *Plot: Main Events* column. Now, as you read the rest of the tale, jot down notes in the *Conclusion* column of your **Foldable.** Write what happens after the men find the money. **0**

186 the Fiend: the devil.

192 perdition: damnation.

196 apothecary: (ə poth′ə ker′ē) one who prepares and sells drugs and medicines.

Your Notes

Reading Coach

👉 **Reading Side Notes**
Read lines 229–232 and the side note that goes with line 231. Using the information in the side note, do you think the two rioters suspect anything is in the wine? **P**

He kept the third one clean, as well he might,
For his own drink, meaning to work all night
Stacking the gold and carrying it away.
220 And when this rioter, this devil's clay,
Had filled his bottles up with wine, all three,
Back to rejoin his comrades <u>sauntered</u> he.
　　Why make a sermon of it? Why waste breath?
Exactly in the way they'd planned his death
225 They fell on him and slew him, two to one.
Then said the first of them when this was done,
"Now for a drink. Sit down and let's be merry,
For later on there'll be the corpse to bury."
And, as it happened, reaching for a sup,
230 He took a bottle of poison up
And drank; and his companion, nothing loth,°
Drank from it also, and they perished both. **P**
　　There is, in Avicenna's long relation°
Concerning poison and its operation,
235 Trust me, no ghastlier section to <u>transcend</u>
What these two wretches suffered at their end.
Thus these two murderers received their due,
So did the treacherous young poisoner too.

📖 **Reading Check**

Vocabulary
saunter (sôn′tər) *v.* to walk at a leisurely pace; stroll
transcend (tran send′) *v.* to go beyond; exceed

231 nothing loth: very willingly.

233 Avicenna's (av´ə sen´əz) **long relation:** a medieval book on medicines by the Arab physician Avicenna (980–1037), which contains a chapter on poisons.

📖 Reading Check

Step 1 Now that you've finished reading, take a moment to think about the poem. Look back at the notes you wrote and the lines you marked. Also review your **Foldable.** Think about the characters—what happened to them, and why. Then explain how the old saying "Be careful what you wish for" applies to this tale.

_____

_____

_____

_____

Step 2 Look back at the Connect activity on page 54. After reading this tale, would you change your responses? Explain why or why not.

_____

_____

_____

_____

_____

_____

Hot Words

Choose three words, either from the underlined vocabulary in the story or from the words you circled as you read. Record them in your **Hot Words Journal** at the back of this book and complete an activity listed there.

READING WRAP UP

Going Solo

Reading Side Notes

Translation, Please Find a passage from the poem that has a side note defining or translating one or two words. On the lines below, rewrite the passage using information from the side note. Be sure to identify the line numbers from the poem.

Line(s): _____

Rewrite: _____

_____

_____

Buddy Up

Question

1. Quiz Kids On the lines below, write one question about the setting, the characters, or an event in the poem. Have your partner answer your question. Then answer your partner's question. If either of you needs help finding answers, review your **Foldable** or look back to the story.

_____

_____

2. Breaking News To stay on top of a major news story, news reporters look for answers to important questions. If you were a TV reporter at the scene at the end of "The Pardoner's Tale," what questions would you try to answer for your viewers? With your partner, come up with at least two important questions that a news report should answer. Write your questions here.

_____

_____

_____

_____

TeamWork

Evaluate

1. Pardon Me, Pardoner Discuss the elements of a good story with your group. Do you agree or disagree that the pardoner has told a good story? Write your group's evaluation on the lines below. Be sure to support your opinions.

_____

_____

_____

_____

_____

2. Where Will It End? Look back at the ending of the poem. In your group, discuss whether the poem would be better if it ended at line 232 or whether the last six lines are necessary. On the lines below, write a reason for ending the poem with line 232 and a reason for ending the poem with line 238.

The poem should end with line 232 because

_____

The poem should end with line 232 because

_____

_____

Standardized Test Practice

Choose the best answer for each multiple-choice question. Fill in the circle in the spaces for questions 1 and 2 on the right.

1. What do the first 50 lines of "The Pardoner's Tale" suggest about the character of the three rioters?

   A. They are liars.

   B. They are thieves.

   C. They are drunkards.

   D. They are murderers

2. Which of these does NOT describe how the rioters react to what they find under the oak tree?

   A. They thank God.

   B. They picture a life of ease.

   C. They forget their hunt for Death.

   D. They agree to divide the treasure.

Write your answer to open-ended question A in the space provided below.

A. How does the poem support the moral that "money is the root of all evil"? Use details from the tale to support your answer.

Multiple-Choice Questions

1. Ⓐ Ⓑ Ⓒ Ⓓ   2. Ⓐ Ⓑ Ⓒ Ⓓ

Open-Ended Question

A. _____

_____

_____

_____

word power   **Vocabulary Check**

From the word list, write the word that belongs in the blank in each sentence.

spry *adj.* lively; agile

adversary *n.* opponent; enemy

prudent *adj.* cautious; careful

gratify *v.* to satisfy; give in to

tarry *v.* to delay in doing something, especially in coming or going

deftly *adv.* quickly and skillfully; nimbly

saunter *v.* to walk at a leisurely pace; stroll

transcend *v.* to go beyond; exceed

1. I had to play twice as hard when the pro was my _____ in tennis.

2. It was amazing to watch her make lace; her fingers moved so _____.

3. When the fire alarm sounds, move rapidly. Don't just _____ towards the door.

4. Nothing could ever _____ the thrill he felt when he won a race for the first time.

5. That woman is still active and _____ at ninety years old.

6. She regularly checked her rearview mirror. She was a _____ driver.

7. I'm sure the birthday party I'm planning for my sister will _____ her.

8. If you _____, you'll be late for the meeting.

GET READY TO READ!

Connect

Small Group Work Imagine that you are writing a screenplay and that one of the characters in your movie is Death. Think about how you'd like the character to look and behave. What personality will you give Death? For example, will Death be a leader or a follower? Will Death be a strong, powerful character, or will Death have weaknesses? In a small group, discuss your ideas and give reasons for them. Work together to write a quick character sketch of Death. Then share your character sketch with the class.

In this poem, the speaker tells what he thinks about death as he speaks directly to Death.

Did You Know?

Building Background John Donne was one of a group of seventeenth-century writers known as the metaphysical poets. In the poem you are about to read, "Death Be Not Proud," Donne uses many devices common to metaphysical poetry:

- The poem makes an **argument** that appeals to the intellect as well as the emotions.
- The poem makes striking **comparisons** (for example, between death and sleep).
- The poem is written in a **plain style** that closely resembles the everyday speech of the time.

The death of Donne's wife and the grief that followed inspired Donne to write "Death Be Not Proud." It is one of nineteen poems in *Holy Sonnets,* a work containing Donne's thoughts on immortality and religious faith.

Reason to Read

Setting a Purpose for Reading Read to find out what the speaker thinks of death.

word power

Vocabulary Preview
Read the definitions of these words from "Death Be Not Proud." Use the pronunciation guides to help you say each word aloud. As you read the poem, use context clues to help unlock the meaning of these words and any others you don't know.

proud (proud) *adj.* displaying an extreme sense of superiority; arrogance; p. 73

overthrow (ō´vər thrō´) *v.* to bring about the downfall of another; defeat; p. 73

fate (fāt) *n.* the unavoidable and predetermined cause of everything that happens; destiny; p. 73

chance (chans) *n.* the seemingly accidental reason that things happen; luck; p. 73

eternally (i tur´ nə lē) *adv.* without end; forever; p. 73

Hot Words Journal

As you read, circle words that you find interesting or that you don't understand. Later you may add them to your **Hot Words Journal** at the back of this book.

What You'll Learn

Key Goals In this lesson, you will learn these key skills, strategies, and concepts.

🔑 **Reading Focus:** Monitor Comprehension

🔑 **Reading Coach:** Understanding Old-Fashioned Language

DEATH
BE NOT PROUD

John Donne

Death, be not <u>proud</u>, though some have called thee
Mighty and dreadful, for thou art not so;
For those whom thou think'st thou dost <u>overthrow</u>
Die not, poor Death, nor yet canst thou kill me. **A**
From rest and sleep, which but thy pictures[1] be,
Much pleasure, then from thee much more must flow,
And soonest our best men with thee do go,
Rest of their bones, and soul's delivery.[2]
Thou art slave to <u>fate</u>, <u>chance</u>, kings, and desperate men,
And dost with poison, war, and sickness dwell,
And poppy[3] or charms can make us sleep as well
And better than thy stroke; why swell'st thou then?[4]
One short sleep past, we wake <u>eternally</u>,
And death shall be no more; Death, thou shalt die. **B**

Reading Check

---

1. *Pictures,* or images, of rest and sleep are similar to images of death.
2. *Soul's delivery* likely means "soul's salvation."
3. *Poppy* is a source of opium, which is a narcotic drug that can produce sleep.
4. *Why swell'st thou then?* can be restated as "Why do you swell with pride?"

Vocabulary

proud (proud) *adj.* displaying an extreme sense of superiority; arrogance

overthrow (ō′ vər thrō′) *v.* to bring about the downfall of another; defeat

fate (fāt) *n.* the unavoidable and predetermined cause of everything that happens; destiny

chance (chans) *n.* the seemingly accidental reason that things happen; luck

eternally (i tur′ nə lē) *adv.* without end; forever

Reading Coach

🢒 **Understanding Old-Fashioned Language**
Seventeenth-century poetry reflects the language of the day. Today this language sounds terribly old fashioned, and the ideas in the poems may be hard to understand. Look at **Mark the text** lines 1–4. Cross out words that sound old-fashioned and write in modern words in their place. Read your new version aloud. Is the meaning clearer? **A**

Reading Focus

🢒 **Monitor Comprehension** When you read a poem, especially a short one, read it once from beginning to end. Pay attention to the punctuation. (Don't stop at the end of a line if there is no punctuation mark.) Then read it again slowly. Use footnotes to clarify any words or phrases you don't understand. Think: What does the speaker mean when he says Death is "slave to fate, chance, kings, and desperate men"? **B**

Reading Check

Why does the speaker say that Death should not be proud?

READING WRAPUP

Buddy Up

➤ Understanding Old-Fashioned Language

1. In Plain English As you read "Death Be Not Proud," you practiced replacing old-fashioned words and phrases with modern language in four lines of the poem. Now try this strategy with a partner. Look at lines 9–12. Replace the old-fashioned words with modern language. Then take turns explaining to one another what this section means. Using your own words, write a sentence telling the meaning of the section.

_____

_____

_____

_____

2. Death Be Not . . . With your partner, write a poem in which you speak directly to Death, imitating the old-fashioned language in "Death Be Not Proud." First, discuss a quality of Death that you could use as an adjective to replace "proud" in the title. You might want to look at the character sketch you wrote with your group in the Connect activity on page 72 for ideas. Write the title and the first two lines of your poem on the lines below.

_____

_____

_____

_____

TeamWork

➤ Monitor Comprehension

1. In Sympathy As you read "Death Be Not Proud," you tried to understand what the poem meant. Now discuss that meaning with your group. How does the speaker view Death? In what way could the poem offer comfort to someone who has suffered the loss of a loved one? Work together to write one or two short sentences to answer these questions.

_____

_____

_____

_____

_____

2. Say Anything With your group, arrange your seats in a circle. Have each student read aloud a line of the poem. Then the student to the right says something about the line just read. For example, he or she may ask a question, tell what the line means, talk about the language, or make a response. Other members of the group may then respond if they wish. When you make it all the way through the poem, discuss its theme, or main message. Write the theme here.

Theme: _____

_____

_____

_____

Standardized Test Practice

Choose the best answer for each multiple-choice question. Fill in the circle in the spaces for questions 1 and 2 on the right.

1. How does the speaker feel about Death?
   A. He thinks Death is almighty.
   B. He fears and respects Death.
   C. He does not consider Death powerful.
   D. He believes that Death is the end of all life.

2. To what does the speaker compare Death?
   A. a king
   B. a slave
   C. a flower
   D. a desperate man

Write your answer to open-ended question A in the space provided below.

A. What conflicting views of Death does the speaker present in the poem? Use details from the poem to support your answer.

Multiple-Choice Questions

1. Ⓐ Ⓑ Ⓒ Ⓓ   2. Ⓐ Ⓑ Ⓒ Ⓓ

Open-Ended Question

A. _____

_____

_____

_____

word power

Vocabulary Check

From the word list, write the word that belongs in the blank in each sentence.

proud *adj.* displaying an extreme sense of superiority; arrogance

overthrow *v.* to bring about the downfall of another; defeat

fate *n.* the unavoidable and predetermined cause of everything that happens; destiny

chance *n.* the seemingly accidental reason that things happen; luck

eternally *adv.* without end; forever

1. A small army of rebels banded together to _____ the cruel leader.

2. Romeo and Juliet believed that their love would live _____ and that nothing could ever destroy it.

3. They met by _____ when they both showed up for a job interview at the same time.

4. The woman was too _____ to admit her mistake.

5. He had no choice in the matter; it was his _____ to live in the shadow of his older brother.

Connect

Quickwrite Think about the trophies that are displayed in your school. Do you ever stop to look at them? Can you remember the students who won them—or the achievements the trophies were meant to honor? Do you think you will remember these details five years from now? Ten years from now? How long do you think the trophies will remain displayed? Take a few minutes to jot down answers to these questions on the lines below. Then share your thoughts with a partner.

_____

_____

_____

_____

In this poem, you'll read about the ruins of a statue that Ozymandias, an ancient ruler, once built to honor himself.

Did You Know?

Building Background *Ozymandias* (ō′ zi man′ dē əs) is the Greek name for Ramses II—the pharaoh, or ruler of Egypt, for much of the thirteenth century B.C. A powerful ruler, Ramses led his armies to several victories and had many temples, monuments, and huge statues of himself built in his honor throughout Egypt. One of these statues, according to one ancient historian, was the largest in Egypt. In the poem you are about to read, Percy Bysshe Shelley writes about the remains of this statue.

Reason to Read

Setting a Purpose for Reading Read to find out how time has destroyed the statue of a once-powerful ruler.

word power

Vocabulary Preview
Read the definitions of these words from "Ozymandias." Use the pronunciation guides to help you say each word aloud. As you read the poem, use context clues to help unlock the meaning of these words and any others you don't know.

vast (vast) *adj.* very large; covering a great space

visage (viz′ ij) *n.* face; outward appearance

sneer (snēr) *n.* a facial expression showing disapproval or contempt

colossal (kə los′ əl) *adj.* huge; gigantic

Hot Words Journal!

As you read, circle words that you find interesting or that you don't understand. Later you may add them to your **Hot Words Journal** at the back of this book.

What You'll Learn

Key Goals In this lesson, you will learn these key skills, strategies, and concepts.

- **Reading Focus:** Visualize
- **Literary Element:** Irony
- **Reading Coach:** Using Footnotes and Definitions

Ozymandias

Percy Bysshe Shelley

I met a traveler from an antique[1] land **A**
Who said: Two <u>vast</u> and trunkless[2] legs of stone
Stand in the desert . . . Near them, on the sand,
Half sunk, a shattered <u>visage</u> lies, whose frown,
And wrinkled lip, and <u>sneer</u> of cold command,   5
Tell that its sculptor well those passions read
Which yet survive, stamped on these lifeless things,
The hand that mocked them, and the heart that fed:[3]
And on the pedestal these words appear:
"My name is Ozymandias, king of kings: 10
Look on my works, ye Mighty, and despair!"
Nothing beside remains. Round the decay
Of that <u>colossal</u> wreck, boundless and bare
The lone and level sands stretch far away. **B**

Reading Check

1. Here, *antique* means "ancient."
2. *Trunkless* means "without a body."
3. The *hand* is the sculptor's. The *heart* is Ozymandias's. Through the sculptor's art, the sculptor *mocked,* or showed exactly, the passions that Ozymandias felt.

Vocabulary

vast (vast) *adj.* very large; covering a great space

visage (viz′ ij) *n.* face; outward appearance

sneer (snēr) *n.* a facial expression showing disapproval or contempt

colossal (kə los′ əl) *adj.* huge; gigantic

Reading Coach

← **Using Footnotes and Definitions** This poem, written almost two hundred years ago, might sound strange to you today. Use the footnotes and definitions to help you make sense of unfamiliar words and ideas. Look at line 1. Underline the footnoted word and then read the footnote. Explain the meaning of line 1 here. **A**

_____

_____

_____

Reading Focus

← **Visualize** This poem describes the remains of a statue in a vast desert. Circle the parts of the statue that remain. What do you see in your mind's eye as you read the description of the statue? **B**

_____

_____

_____

_____

_____

Reading Check

Review the poem. How has time affected the statue?

_____

_____

_____

READING WRAPUP

Going Solo

⚬— Using Footnotes and Definitions

On Solid Footing Read the passage "Two vast . . . in the desert" (lines 2–3). Which words or phrases from this passage are explained at the bottom of page 77? List them here.

_____

Now paraphrase the passage. That is, put the passage into your own words. Write your paraphrase below.

_____

_____

TeamWork

⚬— Visualize

Everyone's an Art Critic Review the description of the ancient statue and your response to the **Visualize** note on page 77. Then draw a picture of the statue—what's left of it—that is based on the description in the poem. With a group, form a "workshop circle." That means that each of you will take turns commenting on each other's picture. Your comments should focus on the details from the poem that were and weren't included in each picture. Below, summarize your group's response to your own picture.

_____

_____

_____

_____

Standardized Test Practice

Choose the best answer for each multiple-choice question. Fill in the circle in the spaces for questions 1 and 2 on the right.

1. In the poem, who describes the ancient statue firsthand?
    A. the traveler
    B. the sculptor
    C. Ozymandias
    D. the speaker of the poem

2. Which of the following statements BEST summarizes the message of the poem?
    A. It's great to be the king.
    B. Nothing lasts forever.
    C. Life's short; art lasts.
    D. It's lonely at the top.

Write your answer to open-ended question A in the space provided below.

A.   What do the words on the pedestal tell you about Ozymandias's character? Use details from the poem to support your answer.

Multiple-Choice Questions

1. Ⓐ Ⓑ Ⓒ Ⓓ   2. Ⓐ Ⓑ Ⓒ Ⓓ

Open-Ended Question

A. _____

_____

_____

_____

_____

Literary Element

← Irony

Irony is the contrast between what is expected and what is real. Writers sometimes use irony for humor—but not always. Sometimes irony helps a reader understand the message of a poem. There are three types of irony.

- **Verbal irony** A person says one thing while meaning another.

- **Situational irony** The outcome of a situation is the opposite of what is expected.

- **Dramatic irony** The audience or the reader knows something that a character or group of characters doesn't know.

Look at the chart below. Read the examples of irony found in "Ozymandias." For each example, tell what kind of irony is used and explain why the passage is ironic.

Example of irony: "Look on my works, ye Mighty, and despair!"

Type: _____

Why it's ironic: _____

_____

_____

_____

Example of irony: Nothing beside remains. Round the decay/
Of that colossal wreck, boundless and bare/
The lone and level sands stretch far away.

Type: _____

Why it's ironic: _____

_____

_____

Reading Drama

Macbeth and *Gilligan's Island* are not titles you often find in the same sentence. Shakespeare's famous tale of ambition, murder, and revenge is a classic poetic tragedy. Hollywood's 1960s sitcom is a light comedy. But these two works have a basic connection. Both are drama.

A **drama** is any story that is meant to be performed by actors for an audience. Drama includes any play, on stage or screen, whether it involves serious dialogue or pies in the face. Drama usually—but not always—starts with a written **script** from which the actors work. This may include stage directions that describe details of the **setting** and of how characters should speak, look, and behave.

Mark the text ▶ **Think of plays, movies, or TV dramas you have seen about the following subjects. Write a few of their titles on the lines provided.**

Revenge _____   Discovering who you are _____

Finding true love _____   Pride before a fall _____

Mistaken identity _____   Loss _____

Mystery _____   Making a difficult decision _____

Why Read Drama?

Why *do* people read drama? After all, drama is meant to be performed by actors. What's the point of leafing through a script? Reading gives you one great advantage: You can go at your own pace, stopping to review difficult passages or lingering over important moments in a way that's impossible during a performance. You can also imagine for yourself what the play would look like on stage.

What's the Plan?

Like other stories, dramas have a **setting, characters,** and a **plot.** But the text of a drama looks different because it's arranged to make the play easier to perform. Some characteristics of drama are listed here.

- The printed version of a drama is called a **script.** The script usually begins with a list of the **cast of characters.**

- The audience follows the story line and learns about the characters through **dialogue,** or **lines** spoken by the characters.

- Story events are usually presented in **chronological order**—that is, in the order that they happen.

- Long plays are broken up into shorter sections called **acts** and **scenes.** A new act or scene shows that the time or place has changed.

What Do I Look For?

The opening of *Everyman*, a religious drama from the 1400s, shows some **text features** and **literary elements** that many plays have.

The **cast of characters** lists all the characters appearing in the play.

A drama's **theme** is the main idea that the author wants to communicate. Here the theme is clearly stated.

A **speaker's name** appears before that character's lines (the words the character speaks).

A **monologue** is a speech delivered directly to the audience by an actor on stage. Conversation between characters is **dialogue**.

Stage directions, which are often printed in italics within brackets, describe the movement of actors on stage. They may also describe what the characters and the **stage set** look like.

 Find it! Circle the names of four characters in the cast of characters.

from *Everyman*

CHARACTERS

GOD
MESSENGER
DEATH
EVERYMAN
FELLOWSHIP

GOODS
GOOD DEEDS
KNOWLEDGE
CONFESSION
BEAUTY

STRENGTH
DISCRETION
FIVE WITS
ANGEL
DOCTOR

Here beginneth a treatise how the High Father of Heaven sendeth Death to summon every creature to come and give account of their lives in this world, and is in manner of a moral play.

MESSENGER.   I pray you all give your audience
      And hear this matter with reverence,
      By figure a moral play:
      The Summoning of Everyman called it is,
5   That of our lives and ending shows
      How transitory we be all day.
      This matter is wondrous precious,
      But the intent of it is more gracious,
      And sweet to bear away.
10   The story saith: Man, in the beginning,
      Look well, and take good heed to the ending,
      Be you never so gay!
      Ye think sin in the beginning full sweet,
      Which in the end causeth the soul to weep,
15   When the body lieth in clay.
      Here shall you see how Fellowship and Jollity,
      Both Strength, Pleasure, and Beauty,
      Will fade from thee as flower in May;
      For ye shall hear how our Heaven King
20   Calleth Everyman to a general reckoning:
      Give audience, and hear what he doth say.

[*Exit* MESSENGER.]
[*Enter* GOD.]

GOD.   I perceive, here in my majesty,
      How that all creatures be to me unkind,
      Living without dread in worldly prosperity.

How Do I Read It?

These **reading strategies** will be especially useful when you read drama.

Predict: Drama is full of surprising twists and turns. Every so often, guess what will happen next. Do any turns of plot surprise you?

Question: Don't take everything for granted. Ask questions as you read. Why did the playwright introduce a character to a scene? What does the action mean? Questioning helps sharpen your understanding.

Respond: The best way to get the most out of reading—or seeing—drama is to respond to the action and ideas. How do you feel about what's going on?

Visualize: Drama is about life and living. As you read, make connections between the events depicted on stage and events in your own life.

For more information on **reading strategies,** see pages 216–222 in the **Reading Handbook.**

Read the drama scenes that follow. Be sure to

• use the **text features, literary elements,** and **author's plan**

• use **reading strategies** to help you get the most from your reading

GET READY TO READ!

Connect

List Ideas Think about a famous person you admire—but have never met. It might be a sports hero, a musician, or someone who is famous for doing good works. What might you find out by getting to know the person that you wouldn't know from media reports or advertising? With your classmates, list some reasons on the board why your opinion of an admired person might change if you actually got to know him or her.

In these scenes from *Macbeth*, you'll "hear" what other characters have to say about the title character. If you were to read the rest of the play, you'd meet Macbeth and learn more about him as he struggles through a strange and difficult time.

Did You Know?

Building Background *Macbeth* is one of William Shakespeare's most famous tragedies. It's a story of pride, ambition, and guilt that has been popular with audiences for hundreds of years.

- Shakespeare based many of his plays on history. For the subject of this tragedy, Shakespeare chose the real-life Macbeth, who was king of Scotland from 1040 to 1057.

- Although Shakespeare wrote about real people and events, he typically changed the facts so his plays would cover the themes and teach the lessons he wanted.

Reason to Read

Setting a Purpose for Reading Read to learn about Macbeth from what other characters say about him.

As you read, use the following **Foldable** to track what you learn about Macbeth from the other characters.

1. Place a sheet of paper in front of you so that the long side is at the top. Fold the top of the paper down, stopping about an inch from the bottom edge, and make a crease.

2. Write **Information About Macbeth** along the bottom edge.

3. Fold the paper in half from side to side and then in half again to make four sections. Unfold. Cut through the top thickness of the paper along the fold lines to make four tabs.

4. Label the tabs **From Witches, From Captain, From Ross,** and **From King Duncan.**

5. As you read, write under the appropriate tab what you learn about Macbeth from each of the characters listed.

Word Power

Vocabulary Preview

Read the definitions of these words from *Macbeth*. Use the pronunciation guides to help you say each word aloud. You may already know the meaning of some of these words, but others might still be unclear. As you read, use context clues to make these words clearer.

plight (plīt) *n.* an unfortunate, difficult, or dangerous situation or condition; p. 84

hardy (här´dē) *adj.* bold; brave; able to endure hardship; p. 86

disdain (dis dān´) *v.* to look on with scorn; consider unworthy; p. 86

valiant (val´yənt) *adj.* courageous; brave; p. 86

mark (märk) *v.* to pay attention to; p. 86

deign (dān) *v.* to lower oneself to give or offer something; p. 90

disburse (dis burs´) *v.* to pay out; make a payment in settlement of; p. 90

Hot Words Journal

As you read, circle words that you find interesting or that you don't understand. Later you may add them to your **Hot Words Journal** at the back of this book.

What You'll Learn

Key Goals In this lesson, you will learn these key skills, strategies, and concepts.

- **Reading Focus:** Clarify

- **Think It Over:** Draw Conclusions

- **Literary Element:** Atmosphere

- **Reading Coach:** Reading Stage Directions

from The Tragedy of
Macbeth

William Shakespeare

CAST OF CHARACTERS

DUNCAN: King of Scotland

MALCOLM: Duncan's older son and heir to the throne

DONALBAIN: Duncan's younger son

MACBETH: Thane of Glamis, a Scottish noble and general in King Duncan's army

LADY MACBETH: Macbeth's wife

BANQUO: a thane of Scotland and general in King Duncan's army

FLEANCE: Banquo's son

MACDUFF: Thane of Fife, a Scottish noble

LADY MACDUFF: Macduff's wife

SON OF MACDUFF AND LADY MACDUFF

LENNOX
ROSS
MENTEITH } thanes and nobles of Scotland
ANGUS
CAITHNESS

SIWARD: Earl of Northumberland and general of the English forces

YOUNG SIWARD: Siward's son

SEYTON: an officer attending Macbeth

THREE WITCHES

HECATE: leader of the witches

PORTER

OLD MAN

THREE MURDERERS

ENGLISH DOCTOR

SCOTTISH DOCTOR

CAPTAIN: an officer serving Duncan

GENTLEWOMAN: an attendant to Lady Macbeth

APPARITIONS

LORDS, GENTLEMEN, OFFICERS, SOLDIERS, MESSENGERS, ATTENDANTS, SERVANTS

SETTING: *Scotland and England during the eleventh century* **A**

Reading Focus

← **Clarify** It's important to keep characters straight as you read. You'll want to **clarify,** or clear up anything that may be confusing. One way to clarify is to reread slowly. Review the cast of characters and statement of the setting. Ask yourself questions about the characters and setting or about unfamiliar words. For example, you might wonder, Who exactly is Macbeth? What is a thane? Where does the action take place? **A**

Model: *It says here that Macbeth is a Scottish noble and a general in the king's army. I think that means he has a position of power both in society and in the military. I see that several of the other characters also have the title of thane, followed by words such as "of Glamis" and "of Fife." A thane must be a member of the upper class, maybe like a lord or an earl. Besides seeing the character list, I see that the action takes place in Scotland and England during the 1000s. Now I'm ready to read.*

Keep This in Mind

Use these symbols to record your reactions as you read.

? I have a question about something here.

! This really caught my attention.

★ This information is important.

from The Tragedy of Macbeth

➤ **Reading Stage Directions** Play scripts include notes called **stage directions** to describe the scene and tell actors what to do and how to speak. Stage directions also help you, the reader, see and hear the action of the play. In most scripts, the stage directions are set in italic type **Mark the text** within brackets [ ]. Circle the first set of stage directions. What do these directions tell you about the weather? **B**

_____

_____

Reading Focus

➤ **Clarify** Make sure you understand what the witches are saying in line 10. Look at the side note for line 10 on page 85. Then use the lines below to restate the witches' message in your own words. **C**

_____

_____

_____

ACT 1

SCENE 1. Scotland. An open place.

[*In the midst of a great storm of thunder and lightning,* THREE WITCHES *appear in a deserted, outdoor place.*] **B**

FIRST WITCH. When shall we three meet again?
  In thunder, lightning, or in rain?

SECOND WITCH. When the hurlyburly's° done,
  When the battle's lost and won.

5 **THIRD WITCH.** That will be ere° the set of sun.

FIRST WITCH. Where the place?

SECOND WITCH.   Upon the heath.°

THIRD WITCH. There to meet with Macbeth.

FIRST WITCH. I come, Graymalkin.°

SECOND WITCH. Paddock° calls.

THIRD WITCH.   Anon!°

10 **ALL.** Fair is foul, and foul is fair.° **C**
  Hover through the fog and filthy air.
[*The* WITCHES *exit.*] **D**

SCENE 2. A military camp near Forres, a town about a hundred miles north of Edinburgh in Scotland.

[*From offstage come the sounds of men fighting, weapons clashing, and trumpets blaring.* DUNCAN, *King of Scotland, enters with his two teenage sons.* MALCOLM, *the older, who is heir to the throne, and* DONALBAIN, *the younger. With them are a Scottish nobleman,* LENNOX, *and other attendants. They meet a* CAPTAIN *bleeding from wounds received in battle between the king's army and the forces of his two rivals, Macdonwald and the Thane of Cawdor.*] **E**

KING. What bloody man is that? He can report,
  As seemeth by his <u>plight</u>, of the revolt
  The newest state.

Vocabulary

plight (plīt) *n.* an unfortunate, difficult, or dangerous situation or condition

3 hurlyburly: commotion.

5 ere: before.

6 heath: uncultivated land covered by small shrubs.

8 Graymalkin: gray cat (the name of a familiar, or spirit in animal form, that serves a witch).

9 Paddock: toad (another familiar). **Anon:** right away.

10 In Shakespeare's time, many people believed that witches reversed normal values and practices, considering ugliness beautiful and vice versa.

Literary Element

━ **Atmosphere** In scene 1, Shakespeare creates a general **atmosphere,** or overall mood, for the play. **D**

Mark the text⟩ In scene 1, underline details of the setting in the stage directions and in the witches' lines. Visualize the scene these words create. Then check the best description of the atmosphere.

_____ mysterious and fun

_____ dark and dangerous

_____ calm and restful

Reading Coach

━ **Reading Stage Directions** On the lines below, describe the event you learn about from these stage directions. **E**

_____

_____

_____

_____

_____

Using Definitions Look at the definition of the underlined vocabulary word at the bottom of the page. Substitute the definition for the underlined word and reread the sentence to make the meaning clearer.

Reading Focus

🔑 **Clarify** Underline or highlight the words in the boxed passage that describe Macbeth and his actions. Then *Mark the text* explain below in your own words what Macbeth has done. **F**

_____

_____

_____

_____

Think It Over

🔑 **Draw Conclusions** When you use several pieces of information to make a general statement about a character or a situation, you are **drawing a conclusion.** In lines 25–33, the Captain explains that just when the king's army seemed safe, the situation changed. (Remember what the witches said?) Below, check any conclusions you could draw from the Captain's words. **G**

❑ The weather is beautiful.

❑ The battle continues to be difficult.

❑ King Duncan has many enemies.

MALCOLM.   This is the sergeant
          Who like a good and <u>hardy</u> soldier fought
5   'Gainst my captivity.° Hail, brave friend!
          Say to the king the knowledge of the broil°
          As thou didst leave it.

          CAPTAIN.   Doubtful it stood,
          As two spent swimmers, that do cling together
          And choke their art.° The merciless Macdonwald—
10   Worthy to be a rebel for to that
          The multiplying villainies of nature
          Do swarm upon him°—from the Western Isles°
          Of kerns and gallowglasses° is supplied;
          And Fortune, on his damnèd quarrel smiling,
15   Showed like a rebel's whore:° but all's too weak:
          For brave Macbeth—well he deserves that name—
          <u>Disdaining</u> Fortune, with his brandished steel,
          Which smoked with bloody execution,
          Like valor's minion° carved out his passage
20   Till he faced the slave;
          Which nev'r shook hands, nor bade farewell to him,
          Till he unseamed him from the nave to th' chops,°
          And fixed his head upon our battlements. **F**

          KING.   O <u>valiant</u> cousin!° Worthy gentleman!

25   **CAPTAIN.**   As whence the sun 'gins his reflection°
          Shipwracking storms and direful thunders break,
          So from that spring whence comfort seemed to come
          Discomfort swells.° <u>Mark</u>, King of Scotland, mark:
          No sooner justice had, with valor armed,
30   Compelled these skipping kerns to trust their heels
          But the Norweyan lord,° surveying vantage,°
          With furbished arms and new supplies of men,
          Began a fresh assault. **G**

          KING.   Dismayed not this
          Our captains, Macbeth and Banquo?

Vocabulary
hardy (här′dē) *adj.* bold; brave; able to endure hardship
disdain (dis dān′) *v.* to look on with scorn; consider unworthy
valiant (val′yənt) *adj.* courageous; brave
mark (märk) *v.* to pay attention to

1–3 The wounded officer **(sergeant)** has returned to King Duncan's military camp near Forres. Duncan hopes the officer can report on the progress of the rebellion.

5 **'Gainst my captivity:** to keep me from being captured.

6 **broil:** battle.

8–9 **As . . . art:** like two tired swimmers who hinder their skill by clinging to each other.

10–12 **Worthy . . . him:** well suited to be a rebel, since he is infested with evil qualities.

12 **Western Isles:** the Hebrides, off Scotland's west coast.

13 **kerns and gallowglasses:** lightly armed Irish foot soldiers and horsemen armed with axes.

14–15 **Fortune . . . whore:** Fortune (luck), approving Macdonwald's cause, appeared to favor the rebel.

19 **minion:** favorite.

21–22 **Which . . . chops:** Macbeth didn't part from Macdonwald until he had cut him open from his navel to his jaw.

24 **cousin:** kinsman (Macbeth and Duncan were both grandsons of King Malcolm).

25 **sun 'gins his reflection:** sun rises.

25–28 **As . . . swells:** The Captain says that Macdonwald's defeat was only a break in the storm.

31 **Norweyan lord:** Sweno, King of Norway. **surveying vantage:** seeing an opportunity for attack.

Hot Words

Mark the text **Choose your own words**
As you continue reading this scene, circle any words that you find interesting or that you don't understand. You may come back to these words later.

FOLDABLES Don't forget about
Graphic Organizer your **Foldable!** As you read, remember to jot down information you learn about Macbeth either from the witches or the Captain. You'll add information from Ross and the king as you read on.

Reading Coach

🔑 **Reading Stage Directions** Read the stage directions on this page. What information do you learn? Write your answer on the lines below. **H**

_____

_____

_____

_____

Think It Over

🔑 **Draw Conclusions** In this passage, Ross talks about the King of Norway, the Thane of Cawdor, and Bellona's bridegroom (*hint:* read the side note to discover who this is). Draw a conclusion about these characters' relationships with King Duncan. Tell whether each character is a friend or an enemy of the king by writing *friend* or *enemy* after each name. **I**

King of Norway _____

Thane of Cawdor _____

Bellona's bridegroom _____

CAPTAIN.   Yes;

35   As sparrows eagles,° or the hare the lion.
      If I say sooth,° I must report they were
      As cannons overcharged with double cracks;°
      So they doubly redoubled strokes upon the foe.
      Except° they meant to bathe in reeking wounds,

40   Or memorize another Golgotha,°
      I cannot tell—
      But I am faint; my gashes cry for help.

KING. So well thy words become thee as thy wounds;
      They smack of honor both. Go get him surgeons.

[*As the* CAPTAIN *exits with the help of attendants, noblemen* ROSS *and* ANGUS *enter.*] **H**

45   Who comes here?

MALCOLM.   The worthy Thane° of Ross.

LENNOX. What a haste looks through his eyes! So should he look
      That seems to° speak things strange.

ROSS.   God save the king!

KING. Whence cam'st thou, worthy Thane?

ROSS.   From Fife, great King;
      Where the Norweyan banners flout the sky

50   And fan our people cold.°
      Norway° himself, with terrible° numbers,
      Assisted by that most disloyal traitor
      The Thane of Cawdor, began a dismal° conflict;
      Till that Bellona's bridegroom, lapped in proof,°

55   Confronted him with self-comparisons,°
      Point against point rebellious, arm 'gainst arm,
      Curbing his lavish° spirit: and, to conclude,
      The victory fell on us. **I**

KING.   Great happiness! **J**

35 As sparrows eagles: as much as sparrows frighten eagles.

36 sooth: truth.

37 cracks: explosive charges.

39 Except: unless.

40 memorize . . . Golgotha: make the field as well known for slaughter as Golgotha, where Christ was crucified.

45 Thane: a Scottish title of nobility.

47 seems to: seems about to.

50 fan . . . cold: filled the Scots with cold fear.

51 Norway: the King of Norway. **terrible:** terrifying.

53 dismal: ominous.

54 Bellona's . . . proof: Ross refers to Macbeth as the husband of Bellona—Roman goddess of war—dressed in strong armor **(proof)**.

55 Confronted . . . self-comparisons: faced him with equal courage and skill.

57 lavish: arrogant.

Reading Focus

◆— **Clarify** Are you sure you know what has happened so far? Think about what you've read. Then number the events below in the order that they occurred. If you are not sure, go back and reread. **J**

___ Macbeth defeated the King of Norway and the Thane of Cawdor.

___ Macbeth killed Macdonwald in battle.

___ The Norwegian army began a new attack.

FOLDABLES *Graphic Organizer* Don't forget about your **Foldable.** Now would be a good time to add information about Macbeth that you learn from Ross.

Draw Conclusions

Reread lines 63–67. Underline the king's directions to Ross. On the lines below, write what the king asks Ross to do. **K**

_____

_____

_____

_____

What can you conclude about the king on the basis of his actions here?

_____

_____

_____

_____

Hot Words

Choose three words, either from the underlined vocabulary in the play or from the words you circled as you read. Record them in your **Hot Words Journal** at the back of this book and complete an activity listed there.

ROSS.   That now
   Sweno, the Norways' king, craves composition;°
60 Nor would we <u>deign</u> him burial of his men
   Till he <u>disbursèd</u>, at Saint Colme's Inch,°
   Ten thousand dollars° to our general use.

KING. No more that Thane of Cawdor shall deceive
   Our bosom interest:° go pronounce his present° death,
65 And with his former title greet Macbeth. **K**

ROSS. I'll see it done.

KING. What he hath lost, noble Macbeth hath won.

[*They exit.*]

Vocabulary
deign (dān) *v.* to lower oneself to give or offer something
disburse (dis burs′) *v.* to pay out; make a payment in settlement of

59 craves composition: begs for terms of peace.

61 Saint Colme's Inch: Inchcolm, an island in the Firth of Forth.

62 dollars: currency that first came into use in the early sixteenth century, about five hundred years after Macbeth's time.

64 Our . . . interest: my dearest concerns. **present:** immediate.

Reading Check

Step 1 Think about the two scenes from *Macbeth* that you just read. Look back at the notes you wrote and review your **Foldable.** On the lines below, summarize briefly what you have learned about Macbeth.

_____

_____

_____

_____

Step 2 How do you feel about the character of Macbeth? Do you think he will change? Be sure to support your thoughts with information from the play.

_____

_____

_____

_____

_____

_____

_____

_____

READING WRAPUP

Going Solo

Clarify

Get the Meaning Use the side notes on page 85 to find the meanings of the following words in scene 1 of the play.

hurlyburly   heath   Graymalkin   Paddock

Now write answers to these questions.

Which word might be used to mean a noisy, chaotic event?

_____

What do Graymalkin and Paddock have in common?

_____

_____

Buddy Up

Draw Conclusions

The Royal Treatment With your partner, review King Duncan's words in scene 2 of the play. Discuss the king's attitude and actions toward the Captain, Macbeth, and the Thane of Cawdor. What general statements can you make about the king's character from what he says and does? Write your conclusions on the lines below.

_____

_____

_____

Atmosphere

That Witchy Feeling During Shakespeare's time, many people believed in witches and witchcraft. With your partner, discuss the witches in scene 1 of *Macbeth*. Why do you think Shakespeare sets the atmosphere of the play by using witches? Write your thoughts on the lines below.

_____

_____

_____

TeamWork

Reading Stage Directions

Set the Stage With your group, take turns reading aloud the stage directions at the beginnings of scenes 1 and 2 on page 84. Now imagine that you are members of the sound and lighting crew for a stage production of *Macbeth*. On the lines below, describe your plans for what the audience will see and hear as each scene begins.

Scene 1: _____

_____

_____

_____

_____

_____

Scene 2: _____

_____

_____

_____

_____

Standardized Test Practice

Choose the best answer for each multiple-choice question. Fill in the circle in the spaces for questions 1 and 2 on the right.

1. When the witches meet Macbeth, they will most likely

   A. sing a song.

   B. give him money.

   C. challenge him to a battle.

   D. give him a threatening message.

2. Which of these men is NOT an enemy of Duncan, King of Scotland?

   A. Banquo

   B. Sweno, King of Norway

   C. Thane of Cawdor

   D. Macdonwald

Write your answer to open-ended question A in the space provided below.

A. Why does the Captain tell King Duncan that Macbeth has ignored Fate while in battle? Use details from the story to support your answer.

Multiple-Choice Questions

1. Ⓐ Ⓑ Ⓒ Ⓓ   2. Ⓐ Ⓑ Ⓒ Ⓓ

Open-Ended Question

A. _____

_____

_____

_____

---

word power   **Vocabulary Check**

Write the word from the word list that belongs in the blank in each sentence.

plight *n.* an unfortunate, difficult, or dangerous situation or condition

hardy *adj.* bold; brave; able to endure hardship

disdain *v.* to look on with scorn; consider unworthy

valiant *adv.* courageous; brave

mark *v.* to pay attention to

deign *v.* to lower oneself to give or offer something

disburse *v.* to pay out; make a payment in settlement of

1. Sam has a tendency to _____ teammates who are not as strong as he is.

2. Only a _____ soldier could survive the harsh winter weather.

3. She plans to _____ the cash bonus among all the workers.

4. You should _____ what I say when I tell you to be careful.

5. We heard of the terrible _____ of these flood victims, and we came to help.

6. The firefighter made a _____ effort to save the puppy from the burning building.

7. The snobbish senior would not _____ to speak to the first-year students.

Reading *Epics and Legends*

An epic tale of intergalactic travel

A legend as a home-run hitter

Words like *epic* and *legend* are familiar to most people. An epic is a story on a grand scale. A legend is a story about someone famous. Those words mean almost the same things when they name kinds of literature.

Type of Story	Characters	Examples
An **epic** is a long narrative poem in formal language that tells the adventures of a hero. Many epics involve supernatural events, long periods of time, journeys to distant places, and struggles between good and evil.	The **epic hero** is often an important, respected man who shows the ideals of his people.	Epics that come from the oral tradition of repeated tellings and retellings, such as *Beowulf* and *Gilgamesh,* are called **folk epics.** Epics such as *Paradise Lost* by John Milton and *The Aenid* by Virgil, which are written by known authors, are called **literary epics.**
A **legend** is a tale that is based on a real person and is handed down from one generation to the next. Although they are based on facts, events and characters in legends are typically exaggerated.	The hero of a legend is generally a real person from the past.	Legends include the stories of Robin Hood, Davy Crockett, and other folk heroes.

Why Read Epics and Legends?

One reason to read epics and legends is to enjoy an exciting adventure that has plenty of action. Another is to follow the experiences of a single hero through a series of adventures. A third reason is to learn about what people found important in a time long ago. Remember, many epics, legends, and romances are based on stories that were told and retold before people were able to write. If a story was worth memorizing and repeating, it must have been important to the people who told it and listened to it again and again.

What's the Plan?

Most legends are organized like other stories. They are usually told in **chronological order**—the order in which events happen. Many epics start in the middle of the action and then tell the background information later. Both kinds of stories have characters, settings, plots, and, most important, a **theme,** or main idea or message.

By understanding a story's theme, you can realize why the story was important enough to pass along from generation to generation.

What Do I Look For?

Epics and legends have some common elements. Look at the beginning of this story about the legendary King Arthur.

The **hero** is often a king, a knight, or another important person.

Point of view refers to who is telling the story. In an epic or legend, an unnamed narrator usually tells the tale and refers to the hero as "he" or "she." This is known as **third-person point of view.**

The **plot** often involves danger, rescue, and a struggle between good and evil.

The **setting** is usually in the distant past. This story is set in the time of kings and knights.

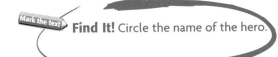 Mark the text ▸ **Find It!** Circle the name of the hero.

---

from Le Morte d'Arthur

Sir Thomas Malory

Upon Trinity Sunday at night King Arthur dreamed a wonderful dream, and that was this: it seemed that he saw upon a platform a chair and the chair was fastened to a wheel, thereupon King Arthur sat in the richest cloth of gold that might be made.

And the king thought that under him, far from him, was hideous deep black water; therein were all manner of serpents and worms and wild beasts, foul and horrible. Suddenly the king thought the wheel turned upside-down and he fell among the serpents, and every beast caught him by a limb. The king cried out as he lay in his bed and slept, "Help, help!"

Then knights, squires, and yeomen awakened the king, and he was so dazed that he knew not where he was. He stayed awake until it was nigh day and then he fell to slumbering again, not sleeping but not thoroughly awake. Then it seemed to the king that Sir Gawain actually came unto him with a number of fair ladies.

When King Arthur saw him he cried, "Welcome, my sister's son; I thought that ye were dead. And now that I see thee alive, much am I beholden unto almighty Jesus. Ah, fair nephew, what are these ladies that have come hither with you?"

"Sir," said Sir Gawain, "all those are ladies for whom I have fought when I was a living man. And all these are those whom I did battle for in righteous quarrels; at their devout prayer, because I did battle for them righteously, God hath given me the grace to bring me hither unto you. Thus God hath given me leave to warn you away from your death: for if ye fight to-morn with Sir Mordred, as ye have both agreed, doubt ye not that ye shall be slain, and the most part of your people on both sides. Through the great grace and goodness that almighty Jesus hath unto you, and through pity for you and many other good men who would be slain there, God in His special grace hath sent me to you to give you warning that in no wise should ye do battle to-morn; but ye should make a treaty for a month. And make this offer generously to-morn so as to assure the delay, for within a month Sir Lancelot shall come with all his noble knights and rescue you worshipfully and slay Sir Mordred and all who ever will hold with him."

Then Sir Gawain and all the ladies vanished; at once the king called upon his knights, squires, and yeoman and charged them quickly to fetch his noble lords and wise bishops unto him. When they had come the king told them of his vision and what Sir Gawain had said to him: that if he fought on the morn, he would be slain. Then the king commanded and charged Sir Lucan le Butler, his brother Sir Bedivere, and two bishops to make a treaty in any way for a month with Sir Mordred: "And spare not; offer him lands and goods, as much as ye think best."

How Do I Read It?

These **reading strategies** will be especially useful when you read epics and legends.

Monitor Comprehension: Don't miss out on the action! Ask yourself questions as you read to make sure that you understand. If you run into trouble, go back and review or ask someone for help.

Predict: After reading a few paragraphs, use the story clues to predict what will happen next. As you continue reading, confirm your predictions and make new ones.

Visualize: These stories were a popular form of entertainment centuries ago, creating graphic, vivid images for their audience. Picturing the scene will enrich your reading experience.

Respond: Epics and legends may be full of amazing, sometimes gruesome, events. As you read, comment on what seems interesting, awful, or simply strange.

For more information on **reading strategies,** see pages 216–222 in the **Reading Handbook.**

 **DO IT!**

As you read the following passages from *Beowulf,* be sure to

- look for the **literary elements**
- use **reading strategies** to get the most from your reading

GET READY TO READ!

Connect

Class Discussion Think of a person whom you would call a hero. What qualities make you admire him or her? As a class, discuss your heroes and the qualities that make them great. Then list five of those qualities on the lines below.

_____

_____

_____

_____

In this selection from the epic _Beowulf,_ you'll meet Beowulf, a brave warrior who travels far from home to help rescue a distant land from an evil monster named Grendel.

Connect

Building Background Imagine a time when kings showered riches on their bravest warriors. Imagine a time when people believed in monsters and dragons. That time was the sixth century—the time when the tale of _Beowulf_ takes place.

- The Anglo-Saxons, people of the land that was later called England, passed the story of Beowulf down from generation to generation.

- The story takes place in the land known as Scandinavia, and it involves the Geats (gēts), a tribe from southern Sweden, and the Danes, a tribe from Denmark.

- Banquet halls, or _mead halls,_ were places where great warriors feasted, drank, and bragged of their bloody conquests. The halls were named after the popular drink called _mead._

- In the action leading up to this part of the epic, the fearsome monster Grendel has been attacking Herot, the Danes' mead hall, for twelve years. In each attack, the monster devours several of King Hrothgar's warriors. The terror the Danes feel brings a time of sadness over the land until, in a faraway land, the heroic warrior Beowulf hears of their troubles.

Reason to Read

Setting a Purpose for Reading Read to find out why Beowulf wants to help the Danes and how he plans to fight Grendel.

word power

Vocabulary Preview

Read the definitions of these words from _Beowulf._ Use the pronunciation guides to help you say each word aloud. As you read, use context clues to help unlock the meanings of these words and any others you don't know.

jut (jut) _v._ to extend out, up, or forward; project; p. 98

errand (er′ ənd) _n._ short trip to do something, usually for someone else; mission; p. 99

afflict (ə flikt′) _v._ to cause great suffering and pain to; distress severely; p. 99

majestic (mə jes′ tik) _adj._ impressive or awesome; dignified; grand; p. 100

purge (purj) _v._ to cleanse or rid of whatever is unclean or undesirable; p. 101

scorn (skôrn) _n._ contempt for someone or something considered vile or inferior; disrespect; p. 102

gorge (gôrj) _v._ to stuff with food; devour greedily; p. 102

Hot Words Journal

As you read, circle words that you find interesting or that you don't understand. Later, you may add them to your **Hot Words Journal** at the back of this book.

What You'll Learn

Key Goals In this lesson, you will learn these key skills, strategies, and concepts.

- **Reading Focus:** Summarize

- **Think It Over:** Analyze

- **Literary Element:** Epic Hero

- **Reading Coach:** Reading Lines of Poetry

FROM BEOWULF

Translated by Burton Raffel

THE COMING OF BEOWULF

So the living sorrow of Healfdane's son[1]
Simmered, bitter and fresh, and no wisdom
Or strength could break it: that agony hung
On king and people alike, harsh
And unending, violent and cruel, and evil. **A**   5

In his far-off home Beowulf, Higlac's
Follower[2] and the strongest of the Geats—greater
And stronger than anyone anywhere in this world—
Heard how Grendel filled nights with horror
And quickly commanded a boat fitted out,   10
Proclaiming that he'd go to that famous king,
Would sail across the sea to Hrothgar,
Now when help was needed. None
Of the wise ones regretted his going, much
As he was loved by the Geats: the omens[3] were good,   15
And they urged the adventure on. So Beowulf
Chose the mightiest men he could find,
The bravest and best of the Geats, fourteen
In all, and led them down to their boat;
He knew the sea, would point the prow[4]   20
Straight to that distant Danish shore. **B**

Then they sailed, set their ship
Out on the waves, under the cliffs.
Ready for what came they wound through the currents,
The seas beating at the sand, and were borne   25
In the lap of their shining ship, lined
With gleaming armor, going safely
In that oak-hard boat to where their hearts took them.

---

1. *Healfdane's son* is Hrothgar.
2. Higlac, king of the Geats, is Beowulf's uncle. *Higlac's follower,* then, refers to Beowulf.
3. An *omen* is a sign or occurrence that predicts good or bad luck.
4. The *prow* is the bow, or forwardmost part of a ship.

Reading Coach

Reading Lines of Poetry
Epic poetry is written in lines and long stanzas. The best way to understand the poem, though, is to read as if you were reading a story, one sentence at a time. If there's no punctuation at the end of a line, keep going! Pause when you come to a comma, a semicolon, or a dash. Stop when you come to a period. Reading this way will help you understand the poem.

Mark the text Draw a slash at the end of the first sentence on this page. Reread the sentence. Below, write the main point that the sentence makes. Hint: The "living sorrow of Healfdane's son" refers to the terror that the monster Grendel is causing among King Hrothgar and his subjects. **A**

_____

_____

_____

_____

Reading Focus

Summarize To figure out what information in the poem is most important, **summarize,** or state the main ideas in your own words. Reread the boxed text. As you read, ask yourself *who* the characters are, *what* is happening, and *where, when,* and *why* the action is taking place. **B**

Model: *In the land of the Geats, Beowulf hears of Hrothgar's troubles with the monster Grendel. Beowulf vows to help Hrothgar. He chooses fourteen of the bravest and best Geats to help him, and they set sail for Denmark.*

Keep This in Mind

Use these symbols to record your reactions as you read.

? I have a question about something here.

! This really caught my attention.

★ This information is important.

Main Idea Reread the boxed

Mark the text text. Underline the lines where the watchman describes what he does on the cliffs. Why is it necessary for the Danes to patrol the shoreline? Check your answer below. **C**

❏ so visitors will know they've reached Denmark

❏ so pirates and raiders won't be able to invade

❏ so Danish soldiers won't help the pirates and raiders

word power

Using the Dictionary If you come across an unfamiliar word that is not explained in a definition or footnote, look it up in a dictionary. Apply the definition that best suits the context of the sentence.

The wind hurried them over the waves,
30 The ship foamed through the sea like a bird
Until, in the time they had known it would take,
Standing in the round-curled prow they could see
Sparkling hills, high and green,
Jutting up over the shore, and rejoicing
35 In those rock-steep cliffs they quietly ended
Their voyage. Jumping to the ground, the Geats
Pushed their boat to the sand and tied it
In place, mail shirts[5] and armor rattling
As they swiftly moored[6] their ship. And then
40 They gave thanks to God for their easy crossing.
    High on a wall a Danish watcher
Patrolling along the cliffs saw
The travelers crossing to the shore, their shields
Raised and shining; he came riding down,
45 Hrothgar's lieutenant, spurring his horse,
Needing to know why they'd landed, these men
In armor. Shaking his heavy spear
In their faces he spoke:

> "Whose soldiers are you,
> 50 You who've been carried in your deep-keeled ship[7]
> Across the sea-road to this country of mine?
> Listen! I've stood on these cliffs longer
> Than you know, keeping our coast free
> Of pirates, raiders sneaking ashore
> 55 From their ships, seeking our lives and our gold. **C**

None have ever come more openly—
And yet you've offered no password, no sign
From my prince, no permission from my people for your landing
Here. Nor have I ever seen,
60 Out of all the men on earth, one greater

---

5. *Mail shirts* are a type of flexible body armor usually made of linked metal loops.

6. To *moor* a ship is to secure it with lines or anchors.

7. A *deep-keeled ship* is a ship that possesses a deep bottom—the *keel* being the main piece of timber that runs the length of the bottom of the ship to support the ship's frame.

Vocabulary

jut (jət) *v.* to extend out, up, or forward; project

Than has come with you; no commoner carries
Such weapons, unless his appearance, and his beauty,
Are both lies. You! Tell me your name,
And your father's; no spies go further onto Danish
Soil than you've come already. Strangers,   65
From wherever it was you sailed, tell it,
And tell it quickly, the quicker the better,
I say, for us all. Speak, say
Exactly who you are, and from where, and why."

   Their leader answered him, Beowulf unlocking   70
Words from deep in his breast:
                       "We are Geats,
Men who follow Higlac. My father
Was a famous soldier, known far and wide
As a leader of men. His name was Edgetho.   75
His life lasted many winters;
Wise men all over the earth surely
Remember him still. **D** And we have come seeking
Your prince, Healfdane's son, protector
Of this people, only in friendship: instruct us,   80
Watchman, help us with your words! Our errand
Is a great one, our business with the glorious king
Of the Danes no secret; there's nothing dark
Or hidden in our coming. You know (if we've heard
The truth, and been told honestly) that your country   85
Is cursed with some strange, vicious creature
That hunts only at night and that no one
Has seen. It's said, watchman, that he has slaughtered
Your people, brought terror to the darkness. Perhaps
Hrothgar can hunt, here in my heart,   90
For some way to drive this devil out—
If anything will ever end the evils
Afflicting your wise and famous lord. **E**
Here he can cool his burning sorrow.

Vocabulary

errand (er´ənd) *n.* short trip to do something, usually for someone else;
mission

afflict (ə flikt´) *v.* to cause great suffering and pain to; distress severely

---

Think It Over

◆ **Analyze** When you **analyze** a story, you look at separate parts of it in order to understand the whole story. For example, looking at different characters or events in *Beowulf* can help you understand its theme or main message. **D**

Mark the text Reread the highlighted text and underline Beowulf's description of Edgetho. From the qualities of Beowulf and Edgetho, what do you think could be one message of the story? Circle the best answer.

Beowulf, coming from the family he does, is likely to be bossy.

Beowulf, coming from the family he does, is likely to fail.

Beowulf, coming from the family he does, is the right person to fight Grendel.

Literary Element

◆ **Epic Hero** The **epic hero** is the main character whose adventures are the subject of an epic. By looking at the epic hero's actions and values, you can learn a lot about the ideals of the people who passed down the hero's story. Reread lines 70–94. What kinds of values do you think were important to Beowulf—and to the Anglo-Saxons? Write down three values on the lines below. **E**

_____

_____

Reading Focus

Sequence It's easier to understand a story if you know the sequence, or order of events. What happens after Beowulf explains his reasons for coming to Denmark? Number the events in the order in which they occur. **F**

_____ The watchman promises that his men will guard Beowulf's boat.

_____ The men march until they catch sight of Herot.

_____ The watchman tells Beowulf to go on into Denmark.

_____ The guide reins in his horse, pointing to Herot.

📖 Reading Check

Step 1 Ask yourself how well you have understood the epic so far. Did you put question marks next to any passages? If so, use one of these strategies to help you clarify the text.

- Reread confusing lines slowly or read them aloud.
- Read on to see whether new information helps make a passage clear.
- Ask a classmate or a teacher, parent, or other adult for help.

Step 2 Once you feel that you understand what you've read so far, write a one- or two-sentence summary of the action on the lines below. If you have trouble, look over the poem again.

_____

_____

_____

_____

_____

95 Or else he may see his suffering go on
    Forever, for as long as Herot towers
    High on your hills."
                        The mounted officer
    Answered him bluntly, the brave watchman:
100   "A soldier should know the difference between words
    And deeds, and keep that knowledge clear
    In his brain. I believe your words, I trust in
    Your friendship. Go forward, weapons and armor
    And all, on into Denmark. I'll guide you
105 Myself—and my men will guard your ship,
    Keep it safe here on our shores,
    Your fresh-tarred boat, watch it well,
    Until that curving prow carries
    Across the sea to Geatland a chosen
110 Warrior who bravely does battle with the creature
    Haunting our people, who survives that horror
    Unhurt, and goes home bearing our love."
        Then they moved on. Their boat lay moored,
    Tied tight to its anchor. Glittering at the top
115 Of their golden helmets wild boar heads gleamed,
    Shining decorations, swinging as they marched,
    Erect like guards, like sentinels, as though ready
    To fight. They marched, Beowulf and his men
    And their guide, until they could see the gables
120 Of Herot, covered with hammered gold
    And glowing in the sun—that most famous of all dwellings,
    Towering majestic, its glittering roofs
    Visible far across the land.
    Their guide reined in his horse, pointing
125 To that hall, built by Hrothgar for the best
    And bravest of his men; the path was plain,
    They could see their way. **F**

📖 Reading Check

····················

Vocabulary
majestic (mə jes´ tik) _adj._ impressive or awesome; dignified; grand

Beowulf arose, with his men
Around him, ordering a few to remain
With their weapons, leading the others quickly   130
Along under Herot's steep roof into Hrothgar's
Presence. **G** Standing on that prince's own hearth,
Helmeted, the silvery metal of his mail shirt
Gleaming with a smith's high art, he greeted
The Danes' great lord: 135

> "Hail, Hrothgar!
> Higlac is my cousin[8] and my king; the days
> Of my youth have been filled with glory. Now Grendel's
> Name has echoed in our land: sailors
> Have brought us stories of Herot, the best   140
> Of all mead-halls, deserted and useless when the moon
> Hangs in skies the sun had lit,
> Light and life fleeing together.
> My people have said, the wisest, most knowing
> And best of them, that my duty was to go to the Danes'   145
> Great king. They have seen my strength for themselves,
> Have watched me rise from the darkness of war,
> Dripping with my enemies' blood. I drove
> Five great giants into chains, chased
> All of that race from the earth. I swam   150
> In the blackness of night, hunting monsters
> Out of the ocean, and killing them one
> By one; death was my errand and the fate
> They had earned. **H** Now Grendel and I are called

Together, and I've come. Grant me, then,   155
Lord and protector of this noble place,
A single request! I have come so far,
Oh shelterer of warriors and your people's loved friend,
That this one favor you should not refuse me—
That I, alone and with the help of my men,   160
May purge all evil from this hall. **I** I have heard,

---

8. In this case, the term *cousin* is used broadly to mean any relative.

Vocabulary
purge (purj) *v.* to cleanse or rid of whatever is unclean or undesirable

---

Reading Coach

🔑 **Reading Lines of Poetry**
Read the first complete sentence on this page. Rewrite the sentence in your own words on the lines below. **G**

_____

_____

_____

Reading Focus

🔑 **Summarize** Reread the boxed text. Circle the place where Beowulf explains what his people said about him. *Mark the text* Underline places where Beowulf describes his amazing feats. Why does Beowulf tell all of this to Hrothgar? Summarize Beowulf's reasons on the lines below. **H**

_____

_____

_____

_____

Reading Focus

Respond What do you think of Beowulf at this point? Is he noble? Generous? Foolish? Jot your thoughts on the lines below. **I**

_____

_____

_____

Analyze What quality do you think Beowulf values most highly? Jot your thoughts on the lines below. **J**

_____

_____

Reading Check

Step 1 Take a moment to review the epic. Then explain in your own words how Beowulf's personal qualities—such as strength and courage—will help him when he battles the monster Grendel.

_____

_____

_____

Step 2 Now think back to the heroic qualities you listed on p. 96. Does Beowulf have those qualities? If he lived in today's world, how would he get along?

_____

_____

_____

_____

_____

Choose three words to record in your **Hot Words Journal** at the back of this book. Complete an activity listed there.

Too, that the monster's <u>scorn</u> of men
Is so great that he needs no weapons and fears none.
Nor will I. My lord Higlac
165 Might think less of me if I let my sword
Go where my feet were afraid to, if I hid
Behind some broad linden shield:9 my hands
Alone shall fight for me, struggle for life
Against the monster. God must decide
170 Who will be given to death's cold grip. **J**
Grendel's plan, I think, will be
What it has been before, to invade this hall
And <u>gorge</u> his belly with our bodies. If he can,
If he can. And I think, if my time will have come,
175 There'll be nothing to mourn over, no corpse to prepare
For its grave: Grendel will carry our bloody
Flesh to the moors, crunch on our bones
And smear torn scraps of our skin on the walls
Of his den. No, I expect no Danes
180 Will fret about sewing our shrouds,10 if he wins.
And if death does take me, send the hammered
Mail of my armor to Higlac, return
The inheritance I had from Hrethel, and he
From Wayland.11 Fate will unwind as it must!"

········· **Reading Check** ·················

_____

9. A *linden shield* is made from the wood of a linden tree.

10. A *shroud* is a burial cloth.

11. The *inheritance* is the armor that Wayland, a blacksmith of Germanic legend, forged for Hrethel, Beowulf's grandfather and former king of the Geats.

_____

Vocabulary

scorn (skôrn) *n.* contempt for someone or something considered vile or inferior; disrespect

gorge (gôrj) *v.* to stuff with food; devour greedily

READING WRAP UP

Going Solo

← Reading Lines of Poetry

Say It Your Own Way! Go back to the passage beginning "God must decide" (lines 169–180). Draw a slash at the end of each sentence; then reread the passage. How many sentences do you count?

_____

Restate one of the sentences in your own words here.

_____

_____

Buddy Up

← Summarize

Beowulf Blurb Imagine that you've been asked to provide a blurb, or brief summary, for the Young Reader's Edition of "The Coming of Beowulf." The blurb will summarize the story for younger readers. With a partner, discuss the story's main ideas and events. Also discuss what kind of language will help the story appeal to younger readers. Then write your blurb on the lines below.

_____

_____

_____

_____

_____

TeamWork

← Analyze

1. **Analyze It!** With a group, review lines 6–21 on page 97. Then discuss these questions: What important information do you first learn in this section? How does this information help you understand the rest of the story? Summarize your discussion on the lines below.

_____

_____

_____

_____

_____

_____

2. **The Way to Live Life** With your group, discuss values that are celebrated in today's movies, television shows, and sporting events. Does Beowulf share those values? Decide which values Beowulf would say a person should try to live by. Write your answer below.

_____

_____

_____

Literary Element

Epic Hero

Epics are long narrative poems that tell a story on a grand scale. The main character in an epic, the **epic hero,** is usually someone with a high rank in society. He's an important man who is celebrated for his skill and courage. An epic hero has miraculous strength, does amazing deeds, and is sometimes boastful of his greatness. His adventures usually involve supernatural events, distant journeys, and life-and-death struggles against evil.

Look at the characteristics of the epic hero listed in the outer ring of the wheel. For each characteristic, write one detail from "The Coming of Beowulf" that shows how Beowulf has that characteristic.

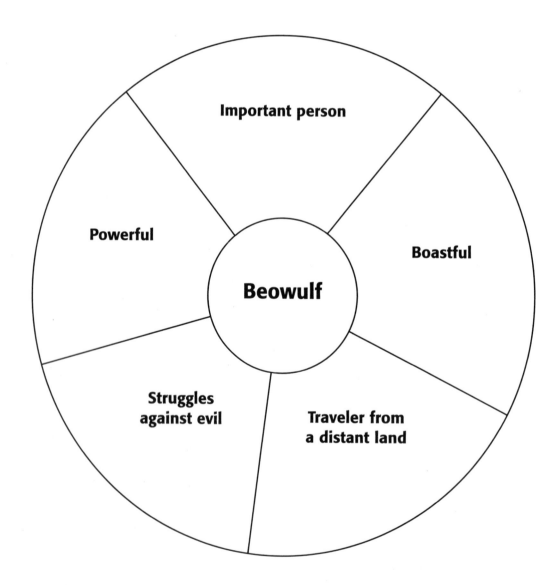

Standardized Test Practice

Choose the best answer for each multiple-choice question. Fill in the circle in the spaces for questions 1 and 2 on the right.

1. How do the Geat elders, or "wise ones," react to Beowulf's decision to go to Denmark?
    A. They try to talk him out of going.
    B. They love him and support his decision to go.
    C. They ask if they can accompany him on his adventure.
    D. They regret his decision but know they can't change his mind.

2. What favor does Beowulf ask of Hrothgar?
    A. to allow him and his men to fight Grendel
    B. to return his body to the Geats if Grendel kills him
    C. to rid the hall of evil before the battle with Grendel
    D. to provide fourteen of his bravest men to help fight Grendel

Write your answer to open-ended question A in the space provided below.

A. Why does Beowulf vow to use no weapons in his fight against Grendel? Use details from the epic to support your answer.

Multiple-Choice Questions

1. Ⓐ Ⓑ Ⓒ Ⓓ   2. Ⓐ Ⓑ Ⓒ Ⓓ

Open-Ended Question

A. _____

_____

_____

_____

_____

word power

Vocabulary Check

Write the word from the word list that belongs in the blank in each sentence.

jut *v.* to extend out, up, or forward; project

errand *n.* short trip to do something, usually for someone else; mission

afflict *v.* to cause great suffering and pain to; distress severely

majestic *adj.* impressive or awesome; dignified; grand

purge *v.* to cleanse or rid of whatever is unclean or undesirable

scorn *n.* contempt for someone or something considered vile or inferior; disrespect

gorge *v.* to stuff with food; devour greedily

1. Bea's cruel behavior made us feel nothing but _____ for her.

2. The Clean City Club has a plan to _____ the city of graffiti.

3. The two diving boards _____ out over the water.

4. The bald eagle is a splendid and _____ bird.

5. You may be hungry, but try not to _____ yourself.

6. Another dry spell would _____ us with more parched grass.

7. Mom asked Pedro to run a quick _____ on his way home.

Reading Novels

Does this sound like you? You read a novel when there's nothing good on television. Novels are what you stuff in your pocket for the bus ride or stretch out with on the beach. If that describes you, have another look. Novels can be rebellious, threatening, and very up-to-date. They challenge popular assumptions about politics, religion, morality, and race. They've been condemned from the pulpit, burned in public, and banned from libraries.

Take your pick. Whether it's for chilling out or changing the world, there's a novel to fit the bill.

A **novel** is a long work of prose fiction, usually about a **protagonist**—or central character—and several minor characters. Because of a novel's length, the writer is often able to include a variety of characters, develop several subplots, and use many details and descriptions. When you read a novel, you can visit a different world.

> **Mark the text** **Think of a novel you've read that provided escape or entertainment or one that challenged your ideas. Briefly explain your choice.**
>
> Title:_____
>
> This novel was entertaining/challenging because _____
>
> _____
>
> _____

Why Read Novels?

You can read novels for many reasons. Novels may simply help to pass the time, or they may challenge your way of looking at life. But there is another reason to read novels, especially those written years before you were born: Novels are a window to the past, a way to experience history without the dates and timelines. Where can you turn to share the energy of the industrial revolution, the elegance of an aristocratic ball, or the squalor of a nineteenth-century slum? To a novel.

What's the Plan?

Novels tell a story. Typically, the events follow each other as they do in life—one after another in **chronological order.** And like other stories, novels have **settings, characters,** and at least one **plot.** Here are the main parts of a plot.

- **Exposition** introduces the characters, the setting, and the conflict.

- In **rising action,** the conflict develops.

- **Climax** brings the action to a point of high excitement, often a turning point.

- **Falling action** describes the results of the climax.

- The **resolution** reveals the final outcome.

The plots of a novel can be shown on a diagram, or plot outline, like this one.

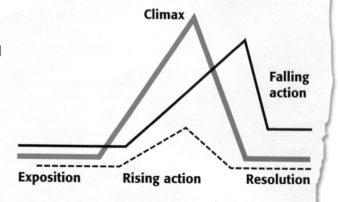

Climax

Falling action

Exposition   Rising action   Resolution

What Do I Look For?

This opening page of *A Tale of Two Cities* by Charles Dickens includes features common to most novels.

> The **author's name** and the **title** may be what first capture your interest.

> **Chapters** are the sections of a novel. They often begin or end with a change of scene or action. The first chapter introduces the **setting**—the time and place of the novel.

> A powerful **opening sentence** catches the reader's interest. This is one of the most famous opening sentences in English literature.

> **Point of view** is the perspective from which the narrator tells the story. In **third-person omniscient** point of view, a narrator who knows everything about the characters and events describes the action from outside the story.

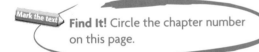 **Mark the text** **Find It!** Circle the chapter number on this page.

Charles Dickens

A Tale of Two Cities

with Related Readings

Chapter 1 # The Period

I**T WAS THE BEST OF TIMES**, it was the worst of times, it was the age of wisdom, it was the age of foolishness, it was the epoch of belief, it was the epoch of incredulity, it was the season of Light, it was the season of Darkness, it was the spring of hope, it was the winter of despair, we had everything before us, we had nothing before us, we were all going direct to Heaven, we were all going direct the other way—in short, the period was so far like the present period, that some of its noisiest authorities insisted on its being received, for good or for evil, in the superlative degree of comparison only.

There were a king with a large jaw and a queen with a plain face, on the throne of England; there were a king with a large jaw and a queen with a fair face, on the throne of France. In both countries it was clearer than crystal to the lords of the State preserves of loaves and fishes, that things in general were settled for ever.

It was the year of Our Lord one thousand seven hundred and seventy-five. Spiritual revelations were conceded to England at that favoured pe-riod, as at this. Mrs Southcott had recently attained her five-and-twentieth blessed birthday, of whom a prophetic private in the Life Guards had heralded the sublime appearance by announcing that arrangements were made for the swallowing up of London and Westminster. Even the Cock-lane ghost had been laid only a round dozen of years, after rapping out its messages, as the spirits of this very year last past (supernaturally deficient in originality) rapped out theirs. Mere messages in the earthly order of events had lately come to the English Crown and People, from a congress of British subjects in America: which, strange to relate, have proved more important to the human race than any communications yet received through any of the chickens of the Cock-lane brood.

France, less favoured on the whole as to matters spiritual than her sister of the shield and trident, rolled with exceeding smoothness down hill, making paper money and spending it. Under the guidance of her Christian pastors, she entertained herself, besides, with such humane achievements as sentencing a youth to have his hands cut off, his

---

How Do I Read It?

These **reading strategies** will help you get the most out of the novels you read.

Predict: Can you predict the next twist in the plot? If you stop to guess every so often, you will be more engaged in your reading.

Connect: Do you recognize yourself in any of the characters? Have you been in similar situations? Making personal connections with your reading will give you a deeper understanding of a novel.

Monitor Comprehension: Don't miss out on the action. If you discover you're confused by what you've

read, go back and review. If you're still stumped, ask a friend or a teacher for help.

Respond: The novel creates a world in miniature. Participate in it as you would in real life. Express what you think or feel as you read.

For more information on **reading strategies,** see pages 216–222 in the **Reading Handbook.**

 **DO IT!**

> **Read *A Tale of Two Cities* or another novel. Be sure to**
> - look for **literary elements** and the **author's plan**
> - use **reading strategies** to help you get the most from your reading

PART 2

NONFICTION AND INFORMATIONAL TEXT

Reading Literary Nonfiction

"Truth is stranger than fiction," people often say. And like lots of other clichés, this one is based in reality. It helps explains why people are eager to hear about travels to strange places, encounters with exotic animals, perilous adventures, original ideas, or unusual childhoods. Of course, not all nonfiction is equally interesting. No one would claim that a catalog description of a pair of jeans can keep a reader's attention for very long. What's the missing ingredient? A single word: *literary.*

Literary nonfiction is the truth dressed up in its party clothes. Authors of literary nonfiction tell their stories or explain their ideas the way writers of fiction do: with skill and passion. Whether it's an **essay** on Islam, a **memoir** of growing up in China, the **biography** of Michael Jordan, or an **autobiography** by a president, a writer will strive to capture the reader's interest by using the tools of the poet or novelist.

> **Mark the text** **Literary nonfiction can be about many topics. This list mentions some of them. Check one subject that you like to read about, or write a subject of your own on the blank line.**
>
> _____ the experiences of a mountain climber   _____ the causes of earthquakes
>
> _____ how people live in a distant part of the world   _____ the history of television
>
> _____ the life story of a famous athlete   _____ a history of an ancient culture
>
> _____

Why Read Literary Nonfiction?

People read literary nonfiction to learn more about the world, to compare their own lives with the lives of other people, and to explore the ideas of people known for their originality or expertise. People read it because the world is very big and life is too short for one person to pack in all the experiences that are interesting. Finally, people read literary nonfiction for the sheer joy of a good story well told.

What's the Plan?

Life stories, such as biographies and autobiographies, along with other nonfiction narratives, are usually told in **chronological order,** events following each other as they do in real life. Essays that explain ideas or present arguments may be in **cause-and-effect** or **comparison-and-contrast** order. Look for **signal words** to point you to each of these **text structures.**

Text Structure	Signal Words
Chronological order	first, then, next, after, later, finally
Cause and effect	therefore, because, so, consequently, as a result of
Comparison and contrast	similarly, in contrast, likewise, on the other hand, but

For more about text structures and their signal words, see pages 222–224 in the **Reading Handbook.**

What Do I Look For?

This page from Dorothy Wordsworth's journals includes elements shared by other works of literary nonfiction.

The **narrator** is the person who speaks to the reader or tells the story. In a journal the narrator is the same as the author.

Imagery—descriptive language that creates "word pictures"—appears in both fiction and literary nonfiction. Images appeal to the five senses: sight, hearing, touch, taste, and smell.

Personification is a figure of speech that gives human characteristics to nonhuman things.

A **metaphor** compares unlike objects without using the words *like* or *as*. Here the author compares the strip of daffodils to a "busy highway."

from *The Journals of*
Dorothy Wordsworth

Dorothy Wordsworth

THURSDAY, APRIL 15. It was a threatening misty morning—but mild. We [Dorothy and William] set off after dinner from Eusemere. Mrs. Clarkson went a short way with us but turned back. The wind was furious, and we thought we must have returned. We first rested in the large boathouse, then under a furze bush opposite Mr. Clarkson's; saw the plough going in the field. The wind seized our breath; the lake was rough. There was a boat by itself floating in the middle of the bay below Water Millock. We rested again in the Water Millock lane. The hawthorns are black and green, the birches here and there greenish, but there is yet more of purple to be seen on the twigs. We got over into a field to avoid some cows—people working, a few primroses by the roadside, wood-sorrel flowers, the anemone, scentless violets, strawberries, and that starry yellow flower which Mrs. C. calls pile wort. When we were in the woods beyond Gowbarrow Park, we saw a few daffodils close to the waterside. We fancied that the lake had floated the seeds ashore and that the little colony had so sprung up. But as we went along there were more and yet more, and at last under the boughs of the trees, we saw that there was a long belt of them along the shore, about the breadth of a country turnpike road. I never saw daffodils so beautiful. They grew among the mossy stones about and about them; some rested their heads upon these stones as on a pillow for weariness, and the rest tossed and reeled and danced and seemed as if they verily laughed with the wind that blew upon them over the lake. They looked so gay, ever glancing, ever changing. This wind blew directly over the lake to them. There was here and there a little knot and a few stragglers a few yards higher up, but they were so few as not to disturb the simplicity and unity and life of that one busy highway. We rested again and again. The bays were stormy, and we heard the waves at different distances and in the middle of the water like the sea.

 Mark the text

Find It! Underline three words or phrases that personify the daffodils.

How Do I Read It?

These **reading strategies** will help you get the most out of literary nonfiction.

Question: Why is the author telling me this? What is the purpose of this story or argument? Asking questions as you read will help you understand the text.

Respond: Literary nonfiction is about the real world. Respond as you would if a friend were telling you a story. "I don't believe it!" "That's terrible!" "What did you do next?"

Connect: Make connections between your reading and your own life. Have you ever felt this way or met someone like that? What do your experiences have in common with those of the author?

Visualize: Make the author's experiences your own by visualizing them as you read.

For more information on **reading strategies,** see pages 216–222 in the **Reading Handbook.**

 DO IT!

Read the literary nonfiction that follows. Be sure to

• enjoy the **literary elements** and recognize the **author's plan**

• use **reading strategies** to help you get the most from your reading

GET READY TO READ!

Connect

Think-Pair-Share Imagine that you come to school one day feeling and looking quite sick. A friend says to you, "You look great today." Your friend doesn't actually mean what he says. He's using **irony**—saying the opposite of what he means to make a point. With a partner, think of ironic comments you might make in the following situations. Write your comments on the line below each situation.

- A rainstorm hits during a picnic you were looking forward to.

  _____

- You see a really bad movie with a friend.

  _____

Share your ironic comments with your class.

In this essay, you'll see how a famous eighteenth-century writer uses irony to draw people's attention to a problem.

Did You Know?

Building Background In the early 1700s Ireland's people experienced desperate times. Many were out of work. Homeless people begged for food. Many Irish believed that English laws were responsible for their economic problems. Ireland was ruled by England, and English laws limited Ireland's ability to trade with other countries. Ireland could buy certain products only from England. And England charged high prices for these products. English taxes on Ireland were also high. English landlords, who owned much of Ireland's best land, charged high rents. Life was especially hard for Irish Catholics. Under England's Protestant rule, Catholics could not own property or hold political office. Jonathan Swift, who was born in Ireland, wrote *A Modest Proposal* to draw attention to the country's problems.

- *A Modest Proposal* is a **satire**—a literary work that uses irony, humor, and other techniques to point out problems and criticize the people who are causing them.
- Swift creates irony with a fictional **speaker.** The speaker who makes the proposal is not Swift. The speaker is an amateur Irish politician who makes ridiculous statements—as you'll see. Swift (the author) does not expect anyone to take the speaker's proposal seriously. He is being ironic—saying the opposite of what he believes in order to make a point.

Reason to Read

Setting a Purpose for Reading Read to see what the "modest proposal" is, how Swift uses irony, and whom and what Swift is really criticizing.

word power

Vocabulary Preview

Read these words from *A Modest Proposal* and their definitions below. Try pronouncing each word aloud. As you read, use context clues to unlock the meaning of these and other words you don't know.

sustenance (sus´ tə nəns) *n.* food or any other item that supports life; p. 113

rudiments (rōō´ də mənts) *n.* basics; p. 115

deference (def´ ər əns) *n.* courteous respect; p. 117

expedient (iks pē´ dē ənt) *n.* a means to an end; p. 118

digress (dī gres´) *v.* to stray from the main subject; p. 119

enumerate (i nōō mə rāt) *v.* to list; p. 120

inevitable (i nev´ ə tə bəl) *adj.* unavoidable; certain; p. 122

Hot Words Journal

As you read, circle words that you find interesting or that you don't understand. Later you may add them to your **Hot Words Journal** at the back of this book.

What You'll Learn

Key Goals In this lesson, you will learn these key skills, strategies, and concepts.

- **Reading Focus:** Monitor Comprehension
- **Think It Over:** Interpret
- **Literary Element:** Satire
- **Reading Coach:** Understanding the Writer's Style

A Modest Proposal

Jonathan Swift

FOR PREVENTING THE CHILDREN OF POOR PEOPLE FROM BEING A *BURTHEN*[1] *TO THEIR PARENTS* OR THE COUNTRY, AND FOR MAKING THEM BENEFICIAL TO THE PUBLIC. **A**

It is a melancholy object to those who walk through this great town,[2] or travel in the country, when they see the *streets*, the *roads*, and *cabin doors* crowded with *beggars* of the female sex, followed by three, four, or six children, *all in rags*, and importuning every passenger for an alms.[3] **B** These *mothers*, instead of being able to work for their honest livelihood, are forced to employ all their time in strolling to beg <u>sustenance</u> for their *helpless infants* who, as they grow up, either turn *thieves* for want[4] of work or leave their *dear Native Country to fight for the Pretender*[5] in Spain or sell themselves to the Barbadoes.[6]

I think it is agreed by all parties that this prodigious number of children, in the arms or on the backs or at the *heels* of their *mothers*, and frequently of their fathers, is, *in the present deplorable*

10

---

1. A *burthen* is a burden.
2. The *town* referred to here is Dublin, Ireland.
3. [*Importuning . . . alms*] means "asking every passerby for a handout."
4. Here, *want* means "lack."
5. *The Pretender* was a name given to James Edward Stuart (1688–1766), the son of England's deposed king, James II. James Edward had the loyalty and sympathy of the Irish people because he was Roman Catholic.
6. [*Sell . . . Barbadoes*] is a reference to the many Irish people who hoped to escape poverty by traveling to the West Indies. They obtained passage by agreeing to work as indentured servants.

Vocabulary

sustenance (sus′tə nəns) *n.* food or any other item that supports life

---

Reading Focus

← Monitor Comprehension When you **monitor comprehension**, you think about whether you're understanding what you're reading. Reread the highlighted subtitle. It tells what problem the proposal is meant to solve. Mark a check next to the statement below that sums up the problem. **A**

_____ how to keep poor Irish kids from being such a burden

_____ how to help poor Irish couples be better parents

Reading Coach

← Understanding the Writer's Style Swift sometimes uses italics, or slanted type, to draw attention to key ideas. **Mark the text** Circle the italicized words in the boxed sentence. On the lines below, tell what the sentence is mainly about. **B**

_____

_____

_____

word power

Using Definitions If you can't figure out the meaning of an underlined vocabulary word, read the definition at the bottom of the page.

Reading Focus 🔑 **Monitor Comprehension** After you read a difficult paragraph like this one, take time to check your understanding. Stop to sum up what you just read. Summarizing will help you make sure that you "get" what you're reading. **C**

Model: *The speaker is mainly talking about why his proposal for making poor Irish kids less of a burden is better than other people's proposals. Under his plan, one-year-olds would help feed and provide clothes for other people.*

Keep This in Mind
Use the following symbols to react to what you are reading or to mark a passage to return to later.

? I have a question about something here.

! This really caught my attention.

★ This information is important.

state of the kingdom, a very great additional grievance; and, therefore, whoever could find out a fair, cheap, and easy method of making these children sound and useful members of the
20 commonwealth would deserve so well of the public as to have his statue set up for a preserver of the nation.

But my intention is very far from being confined to provide only for the children of *professed beggars;* it is of a much greater extent and shall take in the whole number of infants at a certain age who are born of parents in effect as little able to support them as those who demand our charity in the streets.

As to my own part, having turned my thoughts for many years upon this important subject, and maturely weighed the several *schemes of other projectors,* I have always found them grossly mistaken
30 in their computation. It is true a child *just dropped from its dam*[7] may be supported by her milk for a solar year with little other nourishment, at most not above the value of two shillings, which the mother may certainly get, or the value in *scraps,* by her lawful occupation of *begging.* And it is exactly at one year old that I propose to provide for them in such a manner as, instead of being a charge upon their *parents* or the *parish,* or *wanting food and raiment*[8] for the rest of their lives, they shall, on the contrary, contribute to the feeding and partly to the clothing of many thousands. **C**

There is likewise another great advantage in my scheme, that
40 it will prevent those *voluntary abortions,* and that horrid practice of *women murdering their bastard children,* alas! too frequent among us, sacrificing the *poor innocent babes,* I doubt, more to avoid the expense than the shame, which would move tears and pity in the most savage and inhuman breast.

The number of souls in this kingdom being usually reckoned one million and a half, of these I calculate there may be about two hundred thousand couples whose wives are breeders, from which number I subtract thirty thousand couples who are able to maintain their own children, although I apprehend there cannot
50 be so many under *the present distresses of the kingdom,* but this being granted, there will remain a hundred and seventy thousand breeders. I again subtract fifty thousand for those women who

---

7. A *dam* is a mother. The word is normally used only to refer to animals.
8. *Raiment* is clothing.

miscarry or whose children die by accident or disease within the year. There only remain a hundred and twenty thousand children of poor parents annually born. The question, therefore, is how this number shall be reared and provided for, which, as I have already said, under the present situation of affairs is utterly impossible by all the methods hitherto proposed, for we can *neither employ them in handicraft* or *agriculture;* we neither build houses (I mean in the country) nor cultivate land. **D** They can   60
very seldom pick up a livelihood *by stealing* till they arrive at six years old, except where they are of towardly parts,[9] although I confess they learn the <u>rudiments</u> much earlier, during which time they can, however, be properly looked upon only as *probationers,*[10] as I have been informed by a principal gentleman in the County of Cavan, who protested to me that he never knew above one or two instances under the age of six, even in a part of the kingdom *so renowned for the quickest proficiency in that art.*

I am assured by our merchants that a boy or a girl, before twelve years old, is no saleable commodity, and even when they come to   70
this age, they will not yield above three pounds, or three pounds and half-a-crown at most, on the Exchange, which cannot turn to account[11] either to the parents or the kingdom, the charge of nutriment and rags having been at least four times that value.

I shall now therefore humbly propose my own thoughts, which I hope will not be liable to the least objection.

I have been assured by a very knowing American of my acquaintance in London that a young healthy child, well nursed, is at a year old a most delicious, nourishing, and wholesome food, whether *stewed, roasted, baked,* or *boiled,* and I make no doubt   80
that it will equally serve in a *fricassee,* or a *ragout.*[12] **E**

I do, therefore, humbly offer it to *public consideration* that, of the hundred and twenty thousand children already computed, twenty thousand may be reserved for breed, whereof only one-fourth part to be males, which is more than we allow to *sheep,*

---

9. *Towardly parts* means "promising talent."
10. *Probationers* are apprentices, or people who are learning a skill.
11. *Turn to account* means "be profitable."
12. *Fricassee* and *ragout* are types of meat stews.

Vocabulary
rudiments (rōō′ də mənts) *n.* basics

Reading Coach

← **Understanding the Writer's Style** Swift often uses long, complicated sentences. To understand these sentences, focus on their main ideas. One way to do this is to identify the most important parts of a sentence and cross out everything else. Look at this thinking model for understanding the sentence in the boxed text. **D**

Model: *The question, ~~therefore,~~ is how this number shall be reared and provided for, ~~which, as I have already said, under the present situation of affairs is utterly impossible by all the methods hitherto proposed,~~ for we can neither employ them in handicraft or agriculture; we neither build houses ~~(I mean in the country)~~ nor cultivate land.*

Literary Element

← **Satire** Remember, this selection is a satire. A **satire** ridicules the faults of people or countries. One method of satire is to present shocking ideas. What shocking idea is the speaker presenting here? Do you think Swift really agrees with what the speaker is saying? Write your responses below. **E**

_____

_____

_____

_____

◆ Interpret Use your knowledge and experience to **interpret,** or make sense of, what the speaker is suggesting about poor children. Then think about what the author, Swift, is suggesting. **F**

Model: *The speaker talks about selling kids as meat. I guess he is suggesting that poor Irish kids are no better than cattle or pigs! I know the proposal is ironic, so Swift must be saying just the opposite—poor kids are treated like animals but should be treated like human beings.*

Literary Element

◆ Satire One purpose of satire is to criticize the people who are causing a problem. Whom is Swift really criticizing in this paragraph? Check one. **G**

_____ poor parents

_____ young children

_____ rich landlords

black cattle, or *swine;* and my reason is that these children are seldom the fruits of marriage, *a circumstance not much regarded by our savages;* therefore *one male* will be sufficient to serve *four females.* That the remaining hundred thousand may at a year old
90 be offered in sale to the *persons of quality* and *fortune* through the kingdom, always advising the mother to let them suck plentifully of the last month, so as to render them plump and fat for a good table. A child will make two dishes at an entertainment for friends, and when the family dines alone, the fore or hind quarter will make a reasonable dish and, seasoned with a little pepper or salt, will be very good boiled on the fourth day, especially in *winter.* **F**

I have reckoned upon a medium, that a child just born will weigh twelve pounds and, in a solar year, if tolerably nursed,
100 increaseth to twenty-eight pounds.

I grant this food will be somewhat dear,[13] and therefore very *proper for landlords,* who, as they have already devoured most of the parents, seem to have the best title to the children. **G**

Infants' flesh will be in season throughout the year, but more plentiful in *March,* and a little before and after, for we are told by a grave author,[14] an eminent French physician, that *fish being a prolific diet,* there are more children born in *Roman Catholic countries* about nine months after *Lent* than at any other season; therefore, reckoning a year after *Lent,* the markets will be more
110 glutted than usual because the number of *Popish*[15] *infants* is at least three to one in this kingdom, and therefore it will have one other collateral advantage by lessening the number of *Papists*[16] among us.

I have already computed the charge of nursing a beggar's child (in which list I reckon all *cottagers, labourers,* and four-fifths of the *farmers*) to be about two shillings *per annum,* rags included, and I believe no gentleman would repine[17] to give ten shillings for the *carcass of a good fat child,* which, as I have said, will make four dishes of excellent nutritive meat when he hath only some
120 particular friend or his own family to dine with him. Thus the

13. Here, *dear* means "expensive."
14. The *grave author* is François Rabelais, a French satirist.
15. *Popish* means "Roman Catholic."
16. *Papists* are Roman Catholics.
17. *Repine* means "complain."

Squire will learn to be a good landlord and grow popular among his tenants; the mother will have eight shillings net profit and be fit for work till she produces another child.

Those who are more thrifty (*as I must confess the times require*) may flay[18] the carcass, the skin of which, artificially[19] dressed, will make admirable *gloves for ladies* and *summer boots for fine gentlemen.*

📖 Reading Check

As to our City of Dublin, shambles[20] may be appointed for this purpose in the most convenient parts of it, and butchers, we may be assured, will not be wanting, although I rather recommend buying the children alive and dressing them hot from the knife, as we do *roasting pigs.*

130

A very worthy person, *a true lover of his country,* and whose virtues I highly esteem, was lately pleased, in discoursing on this matter, to offer a refinement upon my scheme. He said that many gentlemen of this kingdom, having of late destroyed their deer, he conceived that the want of venison[21] might be well supplied by the bodies of young lads and maidens not exceeding fourteen years of age, nor under twelve, so great a number of both sexes in every country being now ready to starve for want of work and service,[22] and these to be disposed of by their parents, if alive, or otherwise by their nearest relations. **H** But with due

140

deference to so excellent a friend and so deserving a patriot, I cannot be altogether in his sentiments; for as to the males, my American acquaintance assured me from frequent experience that their flesh was generally tough and lean, like that of our schoolboys, by continual exercise, and their taste disagreeable, and to fatten them would not answer the charge. Then as to the females, it would, I think, with humble submission, *be a loss to the public* because they soon would become breeders themselves. And

---

18. To *flay* is to strip off the skin.
19. Here, *artificially* means "skillfully."
20. *Shambles* were slaughterhouses.
21. Here venison (veʹnə sən) means "deer meat."
22. *Service* is work as a servant.

Vocabulary
deference (defʹər əns) *n.* courteous respect

📖 Reading Check

Step 1 If you put a question mark next to any confusing passages, choose one or more of these strategies to better understand the marked passages.

- Reread confusing parts slowly or aloud.
- Ask a classmate or a teacher, parent, or other adult for help.

Step 2 Now answer this question on the lines provided. What are the problem and the solution the speaker in *A Modest Proposal* presents?

Problem:

_____

_____

Solution:

_____

_____

> **Reading Coach**

🔑 **Understanding the Writer's Style** Swift writes in long, complicated sentences. **Mark the text** Cross out the less important parts of the boxed sentences. Now write their main ideas in your own words below. **H**

_____

_____

_____

_____

_____

Literary Element

Satire Satire often contains irony. When people are ironic, they say or do the opposite of what you expect. Here, the speaker says that the plan to use children as a substitute for deer meat might seem cruel. And he insists that he is against cruelty. What is ironic about the speaker's saying that he is against cruel plans? Answer on the lines below. **I**

_____

_____

Reading Focus

Monitor Comprehension Check to make sure you understand what the speaker is saying in this paragraph. Then put a check next to the summary below that sums up what he says. **J**

_____ I'm not worried about how much it costs to take care of old Irish people because my plan would make old people work for a living.

_____ I'm not worried about the cost of helping Irish who are old, sick, or disabled because terrible living conditions will kill them off.

---

150 besides, it is not improbable that some scrupulous people might be apt to censure such a practice (although indeed very unjustly) as a little bordering upon cruelty, which, I confess, hath always been with me the strongest objection against any project, however so well intended. **I**

But in order to justify my friend, he confessed that this **expedient** was put into his head by the famous *Psalmanazar,*[23] a native of the island Formosa, who came from thence to London above twenty years ago and in conversation told my friend that in his country when any young person happened to be put to death, 160 the executioner sold the carcass to *persons of quality* as a prime dainty, and that in his time, the body of a plump girl of fifteen, who was crucified for an attempt to poison the emperor, was sold to his Imperial *Majesty's Prime Minister of State* and other great *Mandarins*[24] of the Court, *in joints from the gibbet,*[25] at four hundred crowns. Neither, indeed, can I deny that if the same use were made of several plump young girls in this town, who, without one single groat to their fortunes, 170 cannot stir abroad without a chair and appear at the *playhouse* and *assemblies* in foreign fineries, which they never will pay for, the kingdom would not be the worse.

Did You Know?
A *groat* was an old British coin worth four pennies.

Some persons of a desponding spirit are in great concern about that vast number of poor people who are aged, diseased, or maimed, and I have been desired to employ my thoughts what course may be taken to ease the nation of so grievous an encumbrance. But I am not in the least pain upon that matter because it is very well known that they are every day *dying* and 180 *rotting* by *cold* and *famine* and *filth* and *vermin* as fast as can be reasonably expected. **J** And as to the younger labourers, they

---

23. George *Psalmanazar* was a French impostor who pretended to be from Formosa (now Taiwan) and wrote about incidences of cannibalism there.
24. *Mandarins* are powerful people.
25. *[Joints from the gibbet]* are pieces of meat from the gallows.

Vocabulary
expedient (iks pē′ dē ənt) *n.* a means to an end

---

are now in almost as hopeful a condition. They cannot get work and consequently pine away for want of nourishment to a degree that if at any time they are accidentally hired to common labour, they have not strength to perform it; and thus the country and themselves are happily delivered from the evils to come.

I have too long digressed and therefore shall return to my subject. I think the advantages by the proposal which I have made are obvious and many, as well as of the highest importance.

For *first,* as I have already observed, it would greatly lessen the number of *Papists,* with whom we are yearly overrun, being the principal breeders of the nation as well as our most dangerous enemies and who stay at home on purpose with a design to *deliver the kingdom to the Pretender,* hoping to take their advantage by the absence of *so many good Protestants,* who have chosen rather to leave their country than stay at home and pay tithes against their conscience to an *Episcopal curate.*[26]

Secondly, the poorer tenants will have something valuable of their own, which by law may be made liable to distress[27] and help to pay their landlord's rent, their corn and cattle being already seized and *money a thing unknown.*

Thirdly, whereas the maintenance of a hundred thousand children, from two years old and upwards, cannot be computed at less than ten shillings a piece *per annum,* the nation's stock will be thereby increased fifty thousand pounds *per annum,* besides the profit of a new dish introduced to the tables of all *gentlemen of fortune* in the kingdom who have any refinement in taste; and the money will circulate among ourselves, the goods being entirely of our own growth and manufacture.

Fourthly, the constant breeders, besides the gain of eight shillings *sterling per annum* by the sale of their children, will be rid of the charge of maintaining them after the first year. **K**

190

200

210

Reading Focus — **Monitor Comprehension** On this page, the speaker lists four main "advantages" of his proposal. Circle the key words that describe each advantage. Then put a check next to each advantage below that is on the speaker's list. **K**

_____ There will be fewer Catholics in Ireland.

_____ Poor parents will have something valuable to sell.

_____ All of Ireland's hungry will be fed.

_____ Ireland's economy will improve.

_____ Taxes will go down.

_____ Poor parents won't have to support their kids after the kids have their first birthday.

26. *[Protestants . . . curate]* Swift is attacking Protestants who have left Ireland and thus avoided paying tithes to the Anglican Church. A *tithe* is one-tenth of a person's annual income.
27. *Distress* is seizure of property for payment of debt.

Vocabulary
digress (dī gres´) *v.* to stray from the main subject

Reading Coach

← **Understanding the Writer's Style** In this paragraph, the speaker tells the fifth main "advantage" of his plan. Cross out the less important parts of the one long sentence in this paragraph. On the lines below, write the main idea in your own words. **L**

Literary Element

← **Satire** This paragraph contains a sixth and final "advantage" of the speaker's plan. In his use of satire, Swift is making the speaker's plan seem ridiculous. Underline one statement that you think seems ridiculous and explain it on the lines below. **M**

Fifthly, this food would likewise bring great *custom to taverns,* where the vintners[28] will certainly be so prudent as to procure the best receipts[29] for dressing it to perfection and consequently have their houses frequented by all the *fine gentlemen,* who justly value themselves upon their knowledge in good eating; and a skillful cook, who understands how to oblige his guests, will contrive to make it as expensive as they please. **L**

220   *Sixthly,* this would be a great inducement to marriage, which all wise nations have either encouraged by rewards or enforced by laws and penalties. It would increase the care and tenderness of mothers toward their children when they were sure of a settlement for life to the poor babes, provided in some sort by the public to their annual profit instead of expense. We should see an honest emulation[30] among the married women, *which of them could bring the fattest child to the market.* Men would become as *fond* of their wives, during the time of their pregnancy, as they are now of their *mares* in foal, their *cows* in calf, or *sows* when they are ready to farrow,[31] nor offer to beat or
230 kick them (as it is too *frequent* a practice) for fear of a miscarriage. **M**

   Many other advantages might be <u>enumerated</u>: for instance, the addition of some thousand carcasses in our exportation of barrelled beef; the propagation of *swine's flesh* and improvement in the art of making good *bacon,* so much wanted among us by the great destruction of *pigs,* too frequent at our tables, which are no way comparable in taste or magnificence to a well-grown, fat yearling child, which, roasted whole, will make a considerable figure at a *Lord Mayor's feast* or any other public entertainment. But this and many others I omit, being studious of brevity.

240   Supposing that one thousand families in this city would be constant customers for infants' flesh, besides others who might have it at *merry-meetings,* particularly *weddings* and *christenings,* I compute that Dublin would take off annually about twenty thousand carcasses, and the rest of the kingdom (where probably they will be sold somewhat cheaper) the remaining eighty thousand.

---

28. *Vintners* are wine merchants.
29. Here, *receipts* are recipes.
30. Here, *emulation* means "competition."
31. *Farrow* means "produce piglets."

Vocabulary
enumerate (i no͞o′ mə rāt) *v.* to list

N I can think of no one objection that will possibly be raised against this proposal, unless it should be urged that the number of people will be thereby much lessened in the kingdom. This I freely own, and it was indeed one principal design in offering it to the world. I desire the reader will observe that I calculate my remedy *for this one individual Kingdom of IRELAND and for no other that ever was, is, or, I think, ever can be upon earth.* Therefore, let no man talk to me of other expedients: *of taxing our absentees*[32] *at five shillings a pound; of using neither clothes, nor household furniture, except what is of our own growth and manufacture; of utterly rejecting the materials and instruments that promote foreign luxury; of curing the expensiveness of pride, vanity, idleness, and gaming in our women; of introducing a vein of parsimony,*[33] *prudence, and temperance; of learning to love our Country, wherein we differ even from LAPLANDERS and the inhabitants of TOPINAMBOO;*[34] *of quitting our animosities and factions; . . . of being a little cautious not to sell our country and consciences for nothing; of teaching landlords to have at least one degree of mercy toward their tenants; lastly, of putting a spirit of honesty, industry, and skill into our shopkeepers, who, if a resolution could now be taken to buy only our native goods, would immediately unite to cheat and exact upon us in the price, the measure, and the goodness, nor could ever yet be brought to make one fair proposal of just dealing, though often and earnestly invited to it.*

Therefore, I repeat, let no man talk to me of these and the like expedients till he hath at least some glimpse of hope that there will ever be some hearty and sincere attempt to put them in practice.

But as to myself, having been wearied out for many years with offering vain, idle, visionary thoughts, and at length utterly despairing of success, I fortunately fell upon this proposal, which, as it is wholly new, so it hath something solid and real, of no expense and little trouble, full in our own power, and whereby we can incur no danger in *disobliging England.* **O** For this kind of commodity will not bear exportation, the flesh being of too tender a consistence to admit a long continuance in salt, *although*

250

260

270

280

---

32. In this context, *absentees* are English people who own land in Ireland but refuse to live on it.
33. *Parsimony* (pär´ sə mō´ nē) is thriftiness.
34. *Topinamboo* was an area in Brazil.

Think It Over

Interpret In this paragraph, the speaker says, "let no man talk to me of other expedients." These expedients are solutions that the speaker doesn't want to hear about. Remember, Swift is being ironic in this essay. So you can figure out that perhaps these are the solutions Swift *really does* believe in.

Mark the text Underline the first two solutions that the speaker does not want to hear about. (Hint: The solutions are in *italic* type, and each begins with the word *of.*) In your own words, describe one more of the remaining solutions on the lines below. **N**

_____

_____

_____

_____

Reading Focus

Respond The speaker calls his proposal "new," "solid and real," and "of no expense and little trouble." Do you agree? What would you call the speaker's proposal? Jot down a few descriptive words on the lines below. **O**

_____

_____

📖 Reading Check

Step 1 Now that you've finished reading *A Modest Proposal,* take a moment to think about it. Look back over the parts that you marked and the questions that you answered. Then answer the questions below on the lines provided.

Does Swift want readers to accept the speaker's proposal? If not, what is one solution Swift might really propose?

_____

_____

_____

_____

Step 2 Now think about your own life and times. If you were writing a satire about today's world, what social problem would you write about? Why?

_____

_____

Choose your own words, either from the underlined vocabulary in the selection or from the words you circled as you read. Record them in your **Hot Words Journal** at the back of this book and complete one of the activities listed there.

perhaps I could name a country which would be glad to eat up our whole nation without it.

After all, I am not so violently bent upon my own opinion as to reject any offer proposed by wise men, which shall be found equally innocent, cheap, easy, and effectual. But before something of that kind shall be advanced in contradiction to my scheme, and offering a better, I desire the author, or authors, will be pleased maturely to consider two points. *First,* as things now stand, how they will be able to find food and raiment for a hundred
290 thousand useless mouths and backs. And *secondly,* there being a round million of creatures in human figure throughout this kingdom, whose whole subsistence[35] put into a common stock would leave them in debt two millions of pounds *sterling;* adding those who are beggars by profession to the bulk of farmers, cottagers, and labourers with their wives and children, who are beggars in effect; I desire those *politicians* who dislike my overture and may perhaps be so bold to attempt an answer, that they will first ask the parents of these mortals whether they would not at this day think it a great happiness to have been sold for food
300 at a year old in the manner I prescribe and thereby have avoided such a perpetual scene of misfortunes as they have since gone through by the *oppression of landlords,* the impossibility of paying rent without money or trade, the want of common sustenance, with neither house nor clothes to cover them from the inclemencies of the weather, and the most <u>inevitable</u> prospect of entailing[36] the like or greater miseries upon their breed for ever.

I profess in the sincerity of my heart that I have not the least personal interest in endeavouring to promote this necessary work, having no other motive than the *public good of my country,*
310 *by advancing our trade, providing for infants, relieving the poor, and giving some pleasure to the rich.* I have no children by which I can propose to get a single penny, the youngest being nine years old and my wife past childbearing.

·················· 📖 **Reading Check** ··················

35. *Whole subsistence* is all their possessions.
36. *Entailing* means "passing on to the next generation."

Vocabulary
inevitable (i nev′ ə tə bəl) *adj.* unavoidable; certain

Going Solo

⚷ Understanding the Writer's Style

Cross Out As you read *A Modest Proposal*, you looked for the main idea of long sentences. Get more practice now. Reread the following sentence from the selection. Cross out the less important parts of the sentence. Then, in your own words, write the main idea.

"I think it is agreed by all parties that this prodigious number of children, in the arms or on the backs or at the *heels* of their *mothers*, and frequently of their fathers, is, *in the present deplorable state of the kingdom*, a very great additional grievance; and, therefore, whoever could find out a fair, cheap, and easy method of making these children sound and useful members of the commonwealth would deserve so well of the public as to have his statue set up for a preserver of the nation." (lines 14–21)

_____

Buddy Up

⚷ Monitor Comprehension

Tell It Fast! Suppose a classmate comes to you just before class and says, "Last night I read *A Modest Proposal*, but I didn't understand it. Tell me really fast what it's about." Think about what you would say. Then, with a partner, think of a two- or three-sentence summary of *A Modest Proposal*. Write your summary on the lines below.

_____
_____
_____
_____
_____

TeamWork

⚷ Interpret

1. Get the Point! In the following passage, Swift uses sarcasm (sharp, bitter irony) to make a point. Discuss the passage with your group. Together, figure out what the passage means and what point Swift is making. Jot down your ideas on the lines provided.

I grant this food will be somewhat dear, and therefore very *proper for landlords*, who, as they have already devoured most of the parents, seem to have the best title to the children. (lines 103–105).

_____
_____
_____

2. A Swift Interview With your group, role-play an interview between Jonathan Swift and a group of reporters. Write up an outline of a script for the interview. Reporters should ask five questions. They should try to find out things like why Swift wrote *A Modest Proposal* and what solutions he *really* proposes for Ireland's problems. Perform your interview for the class. Write one of your questions and Swift's answer on the lines below.

_____
_____
_____
_____
_____

Literary Element

➤ Satire

A **satire** is a work in which an author uses literary devices to point out problems and criticize the people who are causing them. Three common satirical devices are as follows:

- **irony:** saying the opposite of what one means in order to make a point. When Swift suggests that poor Irish families should sell their children for food, he really wants Britain to end laws that keep Ireland's people so poor.
- **exaggeration:** language that makes something seem greater or more important than it really is, as when Swift suggests that landlords have "devoured" poor people
- **understatement:** language that makes something seem smaller or less important than it really is, as when Swift's speaker calls his outrageous proposal "modest"

Review *A Modest Proposal* to find at least one other example of each device. On the chart below, jot down each example and the line numbers in which it appears.

Irony	Exaggeration	Understatement

Standardized Test Practice

Choose the best answer for each multiple-choice question. Fill in the circle in the spaces for questions 1 and 2 on the right.

1. What problem does the speaker of *A Modest Proposal* hope to solve with his plan?

    A. landlords who charge high rents

    B. armers who produce too few crops

    C. parents who are too poor to support their children

    D. store owners who charge very high prices for food

2. The speaker's "modest proposal" is that children should be

    A. employed as craft workers.

    B. employed as farmers.

    C. sold as servants.

    D. sold as food.

Write your answer to open-ended question A in the space provided below.

A. In your opinion, does Jonathan Swift expect readers to take the speaker's solution seriously? Explain.

Multiple-Choice Questions

1. Ⓐ Ⓑ Ⓒ Ⓓ   2. Ⓐ Ⓑ Ⓒ Ⓓ

Open-Ended Question

A. _____

_____

_____

_____

Vocabulary Check

From the word list, write the word that belongs in the blank in each sentence.

sustenance *n.* food or any other item that supports life

rudiments *n.* basics

deference *n.* courteous respect

expedient *n.* a means to an end

digress *v.* to stray from the main subject

enumerate *v.* to list

inevitable *adj.* unavoidable; certain

1. The rangers gave the hungry backpacker _____ to restore her strength.

2. Please stay on the topic and do not _____ to other subjects.

3. His deep admiration and _____ for the teacher showed in everything he did.

4. We applauded Carl's idea for an _____ that would get the job done.

5. Since I didn't study for the exam, I knew that flunking was _____.

6. He knew only the _____ of math when he entered college.

7. Sally is good at so many sports that it would take an hour to _____ all her awards.

GET READY TO READ!

Connect

Think-List-Discuss Think for a moment about recent events you might write about in a diary (a school dance, sporting event, natural disaster—anything that interests you). Then form a circle with two or three other students and pass a piece of paper around for one minute. Each time you receive the paper, quickly write one of your ideas on it. When the time's up, share your list with those of other groups. Discuss how your lists compare and contrast.

In these selections from a diary, you'll "see" two important historical events through the eyes of an Englishman who wrote about them.

Did You Know?

Building Background Samuel Pepys (pēps) lived in London and held a high-level job in the English navy. From 1660 until 1669, he wrote in his diary about his private life and public events. The entries you are about to read describe two important events of the period.

- **The Restoration:** After a bloody civil war, England went eleven years without a king. Then, in April 1661, the monarchy was "restored" when Charles II was crowned king. Samuel Pepys was at the coronation.

- **The Great Fire of London:** In 1666 a huge fire broke out in London. Over the course of four days, Pepys fearfully watched as the fire raged out of control and destroyed four-fifths of the central city.

Reason to Read

Setting a Purpose for Reading Read to learn what happened during Charles II's coronation and during the Great Fire.

 As you read, use the following **Foldable** to keep track of the events in *The Diary of Samuel Pepys.*

1. Place a sheet of paper in front of you with the short end at the top. Fold it in half from side to side.

2. Turn the paper horizontally and fold it in half from side to side again. Then fold it in half two more times.

3. Unfold the paper and position it with the short end at the top. It should form two columns with eight rows. Label the left column **The Coronation** and the right column **The Fire.**

4. As you read, jot down the main things that happen during each event. Put your notes in time order, or the order in which things actually happened. Use as many or as few of the rows as you need.

word power

Vocabulary Preview

Read these words from *The Diary of Samuel Pepys* and their definitions below. Try pronouncing each word aloud. As you read, use context clues to unlock the meaning of these and other words you don't know.

scaffold (skaf′əld) *n.* a raised platform; p. 127

cavalcade (kav′əl kād′) *n.* a ceremonial procession; p. 128

loath (lōth) *adj.* reluctant; unwilling; p.131

quench (kwench) *v.* to put out; extinguish; p. 131

malicious (mə lish′əs) *adj.* deliberately harmful; p. 134

Hot Words Journal

As you read, circle words that you find interesting or that you don't understand. Later you may add them to your **Hot Words Journal** at the back of this book.

What You'll Learn

Key Goals In this lesson, you will learn these key skills, strategies, and concepts.

- **Reading Focus:** Identify Sequence

- **Think It Over:** Infer

- **Literary Element:** Diary

- **Reading Coach:** Understanding Long Sentences

from
The Diary of
Samuel Pepys

Samuel Pepys

The Coronation of Charles II

APRIL 23, 1661. Coronation Day. About four I rose and got
to the Abbey,[1] where I followed Sir J. Denham, the surveyor,
with some company that he was leading in. And with much ado,
by the favor of Mr. Cooper, his man, did get up into a great
<u>scaffold</u> across the north end of the Abbey, where with a great
deal of patience I sat from past four till eleven before the King
came in. And a great pleasure it was to see the Abbey raised in
the middle, all covered with red, and a throne (that is a chair)
and footstool on the top of it; and all the officers of all kinds,   10
so much as the very fiddlers, in red vests.

At last comes in the dean and prebends[2] of Westminster, with
the bishops (many of them in cloth-of-gold copes[3]), and after
them the nobility, all in their Parliament robes, which was a most
magnificent sight. Then the Duke,[4] and the King with a scepter
(carried by my Lord Sandwich) and sword and mond[5] before
him, and the crown, too. **A** The King in his robes, bare-headed,
which was very fine. And after all had placed themselves, there

---

1. The *Abbey* is Westminster Abbey, the London church that is the
   traditional site of coronations.
2. The *dean* and *prebends* (**preb´əndz**) are high church officials.
3. *Copes* are long capes worn by church officials during processions
   and other religious ceremonies.
4. The *Duke* is the Duke of York—the king's brother and later King James II.
5. A *mond* is a ball of gold or other precious material with a cross on
   top, representing the globe of the earth. It is meant to be a symbol
   of royal power.

Vocabulary
scaffold (skaf´əld) *n.* a raised platform

---

word power

Using Related Meanings
When you see a word used in an
unusual way, think of a definition
you do know for the word. That
definition may be related, or
similar, to the unusual one. For
example, you may have heard
the word "scaffold" used to refer
to a framework that people stand
on to work on tall buildings. You
might then guess Pepys was
sitting on a raised structure, and
you'd be right!

Reading Focus

Identify Sequence
As you read, note the order,
or **sequence,** of events.
Pepys usually describes events in
chronological order—the order
in which events actually
occurred. Look for time-order
words that signal when
something happened. **A**

Model: *I see that the nobles
entered the church <u>after</u> the
church officials. <u>Then</u> came the
duke and the king. So this is the
sequence of events:*

(1) The church officials entered.

(2) The nobles entered.

*(3) The duke and the king
entered.*

Reading Coach

⬅ Understanding Long Sentences To understand long sentences, pause when you get to a comma and ask yourself what you have learned so far. Reread the highlighted sentence up to the first comma. What does that part tell you? **B**

_____

_____

Now read up to the next comma. What have you learned?

_____

_____

_____

What kind of medals were they?

_____

_____

Did Pepys get one?

_____

_____

Reading Focus

Visualize Underline any descriptions in this paragraph that help you **visualize,** or picture, what's happening. **Mark the text** Write what you see in your mind's eye on the lines below. **C**

_____

_____

_____

was a sermon and the service; and then in the choir at the high
20 altar, the King passed through all the ceremonies of the
coronation, which to my great grief I and most in the Abbey
could not see. The crown being put upon his head, a great shout
begun, and he came forth to the throne, and there passed more
ceremonies: as taking the oath and having things read to him by
the bishop; and his lords (who put on their caps as soon as the
King put on his crown) and bishops come and kneeled before
him. And three times the King at Arms[6] went to the three open
places on the scaffold and proclaimed that if anyone could show
any reason why Charles Stuart should not be King of England,
30 that now he should come and speak. And a general pardon also
was read by the Lord Chancellor, and medals flung up and down
by my Lord Cornwallis, of silver, but I could not come by any. **B**
But so great a noise that I could make but little of the music; and
indeed, it was lost to everybody. . . .

I went out a little while before the King had done all his
ceremonies and went round the Abbey to Westminster Hall,[7] all
the way within rails, and ten thousand people, with the ground
covered with blue cloth; and scaffolds all the way. Into the hall
I got, where it was very fine with hangings and scaffolds one
40 upon another full of brave[8] ladies; and my wife in one little one
on the right hand. Here I stayed walking up and down, and at
last, upon one of the side stalls, I stood and saw the King come
in with all the persons (but the soldiers) that were yesterday in
the cavalcade; and a most pleasant sight it was to see them in
their several robes. And the King came in with his crown on, and
his scepter in his hand, under a canopy borne up by six silver
staves,[9] carried by barons of the Cinque Ports,[10] and little bells
at every end. **C**

_____

6. The *King at Arms* is the chief herald, an officer whose duties include making royal proclamations and arranging public processions and ceremonies.

7. *Westminster Hall* is the court of justice.

8. As it is used here, *brave* means "finely dressed."

9. *Staves* is the plural of *staff.*

10. *Cinque* (**singk**) *Ports* are the five seaports along the English Channel that jointly provided England's naval defense.

Vocabulary
cavalcade (kav ´ əl kād ´) *n.* a ceremonial procession

And after a long time, he got up to the farther end, and all set themselves down at their several tables; and that was also a brave sight; and the King's first course carried up by the Knights of the Bath. And many fine ceremonies there was of the herald's leading up people before him and bowing; and my Lord of Albemarle's going to the kitchen and eat a bit of the first dish that was to go to the King's table. **D** But, above all, was these three Lords, Northumberland and Suffolk and the Duke of Ormond, coming before the courses on horseback and staying so all dinnertime, and at last to bring up [Dymock] the King's champion,[11] all in armor on horseback, with his spear and target carried before him. And a herald proclaims, "That if any dare deny Charles Stuart to be lawful King of England, here was a champion that would fight with him"; and with these words, the champion flings down his gauntlet, and all this he do three times in his going up towards the King's table. At last when he is come, the King drinks to him and then sends him the cup, which is of gold, and he drinks it off and then rides back again with the cup in his hand. I went from table to table to see the bishops and all others at their dinner and was infinitely pleased with it. And at the Lords' table, I met with William Howe, and he spoke to my Lord[12] for me, and he did give me four rabbits and a pullet, and so I got it, and Mr. Creed and I got Mr. Michell to give us some bread, and so we at a stall eat it, as everybody else did what they could get. I took a great deal of pleasure to go up and down and look upon the ladies and to hear the music of all sorts, but above all, the twenty-four violins.

50

60

70

Did You Know?

A *gauntlet* is a protective glove, usually made of leather or metal, worn with medieval armor. Throwing down a gauntlet symbolized a challenge.

📖 Reading Check

---

11. At coronations, the *King's champion* ceremoniously defended the new king's title to the crown. This office had been held by the *Dymock* family since Richard II was crowned in 1377.

12. *My Lord* is Edward Montagu, the Earl of Sandwich, who was Pepys's cousin and lifelong patron.

Think It Over

🗝 **Infer** Since Pepys is writing in his private diary, he doesn't give explanations of some events. To understand them, "read between the lines," or **infer** ideas. For example, why do you think Lord Albemarle ate some of the king's food before the king did? **D**

Model: I know kings had a lot of enemies in those days. Maybe the lord was checking for poison.

📖 Reading Check

Step 1 Have you understood what you've read so far? If not, use these strategies:

• Reread hard parts slowly or aloud.

• Ask a classmate or a teacher, parent, or other adult for help

Step 2 Now answer this question: If TV had existed in Pepys's day, what scenes from the coronation might be on the news? On the lines below, list four sights you would expect to see.

_____

_____

_____

_____

_____

Hot Words

Choose your own words As you continue reading from Pepys's diary, circle any words that you find interesting or that you don't understand. You'll come back to these words later.

Mark the text

Literary Element

➤ **Diary** A **diary** is a person's private, day-to-day written record of experiences, thoughts, and feelings. Reread the boxed text. Circle a description that you might find in a "facts-only" newspaper report. Then underline a description that is more personal and typical of a diary. Jot down the descriptions on the lines below. **E**

Factual:

_____

_____

_____

Personal:

_____

_____

_____

80 **The London Fire**

SEPTEMBER 2, 1666. Lord's Day.[13] Some of our maids sitting up late last night to get things ready against our feast today, Jane called us up about three in the morning to tell us of a great fire they saw in the city. So I rose and slipped on my nightgown and went to her window and thought it to be on the back side of Mark Lane at the farthest; but, being unused to such fires as followed, I thought it far enough off and so went to bed again and to sleep. About seven rose again to dress myself and there looked out at the window and saw the fire not so much as it was 90 and further off. So to my closet[14] to set things to rights after yesterday's cleaning.

By and by Jane comes and tells me that she hears that above three hundred houses have been burned down tonight by the fire we saw and that it is now burning down all Fish Street, by London Bridge.[15] So I made myself ready presently and walked to the Tower[16] and there got up upon one of the high places, Sir J. Robinson's little son going up with me; and there I did see the houses at the end of the bridge all on fire and an infinite great fire on this and the other side the end of the bridge, which, 100 among other people, did trouble me for poor little Michell and our Sarah on the bridge. So down, with my heart full of trouble, to the lieutenant of the Tower, who tells me that it begun this morning in the King's baker's house in Pudding Lane and that it hath burned St. Magnus's Church and most part of Fish Street already. **E** So I down to the waterside and there got a boat and through bridge and there saw a lamentable fire. Poor Michell's house, as far as the Old Swan,[17] already burned that way, and the fire running further, that in a very little time it got as far as the Steel Yard, while I was there. Everybody endeavoring to remove 110 their goods and flinging into the river or bringing them into

13. *Lord's Day* is Sunday.
14. A *closet* was a private room used especially for study or prayer.
15. *London Bridge* was the only bridge over the Thames River at that time. It was lined with shops and houses.
16. The *Tower* of London actually consists of a group of buildings on the Thames River constructed as a fortress and later used as a royal residence and prison.
17. The *Old Swan* was a tavern near London Bridge.

lighters[18] that lay off; poor people staying in their houses as long as till the very fire touched them and then running into boats or clambering from one pair of stairs by the waterside to another. **F** And among other things, the poor pigeons, I perceive, were loath to leave their houses, but hovered about the windows and balconies till they were, some of them burned, their wings, and fell down. Having stayed, and in an hour's time seen the fire rage every way, and nobody, to my sight, endeavoring to quench it, but to remove their goods, and leave all to the fire, and having seen it get as far as the Steel Yard, and the wind mighty high and driving it into the City; and everything, after so long a drought, proving combustible, even the very stones of churches, and among other things the poor steeple by which pretty Mrs. —— lives, and whereof my old schoolfellow Elborough is parson, taken fire in the very top and there burned till it fell down. I to Whitehall[19] (with a gentleman with me who desired to go off from the Tower, to see the fire, in my boat); to Whitehall, and there up to the King's closet in the Chapel, where people come about me, and I did give them an account dismayed them all, and word was carried in to the King. So I was called for and did tell the King and Duke of York what I saw, and that unless his Majesty did command houses to be pulled down, nothing could stop the fire. They seemed much troubled, and the King commanded me to go to my Lord Mayor from him and command him to spare no houses, but to pull down before the fire every way. **G** The Duke of York bid me tell him that if he would have any more soldiers, he shall; and so did my Lord Arlington afterwards, as a great secret. Here meeting with Captain Cocke, I in his coach, which he lent me, and Creed with me to Paul's,[20] and there walked along Watling Street, as well as I could, every creature coming away laden with goods to save, and here

120

130

140

---

18. *Lighters* are large, open barges.
19. *Whitehall* was the king's residence in Westminster, London, as well as the location of several government offices.
20. *Paul's* is St. Paul's Cathedral, which was destroyed in the fire and later rebuilt.

Vocabulary
loath (lōth) *adj.* reluctant; unwilling
quench (kwench) *v.* to put out; extinguish

Think It Over

Infer Pepys doesn't say why people stayed in their houses for so long, but if you draw on what you know about human nature, you can guess why. On the lines below, jot down a reason that the people might have wanted to stay. **F**

_____

Reading Focus
Identify Sequence Several events are described on this page. On the lines below, number them in the order in which they happened. **G**

_____ Pepys warned the king.
_____ The fire reached the Steel Yard.
_____ Pepys went to Whitehall.

Think It Over

➤ **Infer** Circle phrases in this paragraph that describe the Lord Mayor. Then put a check next to the phrase below that best tells what the Lord Mayor is like. **H**

❏ strong and calm

❏ tired and frightened

Reading Coach

➤ **Understanding Long Sentences** To help you deal with a long sentence, break it up into smaller chunks. A good place to break is at a semicolon (;) or colon (:).

Try breaking the highlighted sentence into three chunks. Then, on the lines below, use your own words to paraphrase each section. **I**

_____

_____

_____

_____

_____

_____

and there sick people carried away in beds. Extraordinary good goods carried in carts and on backs. At last met my Lord Mayor in Canning Street, like a man spent, with a handkerchief about his neck. To the King's message he cried, like a fainting woman, "Lord! What can I do? I am spent: people will not obey me. I have been pulling down houses, but the fire overtakes us faster than we can do it." That he needed no more soldiers and that, for himself, he must go and refresh himself, having been up
150 all night. **H**

So he left me, and I him, and walked home, seeing people all almost distracted, and no manner of means used to quench the fire. The houses, too, so very thick thereabouts and full of matter for burning, as pitch and tar, in Thames Street; and warehouses of oil and wines and brandy and other things. Here I saw Mr. Isaake Houblon, the handsome man, prettily dressed and dirty, at his door at Dowgate, receiving some of his brothers' things, whose houses were on fire, and, as he says, have been removed twice already; and he doubts (as it soon proved) that
160 they must be in a little time removed from his house also, which was a sad consideration. And to see the churches all filling with goods by people who themselves should have been quietly there at this time.

By this time it was about twelve o'clock; and so home and there find my guests, which was Mr. Wood and his wife, Barbary Sheldon, and also Mr. Moone: she mighty fine, and her husband, for aught I see, a likely man. **I** But Mr. Moone's design and mine, which was to look over my closet and please him with the sight thereof, which he hath long desired, was wholly disappointed; for
170 we were in great trouble and disturbance at this fire, not knowing what to think of it. However, we had an extraordinary good dinner, and as merry as at this time we could be. While at dinner, Mrs. Batelier come to enquire after Mr. Woolfe and Stanes (who, it seems, are related to them), whose houses in Fish Street are all burned, and they in a sad condition. She would not stay in the fright. Soon as dined, I and Moone away and walked through the City, the streets full of nothing but people and horses and carts laden with goods, ready to run over one another, and removing goods from one burned house to another. They now removing
180 out of Canning Street (which received goods in the morning)

into Lombard Street and further; and among others I now saw my little goldsmith, Stokes, receiving some friend's goods, whose house itself was burned the day after. **J** We parted at Paul's; he home, and I to Paul's Wharf, where I had appointed a boat to attend me, and took in Mr. Carcasse and his brother, whom I met in the street, and carried them below and above bridge to and again to see the fire, which was now got further, both below and above, and no likelihood of stopping it. Met with the King and Duke of York in their barge, and with them to Queenhithe, and there called Sir Richard Browne to them. 190

Their order was only to pull down houses apace,[21] and so below bridge at the waterside; but little was or could be done, the fire coming upon them so fast. Good hopes there was of stopping it at the Three Cranes above, and at Buttolph's Wharf below bridge, if care be used; but the wind carries it into the City, so as we know not by the waterside what it do there. River full of lighters and boats 200 taking in goods, and good goods swimming in the water, and only I observed that hardly one lighter or boat in three that had the goods of a house in but there was a pair of virginals in it. **K**

Having seen as much as I could now, I away to Whitehall by appointment and there walked to St. James's Park and there met my wife and Creed and Wood and his wife and walked to my boat; and there upon the water again, and to the fire up and down, it still increasing, and the wind great. So near the fire as we could for smoke; and all over the Thames, with one's face in 210 the wind, you were almost burned with a shower of firedrops. This is very true; so as houses were burned by these drops and flakes of fire, three or four, nay, five or six houses, one from another. When we could endure no more upon the water, we to a little alehouse on the Bankside, over against the Three Cranes, and there stayed till it was dark almost and saw the fire grow; and as it grew darker, appeared more and more and in corners and upon steeples and between churches and houses as far as we

Did You Know?

A *pair of virginals* is actually a single musical instrument: a small, rectangular, legless sixteenth-century harpsichord that is placed on a table or held in the lap to play.

FOLDABLES *Graphic Organizer* Don't forget your **Foldable!** As you continue reading, remember to list events in the order that Pepys describes them. **J**

READ ALOUD

Build Fluency Find a quiet place and practice reading the boxed passage aloud. Reread the passage until you can read it comfortably and smoothly. **K**

Your Notes

---

21. *Apace* means "swiftly."

Visualize What do you think the fire looks like? Draw a quick sketch in the frame below. **L**

Your Sketch

Literary Element

Diary Imagine that you are Mr. Hater. On the lines below, write what you would say in your diary about the day's events. **M**

could see up the hill of the City in a most horrid <u>malicious</u>
220 bloody flame, not like the fine flame of an ordinary fire. Barbary and her husband away before us. We stayed till, it being darkish, we saw the fire as only one entire arch of fire from this to the other side the bridge and in a bow up the hill for an arch of above a mile long: it made me weep to see it. The churches, houses, and all on fire and flaming at once; and a horrid noise the flames made and the cracking of houses at their ruin. **L**

So home with a sad heart, and there find everybody discoursing and lamenting the fire; and poor Tom Hater come with some few of his goods saved out of his house, which is
230 burned upon Fish Street Hill. I invited him to lie at my house and did receive his goods, but was deceived in his lying there, the news coming every moment of the growth of the fire; so as we were forced to begin to pack up our own goods and prepare for their removal and did by moonshine (it being brave dry and moonshine and warm weather) carry much of my goods into the garden, and Mr. Hater and I did remove my money and iron chests into my cellar, as thinking that the safest place. And got my bags of gold into my office, ready to carry away, and my chief papers of accounts also there, and my tallies[22] into a box
240 by themselves. So great was our fear, as Sir W. Batten hath carts come out of the country to fetch away his goods this night. We did put Mr. Hater, poor man, to bed a little; but he got but very little rest, so much noise being in my house, taking down of goods. **M**

3rd.[23]   About four o'clock in the morning, my Lady Batten sent me a cart to carry away all my money and plate[24] and best things to Sir W. Rider's at Bednall Green. Which I did, riding myself in my nightgown in the cart; and, Lord! to see how the streets and the highways are crowded with people running and
250 riding and getting of carts at any rate to fetch away things. I find

---

22. *Tallies* were sticks marked with notches representing amounts of money. The tallies served as records of money paid or owed.

23. The abbreviation *3rd* refers to the date, September 3.

24. *Plate* refers to tableware or decorative objects made of a precious metal, such as silver or gold.

Vocabulary
malicious (mə lish´əs) *adj.* deliberately harmful

Sir W. Rider tired with being called up all night, and receiving things from several friends. His house full of goods, and much of Sir W. Batten's and Sir W. Pen's. I am eased at my heart to have my treasure so well secured. Then home, with much ado to find a way, nor any sleep all this night to me nor my poor wife.

·················· ✓ **Reading Check** ··················

Reading Check

Step 1 Take a moment to think about the two selections from Pepys's diary that you have read. Look back over the passages you marked and the events you listed in your **Foldable.** How are Pepys's descriptions of the coronation and the fire similar? How are the descriptions different? Write your ideas on the lines below.

_____

_____

_____

_____

Step 2 Now think about your own life and times. If you were keeping a diary similar to Samuel Pepys's, what recent U.S. or world event would you write about? Why?

_____

_____

_____

_____

Hot Words

Choose three words, either from the underlined vocabulary in the story or from the words you circled as you read. Record them in your **Hot Words Journal** at the back of this book and complete one of the activities listed there.

The Glencoe Reader **135**

READING WRAP UP

Going Solo

Understanding Long Sentences

Making Sense While you were reading the selections from Samuel Pepys's diary, you practiced dividing long sentences into shorter chunks. Get more practice now. Reread the following sentence about the coronation. Then divide the sentence into four shorter chunks and paraphrase them on the lines provided.

> The crown being put upon his head, a great shout begun, and he came forth to the throne, and there passed more ceremonies: as taking the oath and having things read to him by the bishop; and his lords (who put on their caps as soon as the King put on his crown) and bishops come and kneeled before him. (lines 22–27)

_____

_____

_____

_____

Buddy Up

Identify Sequence

First Things First Choose one of the selections from the diary—either the coronation or the fire. Have a partner work with the other selection. Tear a piece of paper into strips. On each strip make a note about an event in your selection. Shuffle your slips of paper and exchange them with your partner. Read the slips that your partner gives you and put them in chronological order. Check with your partner to see if you put the slips in the correct order. On the lines below, write the events in the correct sequence.

_____

_____

_____

_____

TeamWork

Infer

What a Character! Take a few minutes to talk about what you learned about Pepys from reading these selections from his diary. Then take turns choosing one adjective (such as _brave_) that you think describes Pepys's character. Be sure to give at least one example from the diary to support your choice. On the lines below, write your adjective and the line numbers from the selection that support it.

Adjective: _____

Line numbers: _____

Diary

Breaking News Imagine that you and your group members are TV reporters reporting on the coronation or the London fire. Together, plan a brief segment giving the facts about the event and a longer segment interviewing Pepys for his "personal account" as an eyewitness. Use the diary as a resource as you plan both segments—find factual details for the first part and personal details for the second part. Choose roles (for example, the anchor, reporters, Pepys), practice, and then perform your news report for the class. On the lines below, explain your part in the sketch.

_____

_____

_____

_____

Standardized Test Practice

Choose the best answer for each multiple-choice question. Fill in the circle in the spaces for questions 1 and 2 on the right.

1. What does Pepys do just after he sees the fire burning in the distance for the first time?

    A. He goes back to bed.

    B. He walks to the Tower of London.

    C. He goes to see the King at Whitehall.

    D. He rides down the Thames in a boat.

2. Which of the following pairs of adjectives best describes what Samuel Pepys is like?

    A. witty and sarcastic

    B. critical and severe

    C. curious and observant

    D. cold-hearted and judgmental

Write your answer to open-ended question A in the space provided below.

A. How does Pepy's diary differ from a history book? Give at least two specific examples to support your answer.

Multiple-Choice Questions

1. Ⓐ Ⓑ Ⓒ Ⓓ   2. Ⓐ Ⓑ Ⓒ Ⓓ

Open-Ended Question

A. _____

_____

_____

_____

_____

word power

Vocabulary Check

From the word list, write the word that belongs in the blank in each sentence.

scaffold *n.* a raised platform

cavalcade *n.* a ceremonial procession

loath *adj.* reluctant; unwilling

quench *v.* to put out; extinguish

malicious *adj.* deliberately harmful

1. They prepared for the parade by building a viewing _____.

2. She set out to hurt him by damaging his reputation with _____ lies.

3. I don't use a leaf blower because I'm _____ to cause noise pollution.

4. The graduates marched in an impressive _____.

5. I drink lemonade in the summer to _____ my thirst.

GET READY TO READ!

Connect

Quickwrite If you're like most people, you probably do more things for yourself and your family than for your country. What could persuade you to put your country first? Think about that for a minute. Then write your response in your journal. Share your ideas with the class.

In this speech, you'll read the words one wartime leader spoke to inspire selflessness and bravery in his fellow citizens.

Did You Know?

Building Background On May 19, 1940, Winston Churchill gave the radio address you're about to read. It was his first speech as Britain's prime minster, and it came at a very scary time. World War II was raging. Within the last twelve months, Nazi Germany had taken over Denmark, Norway, and Poland. A few days before Churchill addressed his country, the German army had invaded Belgium and Holland and had broken through the French border. People knew that if Germany defeated France, it would probably attack Britain next.

Reason to Read

Setting a Purpose for Reading Read to learn how Winston Churchill persuaded the British public to sacrifice for their country during a dangerous time.

 As you read, use the following **Foldable** to help you keep track of what Churchill is asking the British public to do and the reasons he gives for why they should do it.

1. Place a sheet of paper in front of you so the short side is at the top. Fold it in half from side to side.

2. Fold the paper down about 1 inch from the top. Then unfold.

3. Label the left column **What they should do.** Label the right column **Why they should do it.**

4. As you read, use the left column to note what Churchill is telling his audience to do. Use the right column to note reasons he gives for why they should do it.

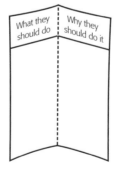

What they should do | Why they should do it

word power

Vocabulary Preview

Read the definitions of these words from "Be Ye Men of Valor." Use the pronunciation guides to help you say each word aloud. When you read these words in the speech, use context clues to help you better understand their meanings.

ravage (rav´ij) *v.* to lay waste to; destroy; p. 139

intimidated (in tim´ ə dāt´ əd) *adj.* influenced or deterred by threats or violence; p. 139

dogged (dô´ gid) *adj.* stubborn; persevering; unyielding; p. 139

grapple (grap´əl) *v.* to attempt to deal with; struggle; p. 140

obstinate (ob´ stə nit) *adj.* difficult to overcome; stubborn; p. 141

indomitable (in dom´ət ə bəl) *adj.* incapable of being subdued or overcome; p. 142

Hot Words Journal

As you read, circle words from the speech that you find interesting or difficult. Later you may add them to your **Hot Words Journal** at the back of this book and complete one of the activities there.

What You'll Learn

Key Goals In this lesson, you will learn these key skills, strategies, and concepts.

Reading Focus: Monitor Comprehension

Think It Over: Infer

Literary Element: Persuasion

Reading Coach: Understanding Dashes

Be Ye Men of Valor

Winston Churchill

BBC, LONDON, 19 MAY 1940

I speak to you for the first time as Prime Minister in a solemn hour for the life of our country, of our Empire, of our Allies,[1] and, above all, of the cause of Freedom. A tremendous battle is raging in France and Flanders. The Germans, by a remarkable combination of air bombing and heavily armored tanks, have broken through the French defenses north of the Maginot Line,[2] and strong columns of their armored vehicles are <u>ravaging</u> the open country, which for the first day or two was without defenders. They have penetrated deeply and spread alarm and confusion in their track. Behind them there are now appearing infantry in lorries,[3] and behind them, again, the large masses are moving forward. The regroupment of the French armies to make head against, and also to strike at, this intruding wedge has been proceeding for several days, largely assisted by the magnificent efforts of the Royal Air Force. **A**

10

We must not allow ourselves to be <u>intimidated</u> by the presence of these armored vehicles in unexpected places behind our lines. If they are behind our Front, the French are also at many points fighting actively behind theirs. Both sides are therefore in an extremely dangerous position. And if the French Army, and our own Army, are well handled, as I believe they will be; if the French retain that genius for recovery and counter-attack for which they have so long been famous; and if the British Army shows the <u>dogged</u> endurance and solid fighting power of which there have been so many examples in the past—then a sudden transformation of the scene might spring into being.

20

---

1. The *Allies* of World War II were mainly the United States, Canada, Great Britain, France, and the USSR.
2. The *Maginot Line* was a heavily fortified line of defense in France that was built to keep away the German army.
3. *Lorries* is a British term for motor trucks.

Vocabulary

ravage (rav′ ij) *v.* to lay waste to; destroy

intimidated (in tim′ ə dāt′ əd) *adj.* influenced or deterred by threats or violence

dogged (dô′ gid) *adj.* stubborn; persevering; unyielding

Reading Focus

← **Monitor Comprehension** When you read, make sure you're not just moving your eyes across the words. **Monitor your comprehension** by asking and answering questions that check your understanding of the text. For example: How well do I understand what Churchill is talking about in this paragraph? Fill in the blanks in the sentences below by writing the name of the correct country—either Germany or France. **A**

_____ invaded _____.

_____ is regrouping its army.

_____ has used armored tanks and bombers.

Using Context Clues If you don't know the meaning of an underlined vocabulary word, look at **context clues**—the words and sentences around the word. If context clues don't help you guess the meaning, reread the whole sentence, substituting the definition at the bottom of the page for the underlined word.

Mark the text ▸ **Choose your own words** As you read, circle words you find interesting or difficult. You will come back to these words later.

Think It Over

➤ **Infer** When you **infer**, you "read between the lines." Have you ever heard that phrase? It means that you use clues from what someone says or writes to understand what he or she *really* means. **B**

Model: Churchill tries to be reassuring by saying what a great army France has and how it won't be beaten in a few weeks or months. But if that's the good news, I can infer that the situation is really, really bad—probably worse than he's admitting, even though he's trying to be honest.

Reading Coach

➤ **Understanding Dashes** Churchill uses dashes to set off and emphasize extra information within his sentences. Sometimes he even uses dashes within dashes to create greater emphasis, as he does in this sentence.

Mark the text ➤ Underline the words that appear between dashes. What is Churchill emphasizing? Show your answer by checking a box below. **C**

❏ the surprising success of the British air force

❏ the unbeatable power of the German air force

❏ the great sacrifice required to shoot down planes

It would be foolish, however, to disguise the gravity[4] of the hour. It would be still more foolish to lose heart and courage or
30 to suppose that well-trained, well-equipped armies numbering three or four millions of men can be overcome in the space of a few weeks, or even months, by a scoop, or raid of mechanized vehicles, however formidable.[5] We may look with confidence to the stabilization of the Front in France, and to the general engagement of the masses, which will enable the qualities of the French and British soldiers to be matched squarely against those of their adversaries.[6] For myself, I have invincible confidence in the French Army and its leaders. Only a very small part of that splendid army has yet been heavily engaged; and only a very
40 small part of France has yet been invaded. **B** There is good evidence to show that practically the whole of the specialized and mechanized forces of the enemy have been already thrown into the battle; and we know that very heavy losses have been inflicted upon them. No officer or man, no brigade or division, which grapples at close quarters with the enemy, wherever encountered, can fail to make a worthy contribution to the general result. The Armies must cast away the idea of resisting behind concrete lines or natural obstacles, and must realize that mastery can only be regained by furious and unrelenting assault.
50 And this spirit must not only animate the High Command, but must inspire every fighting man.

In the air—often at serious odds—often at odds hitherto thought overwhelming—we have been clawing down three or four to one of our enemies; and the relative balance of the British and German Air Forces is now considerably more favorable to us than at the beginning of the battle. **C** In cutting down the German bombers, we are fighting our own battle as well as that of France. My confidence in our ability to fight it out to the finish with the German Air Force has been strengthened
60 by the fierce encounters which have taken place and are taking place. At the same time, our heavy bombers are striking nightly at

---

4. Here, *gravity* means "seriousness" or "importance."
5. *Formidable* means "arousing fear or dread."
6. *Adversaries* are opponents.

Vocabulary
grapple (grap′ əl) *v.* to attempt to deal with; struggle

the taproot[7] of German mechanized power, and have already inflicted serious damage upon the oil refineries on which the Nazi effort to dominate the world directly depends.

📖 Reading Check

We must expect that as soon as stability is reached on the Western Front, the bulk of that hideous apparatus of aggression which gashed Holland into ruin and slavery in a few days, will be turned upon us. I am sure I speak for all when I say we are ready to face it; to endure it; and to retaliate against it—to any extent that the unwritten laws of war permit. There will be many men, and many women, in this island who when the ordeal comes upon them, as come it will, will feel comfort, and even a pride— that they are sharing the perils of our lads at the Front—soldiers, sailors, and airmen, God bless them—and are drawing away from them a part at least of the onslaught they have to bear. Is not this the appointed time for all to make the utmost exertions in their power? If the battle is to be won, we must provide our men with ever-increasing quantities of the weapons and ammunition they need. We must have, and have quickly, more airplanes, more tanks, more shells, more guns. There is imperious[8] need for these vital munitions. They increase our strength against the powerfully armed enemy. They replace the wastage of the obstinate struggle; and the knowledge that wastage will speedily be replaced enables us to draw more readily upon our reserves and throw them in now that everything counts so much.

Our task is not only to win the battle—but to win the War. After this battle in France abates[9] its force, there will come the battle for our island—for all that Britain is, and all that Britain means. That will be the struggle. In that supreme emergency we shall not hesitate to take every step, even the most drastic, to call forth from our people the last ounce and the last inch of effort of which they are capable. **D** The interests of property, the hours

70

80

90

---

7. As it is used here, *taproot* means "the most important part."
8. As it is used here, *imperious* means "urgent."
9. *Abates* means "reduces in intensity."

Vocabulary
obstinate (ob′ stə nit) *adj.* difficult to overcome; stubborn

📖 Reading Check

Step 1 Ask yourself how well you understand the speech so far. If you put question marks next to anything, these strategies can help you answer your questions.

- Reread confusing passages or read them aloud.
- Think about connections between the speech and your own life.
- Ask a classmate or a teacher, parent, or other adult for help.

Step 2 Now think about what Churchill has said so far. What reasons does he give the British public for being hopeful even though Germany is winning the war? Write at least two reasons below.

_____

_____

_____

_____

_____

Literary Element

➤ **Persuasion** In **persuasion,** the writer or speaker tries to influence other people to think or act in a certain way. What is Churchill trying to persuade people to do on this page? Check all that apply. **D**

❏ to do without electricity

❏ to make weapons

❏ to make extreme sacrifices

❏ to enlist in the army

❏ to be brave during bombing

Reading Check

Step 1 Take a moment to think about Churchill's speech and the dramatic events that were unfolding when he delivered it. Look over your **Foldable** and review any notes you made on these pages. Then, on the lines below, explain why Churchill gave this speech.

_____

_____

_____

_____

_____

Step 2 If the leader of your country gave a speech like this today, would you be persuaded to sacrifice everything—even your life—for your country? Explain why or why not on the lines below.

_____

_____

_____

_____

Choose three words, either from the underlined vocabulary in the speech or from the words you circled as you read. Record them in your **Hot Words Journal** at the back of this book and complete an activity listed there.

of labor, are nothing compared with the struggle for life and honor, for right and freedom, to which we have vowed ourselves.

I have received from the Chiefs of the French Republic, and in particular from its <u>indomitable</u> Prime Minister, M. Reynaud, the most sacred pledges that whatever happens they will fight to the end, be it bitter or be it glorious. Nay, if we fight to the end, it can only be glorious.

100   Having received His Majesty's commission, I have found an administration of men and women of every party and of almost every point of view. We have differed and quarreled in the past; but now one bond unites us all—to wage war until victory is won, and never to surrender ourselves to servitude and shame, whatever the cost and the agony may be. This is one of the most awe-striking periods in the long history of France and Britain. It is also beyond doubt the most sublime. Side by side, unaided except by their kith and kin in the great Dominions and by the wide Empires which rest beneath their shield—side by side, the

110 British and French peoples have advanced to rescue not only Europe but mankind from the foulest and most soul-destroying tyranny which has ever darkened and stained the pages of history. Behind them—behind us—behind the armies and fleets of Britain and France—gather a group of shattered States and bludgeoned[10] races: the Czechs, the Poles, the Norwegians, the Danes, the Dutch, the Belgians—upon all of whom the long night of barbarism will descend, unbroken even by a star of hope, unless we conquer, as conquer we must; as conquer we shall.

Today is Trinity Sunday.[11] Centuries ago words were written to

120 be a call and a spur to the faithful servants of Truth and Justice: "Arm yourselves, and be ye men of valor, and be in readiness for the conflict; for it is better for us to perish in battle than to look upon the outrage of our nation and our altar. As the Will of God is in Heaven, even so let it be."

Reading Check

---

10. As it is used here, *bludgeoned* means "bullied or beaten."
11. *Trinity Sunday* is the first Sunday after Pentecost, in the Christian year.

Vocabulary
indomitable (in dom′ ə tə bəl) *adj.* incapable of being subdued or overcome

Reading WrapUp

Going Solo

← Infer

1. Us and Them Reread lines 100–180. From the clues in this paragraph, what can you infer about how Churchill views the relationship between Britain and France and the other countries in Europe? Check your answer.

❏ Britain and France must demand sacrifices from the rest of Europe.

❏ Britain and France must be the saviors for the rest of Europe.

On the lines below, copy a sentence or phrase that helped you make your inference.

_____

_____

2. Give Your All Churchill talks in grand but often general ways about what the British public must do to help win the war. Review the speech and your **Foldable** to help you make an inference about the *specific* things people might have to do. Write an example on the lines below.

_____

_____

Buddy Up

← Understanding Dashes

Gotta Dash With a partner, study the sentence that begins on line 70 with "There will be many men. . . ." Talk about what kind of information is included between dashes. What effect do the dashes have on the meaning of the sentence? Work together to rewrite the sentence in your own words. Break it into as many sentences as you want to, but try not to change Churchill's meaning.

_____

_____

_____

_____

_____

TeamWork

← Monitor Comprehension

1. Question Everything With your group, turn to page 141. Beginning with the first paragraph under the Reading Check, number the paragraphs in the rest of the selection from one to five. Then take turns reading this part of the speech aloud. Let one person read an entire paragraph. When he or she is finished reading, the person sitting to the right should ask a question that can help check everyone's understanding of the paragraph. The group should make sure they can answer the question before the next person begins reading.

On the lines below, write the number of the paragraph you asked a question about. Then write the question.

_____

_____

_____

_____

2. Do You Get It? For each page of this speech, work with your group to come up with a question that checks a reader's basic understanding of the content. Write the questions and their answers below and use them to quiz another group.

_____

_____

_____

_____

_____

_____

_____

Literary Element

☞ Persuasion

Persuasion is writing or speech that tries to influence an audience to think or act in a particular way. Persuasive writers or speakers try to convince their audience through appeals to logic, appeals to emotion, or both.

- **Appeals to logic** use clear and organized thinking to show why the audience should think or act in a certain way. These appeals often rely on facts and evidence to persuade the audience.

- **Appeals to emotion** use images, language, or symbols that bring up strong feelings. For example, words and images that connect to ideas such as innocence, freedom, honor, and patriotism are often used in emotional appeals. The writer or speaker encourages the audience to think or act according to their feelings.

Churchill uses both appeals to logic and appeals to emotion in "Be Ye Men of Valor." Look through the speech to find at least two examples of each kind of appeal. In the left column of the chart, give the line numbers of sections of the speech that contain appeals to logic. Describe the appeals. In the right column, give the line numbers of appeals to emotion. Describe the appeals. Use quotations if it helps you. An example has been done for you.

Appeals to Logic	Appeals to Emotion
Lines 17-27: Churchill tries to persuade his audience not to be intimidated by giving facts about the position of the German army and by talking logically about the abilities of the French and British armies.	

Standardized Test Practice

Choose the best answer for each multiple-choice question. Fill in the circle in the spaces for questions 1 and 2 on the right.

1. Which phrase best describes Churchill's main purpose in making this speech?
   A. inspire his listeners to resist Germany
   B. promise his listeners that France is their ally
   C. create a climate of fear in Britain
   D. convince his listeners that God is on their side

2. How does Churchill think Britain can win the war?
   A. by signing a treaty with Germany so they will stop the bombing
   B. by working together with all the countries of northern Europe
   C. by a heroic effort on the part of all citizens and soldiers
   D. by helping France defend its borders

Write your answer to open-ended question A in the space provided below.

A. How do you think a typical listener to this speech would have responded? Imagine that you were in Britain, listening to your radio in 1940. Write your immediate thoughts after hearing Churchill speak.

Multiple-Choice Questions

1. Ⓐ Ⓑ Ⓒ Ⓓ   2. Ⓐ Ⓑ Ⓒ Ⓓ

Open-Ended Question

A. _____

_____

_____

_____

_____

word power   Vocabulary Check

Write the word that best completes each sentence.

ravage *v.* to lay waste to; destroy

intimidated *adj.* influenced or deterred by threats or violence

dogged *adj.* stubborn; persevering; unyielding

grapple *v.* to attempt to deal with; struggle

obstinate *adj.* difficult to overcome; stubborn

indomitable *adj.* incapable of being subdued or overcome

1. Lars's opponents were _____ by his bullying and blustering.

2. The _____ passenger refused to sit down even when the driver insisted for the third time.

3. If you don't get rid of those spider mites, they will _____ the tomato plant.

4. My problems are not the worst, but they are hard to _____ with.

5. Day after day, hour after hour, Ron continued his steady, _____ work.

6. Thanks to their good attitudes and faith, the refugees remained _____.

Reading Mass Media

Here's a scene that might be familiar: Dad's watching the ball game on TV; Mom's reading the newspaper; your sister is going through a summer sale catalog; and you've logged on to a favorite Web site. Across the street, someone has the stereo on loud. Recognize the common theme here? The answer in two words is *mass media.*

Mass media are the whole extended family of methods (*media*) for communicating with large numbers of people (the *masses*). Some media use print, some use video, some use sound. Mass media take the form of newspapers, magazines, movies, TV and radio, advertisements of all sorts, Web sites, old-fashioned books, and every new-fangled device the recording industry comes up with. Whatever the method, whatever the message, if it reaches lots of people, you can label it part of the mass media.

In the table below, make note of four forms of mass media you used for entertainment during the last twenty-four hours.

Time	Mass Media Used	Purpose

Why Read Mass Media?

This question is a little more complex than it seems. Of course, you read mass media for information or entertainment. But you also read forms of mass media just because they are there! Try sitting in traffic without reading those billboards towering over the highway. Try asking television news producers to stop airing banner headlines during your favorite show. In spite of these occasional nuisances, however, mass media can be a uniting force. Just ask anyone who has ever given money to a charity during a TV telethon. To use a phrase borrowed from one of their many forms, mass media can get people on the same wavelength.

What's the Plan?

Most people don't have the time to read a newspaper or news magazine from beginning to end. For this reason, writers of news stories follow a structure that helps readers find important details quickly and easily. That structure, or form, is known as the inverted pyramid. It is pictured here.

Lead
the main facts of a story

Body
further information on the topic; may include direct quotations and other supporting details

less important information

What Do I Look For?

Newspaper and magazine articles often have elements like the **text features** and **text structures** in this article from *inTIME* magazine.

> The **headline,** or **title,** catches the eye with large print and often witty wording.

> The **deck,** or **subtitle,** includes lively information, inviting readers to continue.

> The **lead** of a news story will often provide a concise summary of the entire article.

> **Quotations** from newsmakers or experts support factual information and lighten the style.

> **Supporting details** occur later in the article and may—as here—include **statistics.**

Mark the text **Find It!** Circle a direct quotation in the article. Underline the name of the person who spoke the words.

WORLD

PORTRAITS OF PLAGUE

Britain's rampaging foot-and-mouth outbreak raises fears of an epidemic in Europe—and throughout the world

By JAMES O. JACKSON

It is called *fièvre aphteuse* in France, *fiebre aftosa* in Spain, *Maul-und-Klauenseuche* in Germany, and *mundog klovsyge* in Denmark. It is harmless to humans and does not kill most infected animals. Yet foot-and-mouth disease has aroused anxiety throughout the world in 2001, and the virus that causes the ailment in pigs, sheep, and cattle has closed borders, destroyed livelihoods, and brought to a standstill much of the world's trade in beef, pork, and lamb.

"We are on red alert," said Chuck Lambert, chief economist at the U.S. National Cattlemen's Beef Association as Department of Agriculture inspectors imposed strict checks on goods and passengers arriving from Britain and France. From Sydney to Seattle, worried officials banned European meat imports, confiscated sandwiches, and decontaminated arriving passengers to prevent inadvertent infection by a disease that, like everything else these days, is going global.

The worldwide foot-and-mouth alert is a sobering demonstration of how quickly a single isolated infection can hop from farm to farm and continent to continent. The current crisis began when a bit of infected meat found its way into a school lunch in Britain's Northumberland in mid-February and then, as leftovers, into swill fed to pigs. Before the first symptoms appeared to warn of the danger, the virus was spreading to farms all across the country. Within a few weeks, it turned up in Northern Ireland and jumped the English Channel to a farm in western France. But before French veterinarians confirmed cases in six cows, authorities from Germany to Portugal were ordering the slaughter of tens of thousands of animals that might have been exposed. Across Europe, traffic backed up for inspection and disinfection at border posts left idle and untended for years. Most of the world banned meat from the European Union, sending already struggling farm businesses into an economic tailspin.

Worst hit is Britain, where the stench of the burning hair, hide, and flesh of slaughtered animals casts gloom across the countryside. Agriculture Minister Nick Brown announced plans for the "preemptive" killing of every pig and sheep within 5 mi. (3 km) of any infected farm in Cumbria and southwest Scotland. By some accounts, the massive slaughter order could doom more than a million animals. The cost: $10 million and rising in compensation to farmers and an estimated $150 million a week in losses to the tourist industry as visitors avoided the countryside.

Death so widespread could bring the virtual collapse of a British agricultural economy already near bankruptcy because of bovine spongiform encephalopathy, or "mad cow" disease, which originated in Britain. An Irish government minister went so far as to call Britain "the leper of Europe," an epithet that brought grim nods of agreement elsewhere in Europe.

Britain's stigma is spreading to the Continent even faster than the virus itself. The U.S. and Canada, two of the European Union's biggest customers, have slapped bans on animal products from all 15 countries. Other countries in Europe and the Middle East also imposed restrictions on E.U. meat products, as did Australia, New Zealand, and parts of Asia.

If the infection spreads as it has in Britain, Europe could be facing its gravest agricultural crisis since the end of World War II.

—From TIME, March 26, 2001

BLACK SHEEP A ewe and lambs in Cumbria are among the 1 million animals due to be slaughtered to help contain the spread of foot-and-mouth disease.

inTIME Glencoe Language Arts Links

147

How Do I Read It?

These **reading strategies** will be especially helpful when you read mass media.

Skim: Do you need to read every word on an article or Web site? Glance over a selection before you commit.

Scan: Looking for specific information? Find the information you need by scanning for key facts or phrases.

Summarize: Describing what you've read in a sentence or two is a good way to test your understanding.

Evaluate: What's a writer's bias? Challenge the facts and opinions you encounter. Learn to read wisely and skeptically.

For more information on **reading strategies,** see pages 216–222 in the **Reading Handbook.**

DO IT!

Read the mass media selections that follow. Be sure to

- look for **text features** and **text structures**
- use **reading strategies** to help you get the most from your reading

GET READY TO READ!

Connect

List Ideas Have you said "thank you" to a plant recently? The idea is not as strange as you might think. Plants do a lot for us. Get together with a partner and, on the lines below, list three ways plants contribute to life on Earth. Share your ideas with the class.

_____

_____

_____

In the magazine article "Britain's Eden," you'll learn about the "Eden Project," which helps people appreciate the beauty and importance of plants.

Did You Know?

Building Background In this article, there are many **allusions,** or references to well-known persons, places, events, literary works or characters, or works of art. Understanding allusions will help you better understand the point the writer is making. If you don't understand an allusion, you can ask a friend or your teacher for help, look it up in a dictionary, or search online for the reference. Below are some of the allusions found in "Britain's Eden."

- According to the Bible, the **Garden of Eden** was the natural paradise where the first man and woman lived happily until they disobeyed God and were forced to leave.

- **James Bond,** also known as **007,** is a fictional British intelligence agent. His mission is usually to save Earth from a madman who is threatening to take over the world.

- **Kubla Khan** ruled over China from 1279. Samuel Taylor Coleridge wrote a poem about the **"pleasure dome"** that Kubla Khan built at a city called **Xanadu.**

- *The Importance of Being Vegetables* is a pun on the title of a play by Oscar Wilde, *The Importance of Being Earnest.*

- The **Hanging Gardens of Babylon** were considered one of the ancient Seven Wonders of the World. King Nebuchadnezzar built a hill in the flat desert of Babylon and covered it with a garden. He created this hilly garden for his wife, who was homesick for her mountainous homeland.

Reason to Read

Setting a Purpose for Reading Read to learn how a man who loves plants is creating a futuristic paradise.

word power

Vocabulary Preview

Read the words and definitions below. Use the pronunciation guides to help you say each word aloud. You may already know the meaning of some of these words, but others might still be unclear. As you read, use context clues to help unlock the meaning of words you find difficult.

scurry (skur´ē) *v.* to go or move hurriedly; p. 149

attest (ə test´) *v.* to be proof or evidence of; p. 150

upstage (up´stāj´) *v.* to draw attention to oneself at the expense of another; p. 150

arid (ar´id) *adj.* dry; parched; p. 150

nurture (nur´chər) *v.* to help make grow or develop; nourish; p. 151

optimize (op´tə mīz´) *v.* to make the most of; p. 152

sustain (sə stān´) *v.* to keep in effect or in existence; p. 152

Hot Words Journal

As you read, circle words that you find interesting or that you don't understand. Later you'll add them to your **Hot Words Journal** at the back of this book.

What You'll Learn

Key Goals In this lesson, you will learn these key skills, strategies, and concepts.

- **Reading Focus:** Summarize

- **Think It Over:** Main Idea

- **Author's Plan:** Author's Craft

- **Reading Coach:** Reading Conversational Style

BRITAIN'S EDEN

Giant domes in a former clay quarry, housing a tropical rain forest and a Mediterranean landscape, reveal the symbiosis[1] between people and plants

Christopher Redman
from *inTIME*, Volume 3, ©2003

At first glance the Eden Project looks like the set for a James Bond movie's doomsday finale. Dwarfed by giant sci-fi structures, workers in helmets and boots scurry around as if they were doing the final bidding of a megalomaniac[2] whose plot to destroy humankind is named for the biblical paradise. Ladies and Gentlemen, take your seats for the last show on Earth, unless 007 can get here on time. **A**

But Bond is not needed. Once inside the vast complex at Bodelva in Britain's Cornwall county, about 210 mi. (350 km) southwest of London, a visitor realizes that the Eden Project is not about destroying the planet but saving it. A modern version of Kubla Khan's legendary pleasure dome in Xanadu, the Eden Project (now nearing completion) is not just the mother of all greenhouses. It is the dramatic setting for a modern morality play[3] whose title could be *The Importance of Being Vegetables*—not to mention fruits and grains or even mangroves. "Plants are the life force of our planet," explains Tim Smit, 46, a former rock 'n' roll impresario[4] turned eco-friend who is the project's procreator[5] and prime mover. "For our own good, they must be treated with the utmost respect." **B** The Eden Project is his medium for getting

10

20

---

1. *Symbiosis* is when two different organisms live together in close union.
2. A *megalomaniac* is obsessed with a grand—often mad—idea.
3. A *morality play* is a drama in which the characters represent concepts, such as love or evil.
4. An *impresario* is a producer, particularly in the music business.
5. A *procreator* is one who has an idea and brings it to life.

Vocabulary

scurry (skur´ē) *v.* to go or move hurriedly

Main Idea Sometimes a paragraph doesn't include a topic sentence that clearly states the main idea. Reread the boxed paragraph. Then check the main idea. **C**

❏ Smit is ambitious and effective.

❏ The Eden Project is very expensive.

Summarize To **summarize** means to state the main idea in your own words. Ask yourself about what you've read so far. Think of questions beginning with *who, what, where, when, why,* and *how.* Answering these questions will help you summarize. On the lines below, write one of your questions and its answer. **D**

Question: _____

_____

Answer: _____

_____

_____

Reading Coach

Reading Conversational Style Sometimes writers use dashes to insert a short explanation in a sentence.

Mark the text Circle the dashes in this paragraph. What does the information inside the dashes tell you? **E**

_____

_____

that message across to the masses without boring them. A real Plant Kingdom rather than a make-believe Magic Kingdom, the Eden Project is Smit's "living theater" for bringing to a global audience "the planet's greatest drama," featuring plants and people and the way they intertwine. "It's not enough simply to display plants," says Smit. "Thousands of botanical gardens already do that. This project is about getting people to think about living with plants and [about] their dependence on them. And we hope to communicate our message to billions. We want

30 the Eden Project to be instantly recognizable around the globe."

Does that make Smit a megalomaniac? Let's hope so, because megalomaniacs get things done, dreaming impossible dreams and turning them into reality. And, as the $120 million Eden Project <u>attests</u>, they do not go in for half measures. When Smit engaged the project's architects—an internationally acclaimed British firm headed by Nicholas Grimshaw—he encouraged them to create the eighth wonder of the world. They may have succeeded: Even the Hanging Gardens of ancient Babylon would be pushed to <u>upstage</u> this latter-day Eden. **C** **D**

40 The geodesic domes (or "biomes"), which contain the project's temperature-sensitive plants, form the world's biggest conservatory. The larger of the biomes contains so much open space it could house the Tower of London with room to spare for a stack of 11 double-decker London buses. The larger biome brings together the plant life of the humid tropics, plants ranging from the towering teak trees of the Amazon rain forest to the oil palms of West Africa and the rice of southeast Asia. The smaller of the biomes is devoted to the flora of the world's warm temperate[6] zones, such as the Mediterranean, South Africa's

50 Cape region, and parts of California. The theme of the third biome—yet to be funded and built—will be the <u>arid</u> semidesert regions. **E** Outside the temperature-controlled greenhouses, the project's remaining land is planted with the more familiar

_____

6. A *temperate* climate is characterized by moderate temperatures.

_____

Vocabulary

attest (ə test´) *v.* to be proof or evidence of

upstage (up´stāj´) *v.* to draw attention to oneself at the expense of another

arid (ar´id) *adj.* dry; parched

Panoramic view of the Eden Project's exterior, where work continues on the landscape.

vegetation of the world's temperate climates. And to help everything grow, the Eden Project has created the world's largest soil factory. **F**

As the Eden Project rises from the ground like a cluster of giant mushrooms, it is difficult to imagine that less than 3 years ago the site was a china-clay quarry—a flooded hole in the ground about as suited to growing plants as a crater on the Moon. But Smit has a way of uncovering hidden potential. A decade ago he moved to Cornwall. There he came upon the overgrown gardens of Heligan, a huge estate that had been abandoned to nature. Recognizing the possibilities of the gardens, Smit and his team restored them. The gardens are now Britain's most-visited private garden attraction. **G**

The Eden Project was a natural extension of Smit's involvement with the gardens. He found himself <u>nurturing</u> the idea of creating a world-class attraction that would bring home to visitors the importance of the plant kingdom and their reliance on it. Better still if he could invest the concept with an approach that would have a real impact, particularly on children. "I'd always been romantically attached to the concept of a lost world," Smit recalls. "Suddenly I realized that was what we should be trying to create here."

60

70

Vocabulary

nurture (nur´chər) v. to help make grow or develop; nourish

Reading **Focus**

Respond From what you have read about the Eden Project, is it a place you'd like to visit? Explain why or why not on the lines below below. **F**

_____

_____

_____

_____

Reading **Focus**

Sequence The order in which events happen is called **sequence.** Writers don't always relate events in the exact order they happened. Smit has done a lot in a short time. Number the actions described below in the sequence in which he accomplished them. **G**

☐ moved to Cornwall

☐ began project in quarry

☐ restored gardens of Heligan

Hot Words

Choose three words, either from the underlined vocabulary in the article or from the words you circled as you read. Record them in your **Hot Words Journal** at the back of this book and complete one of the activities listed there.

Think It Over

Evaluate To **evaluate** means to form your own opinion about something. Smit believes that people will visit the Eden Project when it is finished. Do you think people will come? Explain your answer on the lines below. **H**

_____

_____

_____

_____

Reading Check

Step 1 Think about the Eden Project and Tim Smit's hopes for educating the public. Look back over the passages you marked. Then explain the main ideas of the Eden Project in two or three sentences. Write your summary on the lines below.

_____

_____

_____

_____

_____

_____

Step 2 How will plants have been part of your life by the end of the day today?

_____

_____

_____

Once Smit saw the clay quarry at Bodelva, he knew that it was the natural arena for the project. A local government grant helped kick start the process. But Smit still needed millions to pay for the architects, builders, and engineers without whom
80 the project was doomed. In 1996 he received a $60 million grant, on the condition that the amount be matched from other sources. Thanks to pledges from the European Union, the project went ahead.

Key to its success has been the dramatic design from the architectural team led by Nicholas Grimshaw. Plants need light and space, and Grimshaw's domes—made up of a latticework of steel surrounding and supporting air-filled hexagonal plastic bubbles—offer masses of both. Lightweight (the domes weigh about the same as the air they contain) and versatile, the biomes
90 have been molded to the uneven sides of the former quarry, optimizing the use of land and light.

Smit is confident his dream will attract 750,000 visitors a year, many more than the 500,000 needed to complete the planting and to sustain the project. Paul Travers, Eden's media director, points out that half a million people paid to visit the project in 2000, even though there was little to see but a building site. Smit is confident that as the biomes open and the visitors return, they will be wowed by the plant kingdom whose very fate they will determine. **H**

From *TIME,* March 26, 2001

Reading Check

_____

Vocabulary
optimize (op´tə mīz´) *v.* to make the most of
sustain (sə stān´) *v.* to keep in effect or in existence

Buddy Up

⟜ Summarize

1. Travel Poster With a partner, create a travel poster advertising the Eden Project. Summarize the main points from the article in the poster's written text and include eye-catching artwork. (Copy the written material below.) Then, as a class, decide whose poster would most persuade travelers to visit the Eden Project.

_____

_____

_____

_____

_____

2. Any Questions? Tim Smit wants everyone to know about the Eden Project. This means giving interviews to the media (radio, television, and the press). With your partner, think of questions an interviewer may ask Smit—and answers he may give. Then take turns playing the roles of Smit and the interviewer. Write one of the questions and answers from the interview on the lines below.

Interviewer: _____

_____

Tim Smit: _____

_____

_____

Standardized Test Practice

Choose the best answer for each multiple-choice question. Fill in the circle in the spaces for questions 1 and 2 on the right.

1. Tim Smit's main purpose in creating the Eden Project was to
   A. protect endangered species.
   B. create a rival Magic Kingdom.
   C. educate and fascinate people about plants.
   D. alert people about harm to the environment.

2. The author portrays Tim Smit as mainly
   A. a brash musician.
   B. a financial wizard.
   C. an artistic escapist.
   D. a practical dreamer.

Write your answer to open-ended question A in the space provided below.

A. When the Eden Project is finished, how might a visitor describe the place to a friend? Write your description using details from the article.

Multiple-Choice Questions

1. Ⓐ Ⓑ Ⓒ Ⓓ   2. Ⓐ Ⓑ Ⓒ Ⓓ

Open-Ended Question

A. _____

_____

_____

_____

_____

GET READY TO READ!

Connect

Whole-Class Discussion "Crazy teenage driver!" You've probably heard someone make a remark like that. But is there any truth to it? Do you and your friends drive carefully? And what makes a good driver, anyway? Spend a few minutes discussing these questions with your classmates. What's your conclusion? Should people be worried about teenagers behind the wheel?

In this article, you'll learn about an electronic device that keeps track of how teenagers drive.

Did You Know?

Building Background Here are some factors that contribute to teen road injuries.

alcohol: In 2000, 30% of teenage drivers who died in auto accidents had been drinking.

passengers: The risk of accidents increases with the number of teenage passengers in a car.

time of day: More than 40% of teenage deaths from car accidents occur between 9 P.M. and 6 A.M.

time of year: July and August are the deadliest months for teenage drivers.

Reason to Read

Setting a Purpose for Reading Read to learn how parents in one California town are keeping an eye on their teenage drivers.

As you read, use the following **Foldable** to help you record your responses to the ideas in this article.

1. Place a sheet of paper in front of you with the short end at the top. Fold it in half from side to side.

2. Turn the paper and fold it in half. Then fold it in half twice more.

3. Open the folds you made in step 2. Through the top thickness of paper, cut along each of the fold lines to form eight tabs.

4. Hold the paper so the fold is on the left. As you read, write down information from the article that surprises or interests you on the front of each tab. Inside the flaps, tell what you think about the information. For example, you might write "That seems like a good idea" or "Oh, please!" Fill in at least five tabs.

word power

Vocabulary Preview

Read the words and definitions below. Try pronouncing each word aloud. As you read, use context clues to help unlock the meaning of words you don't know.

monitor (mon´ə tər) *v.* to check; watch; keep track of; p. 155

data (dā´ tə) *n. pl.* information that conclusions can be drawn from; facts and figures; p. 155

exuberant (ig zōō´ bər ənt) *adj.* overflowing with high spirits or vigor; p. 156

mandate (man´ dāt) *v.* to require; make compulsory; p. 156

revelation (rev´ ə lā´ shən) *n.* something suddenly revealed that was not known before; p. 161

Hot Words Journal

As you read, circle words from the article that you find interesting or difficult. Later you may add them to your **Hot Words Journal** at the back of this book.

What You'll Learn

Key Goals In this lesson, you will learn these key skills, strategies, and concepts.

➤ **Reading Focus:** Connect

➤ **Think It Over:** Evaluate

➤ **Author's Plan:** Reading Sidebars

➤ **Reading Coach:** Understanding Facts and Statistics

Teen at wheel makes driving doubly deadly

Monitoring devices tell parents how their teen is driving: 'It's like having a babysitter in the car'

By Robert Davis
Contributing: Anthony DeBarros
USA TODAY.
July 05, 2002

CAMARILLO, Calif.—When 17-year-old Mallory Gompert's friends learn that the weird growl in her car comes from a black box her folks use to <u>monitor</u> every second of her driving, they all say the same thing: "Don't tell my parents about that thing!"

But the secret is out. In this Southern California town— rocked recently by fatal crashes involving teens—parents are increasingly asking Mallory's dad and his co-workers at Road Safety International when they can get a black box for their own kid's car.

The Camarillo-based company says the $280 device will be in stores nationwide by November. Called SafeForce, it records <u>data</u> like the car's speed and growls warnings when the driver is going too fast or turning too hard. Parents can check the box later and see for themselves just how fast their teenager was driving. **A**

It's far too soon to tell if the new tool will help teens drive more safely. Prototypes,[1] developed from a more complicated device used on emergency vehicles, have been installed in only a handful of private passenger cars. But evidence shows that the devices on emergency vehicles have reduced accidents in ambulances and fire trucks.

10

20

---

1. A *prototype* is a model something is based on.

Vocabulary

monitor (mon´ ə tər) *v.* to check; watch; keep track of
data (dā´ tə) *n.* information that conclusions can be drawn from; facts and figures

Reading Focus

🔑 **Connect** A black box that growls when you're driving too fast? How would you feel if your parent or guardian installed one in the car you drive? **A**

Model: *Well, I wouldn't like being spied on, but something that reminded me not to speed wouldn't be that bad.*

word power

Discovering Definitions
Sometimes the meaning of an unfamiliar word becomes clear when you read ahead a bit. For example, if you aren't sure what *monitor* means (line 3), all you have to do is keep reading! When you read on, you learn that the black box records information about a person's driving. It *keeps track of* what the driver's doing. And that's what *monitor* means!

Keep This in Mind
Use the following symbols to record your reactions as you read.

? I have a question about something here.

! This really caught my attention.

★ This information is important.

Reading Coach

◆ **Understanding Facts and Statistics** When an author use facts and numbers, pay attention! Slow down and read carefully. Rereading may help you figure out what the author is saying.

For example, reread the boxed paragraph. What do these statistics tell you? Check the correct statement below. **B**

❏ Teens need more drivers' education to learn to drive safely.

❏ Teens are more at risk on the road than other drivers.

❏ Teens are careless drivers.

◆ **Evaluate** When you **evaluate,** you judge something for yourself. Reread the highlighted sentence. Have the things you've read here convinced you that this is a public health issue? Mark your evaluation on the scale below. Then briefly explain your answer. **C**

No, I'm not convinced.			Yes, I'm convinced!

```
+    +    +    +    +
1    2    3    4    5
```

_____

_____

_____

_____

The black box is the latest of various tools the nation is using to steer teens into safer driving. About a dozen services have cropped up that allow parents, for a fee, to slap a bumper sticker on the family car that asks other drivers to report teen driving behavior on a toll-free telephone line. And many states use graduated drivers' license programs to give teens more road experience and adult supervision before they are granted unrestricted licenses.

30 Summer is when kids need that oversight most. With school out, these inexperienced and <u>exuberant</u> drivers are behind the wheel more. That makes July and August the deadliest months for teenage drivers. At greatest risk are the youngest drivers: They die at higher rates than any other drivers. A USA TODAY analysis of federal data has found that while the 1,134 drivers ages 15, 16 and 17 who were killed in crashes in 2000 made up only a small part of the 25,492 drivers killed in vehicle crashes, those ages represent the smallest number of licensed drivers. Teen drivers die at more than twice the rate of all drivers. **B**

40 "This is really a public health issue," says Bella Dinh-Zarr, a former traffic safety researcher for the Centers for Disease Control and Prevention who now is the director of road safety policy for the American Automobile Association (AAA). "Motor vehicle crashes are the leading cause of death for people 1 to 35." **C**

States are struggling to keep kids safe. Some states do better than others. The USA TODAY analysis found that Alaska, for instance, has a death rate among teen drivers that is more than twice the national average. North Dakota and Rhode Island have rates less than half the national average.

More than 30 states have passed laws—known as graduated 50 license laws—that attempt to force kids to drive more with a parent before they get their own licenses. The teens may get a provisional license[2] until they've spent a certain number of hours behind the wheel, accompanied by a parent or guardian. At the same time, laws prohibiting drunken driving and <u>mandating</u> seat

_____

2. In some states, a young driver gets a *provisional,* or restricted, license before being issued with a full license.

_____

Vocabulary
exuberant (ig zōō′bər ənt) *adj.* overflowing with high spirits or vigor
mandate (man′dāt) *v.* to require; make compulsory

belt use are tougher now than any time in driving history. But the key, Dinh-Zarr and others say, is enforcement.

"Even when states do have tougher teen driving laws," Dinh-Zarr says, "the problem may be that parents don't know they have this tool. Or the enforcement of these laws may not be very good in these states."

60

Watching the rescuers

For 10 years, some ambulances, fire trucks and other emergency vehicles have been equipped with the Road Safety black box that monitors the performance of drivers. Emergency crews call the boxes growlers—or worse—because they squawk when the rig[3] exceeds pre-set parameters[4] for speed, acceleration, braking and more.

Their supervisors call the boxes their eyes and ears.

"People drive perfectly when their supervisor is riding with them," says Larry Selditz, president of Road Safety. "This device allows the supervisor to stay in that front seat all the time."

70

Those $2,500 devices are credited with reducing accident rates and saving maintenance costs in rescue fleets across the nation. But they also have surprised even their makers by spotting trends that are otherwise hard to detect. **D**

For instance, occasionally, a paramedic who ranks among the best drivers in an ambulance corps based on black box monitoring for months on end will pop up on a supervisor's hit list for overly aggressive driving. When the supervisor confronts the medic about the change in driving patterns, the root cause is often marital trouble or some other stress at home.

80

"They say, 'I never realized it was bleeding over to my work,'" says Scott Springstead, operations supervisor for Sunstar ambulance in Pinellas County, Fla. "Without the system, they would be out there driving that way, and we would never know it."

Jeff Gompert, Road Safety's vice president, wondered as he traveled around the nation selling boxes to rescuers whether the same system might work as well for his teenage daughter, Mallory. **E**

The company (at www.roadsafety.com) found a way to make the device cheaper for family use. The emergency rigs

90

---

3. A *rig*, here, is a vehicle, such as a fire truck or an ambulance.
4. *Parameters* refers to boundaries or limits.

Reading Focus

🔑 **Connect** According to the author, drivers of emergency vehicles perform better when their supervisor (or the black box) is riding with them. How do you respond when you're under supervision? Check the statement that best describes your response. **D**

❑ I get nervous.

❑ I'm more careful.

❑ It doesn't make any difference.

Think It Over

Mark the text ▸ **Main Idea** Put a check next to the paragraph in the box whose main idea can be summarized by the following statement: *Emotions affect the way you drive.* **E**

Hot Words

Mark the text ▸ **Choose your own words** Don't forget to circle words you find interesting or difficult. You'll come back to these words later.

automatically transmit the driving data via radio to a computer at their home base whenever the rig returns from a tour. The family version uses a flash memory card—the postage-stamp-sized memory card that drives everything from digital cameras to handheld organizers—to record the data in the car. It must be carried inside and plugged into an inexpensive reader on the family PC. Otherwise, the devices are nearly identical.

"This is something that every car should have," says Janice Manzer of Camarillo. By word of mouth, she managed to get a
100 prototype of the box in her 17-year-old son's car after he had an accident in the school parking lot and got a speeding ticket on a city street. "It's like having a babysitter in the car."

.... ## Reading Check ....

The early results from the device's recordings have been eye-popping for parents.

The box showed that Mallory Gompert—both smart and polite as she addresses a reporter—had a lead foot.[5] She routinely cruised in the family's Ford Explorer at more than 80 mph, and she took turns dangerously fast. She had no idea, she says, that she was over the limit. Neither, of course, did her parents.
110 "I used to dread it when my dad would come home with his PC and say, 'Let's see how your driving is,'" Mallory says.

"She said, 'My life is terrible,'" her mother Donna recalls. "'Why does Dad have to work for Road Safety? I hate my life!'"

Now she likes the way the box reminds her to pay attention when she "spaces out." Because of her improved driving, she says, other parents ask her to drive their kids, and she hauls her siblings to practices and other places. "I was a soccer mom at age 16," she says. **F**

And the box has spotted a teen driving trend much the same
120 way it identified stressed-out ambulance drivers. The device has shown that Mallory and almost every other teen who has tested the box drive worse when they're racing to get home before curfew.

----

5. Having a *lead foot* means that a driver's foot is very heavy on the accelerator. In other words, Mallory drives too fast!

That finding in particular rattles the nerves of parents who still ache for the local families who lost their two teens in a late-night crash just before Christmas.

The tragic deaths were not unlike other teen driving fatalities[6] that occur, on average, three times a day across the USA. Feeling good after his high school team won its basketball game, the teenage driver was tearing through town in a luxury SUV. He hit a wall at 107 mph. He was 16. The driver and one passenger died. Two other passengers survived.

"They were just trying to have fun," says Ryan Evans, 17, who knew them and now has the black box in his car. Does he think the box would have saved them? "It might have," he says. **G**

Inexperience kills

Charles Butler, director of safety services at AAA, says the Road Safety black box is a potentially useful, one-of-a-kind device. But he says parents would be mistaken to believe they could install the box in a car and automatically make their teenager a safer driver.

The biggest threat to young drivers, Butler says, is something the box can't fix—inexperience. Teen crashes, he says, are most often caused by three factors: not looking in the right place at the right time; being distracted behind the wheel by conversations, music, cellphones or even daydreams; and not being able to "manage the space around their car."

"It takes two to four years" of driving to become proficient, he says. Somewhere between 750 and 1,500 miles of driving in various conditions, he says, the "crash probability" begins to drop.

"Inexperienced 16-year-olds have three times as many crashes as 18-year-olds," Butler says. "If the box helps give parents peace of mind, maybe it's worth it. But if you really want peace of mind, don't let your kid drive alone. You can be the black box." **H**

AAA offers tips for parents on how to teach driving. The video and a handbook, called *Teaching Your Teens to Drive: A partnership for survival,* cost $21.95 (members get a discount) and are available to everyone through local AAA chapters or at www.aaa.com.

Bryce Riach, 17, says the black box in his 1998 Toyota Tacoma has no impact on his driving. "I pretty much beep on every turn,"

130

140

150

160

6. *Fatalities* means "deaths."

Think It Over

◆ **Evaluate** The author appeals to your emotions with the story of the teenage boy who died. Evaluate the use of this story by checking the statement below that you agree with. **G**

❑ The story made me think that teens should have the box in their cars.

❑ I don't think one driver's accident applies to all teen drivers.

❑ I think the story is sad, but I need to read more before deciding if teens need the box.

Reading Coach

◆ **Understanding Facts and Statistics** This section (Inexperience kills) contains many facts and statistics. Mark the text ▶ Underline the fact or statistic that you find the most persuasive. Then explain how it supports the idea that inexperience is the biggest threat to young drivers. **H**

_____

_____

_____

_____

Author's Plan

Reading Sidebars Notice the **sidebar**—the box with information off to the side. A sidebar doesn't have to interrupt your reading. Briefly scan its contents and decide whether to read the sidebar now or after finishing the article. **I**

Model: *This sidebar seems to sum up information about the SafeForce monitor. I think I'll read it after I finish the article.*

Reading Focus

Connect Underline the sentences that tell how Bryce Riach was driving. If you were Bryce's friend, would you say [Mark the text] anything to him about his driving? Explain your answer below. **J**

_____

_____

_____

_____

he says, one week after the box was installed. "It's funny. . . . When it starts making noise, I just turn the (punk) music up," he says. "If my parents were looking at my results, it would be a bigger factor."

His parents know he has the box in his car as part of a study for Road Safety, but they have not yet seen any of his performance reports. Bryce says his parents don't know how he drives. "When I drive with them, I drive a lot safer, so they don't really know," he says.

170

Monitor your teen's driving **I**

SafeForce, which monitors driving performance of emergency vehicle operators, has been redesigned to help parents keep teen drivers safe. Here's how the black box works:

- The box monitors seat belt use, engine speed, tire traction and other parameters.
180
- Second-by-second information is recorded on a flash memory card.
- When the driver exceeds preset limits for speed, braking or sharp turns, the box growls first, then beeps that a violation has been recorded. The audible cues help drivers learn to drive within safe limits.
190
- Back home, when the flash memory card is put into the home computer, parents can see how their teen has been driving in recent days.

Source: RoadSafety

Road Safety's Selditz agreed to display the previous five days of Bryce's driving on the company computer. The screen is full of red violations. There are 34 turns where at least half of the tires' traction[7] was lost to high speed. There are more than 70 minutes of driving faster than 80 mph.

But one moment stands out. At 8:55 p.m. on the previous Thursday, he had lost nearly 70% of his traction while making a hard left turn. He had his headlights on, but he was not wearing his seat belt. **J**

_____

7. *Traction,* here, refers to the ability of a tire to stick to the road.

Bryce grins. "That is the island by my house," he explains. "It's an illegal turn, but if I don't make that turn I have to go up a mile and make a U-turn."

When a reporter tells his father, Ron Riach, a former firefighter, about the turn, the father of four young drivers is shocked: "That is a <u>revelation</u>. Especially about the seat belt. I have drilled that into their heads."

200

Bryce has heard the horror stories his dad has brought home from years on the street as a firefighter. But the boy says he doesn't worry about getting hurt.

"After I come close to getting into an accident, I think about what happened to those other people," he says. "But when I'm speeding, I don't really think about it."

Nearly two months have passed since Bryce got the black box. His parents still haven't looked at his black box reports, but constant reviews by Road Safety officials—who have threatened to remove the box and a $50-a-week payment for his participation— have begun to tame his driving.

210

"My driving has changed a lot," he says. "I don't really like it, but it's good for me. It was hard to get used to, but now that I am used to it, I can still get around quickly."

His dad says Bryce has learned to drive within the box's parameters. "He's safer," Ron Riach says, "but to what extent, who knows."

 **Reading Check**

Reading Check

Step 1 Take a moment to think about teen drivers, their parents, and the black box that checks up on them. Look back over the passages you marked and the responses you wrote in your Foldable. From the evidence presented in this article, do you think the black box makes teen drivers safer? Explain your answer.

_____

_____

_____

_____

Step 2 How do you think the black box would go over with your friends? What do you think of it? Write your ideas below.

_____

_____

_____

_____

Hot Words

Choose three words to record in your **Hot Words Journal** at the back of this book. Then complete one of the activities listed there.

Vocabulary

revelation (rev´ ə lā´ shən) *n.* something suddenly revealed that was not known before

Reading WrapUp

Going Solo

Connect

1. Safety First, or Last? How safe are your teenage friends as drivers? Do you think they might be twice as likely to have accidents as others on the road, as this article suggests? Rate three young drivers you know (call them A, B, and C) on a scale of 1 to 10, with 1 meaning they're terrible drivers and 10 meaning they're great. Then, on the lines below, explain why you gave them these ranks.

Rank: A _____ , B _____ , C _____

Reasons: _____

_____

_____

2. Outside the Box The kids mentioned in this article have mixed feelings about the use of the black box. Imagine that your parents have put a black box in the car you drive. Write a brief e-mail to a friend explaining what's happened and how you feel about it. Write your message below.

_____

_____

_____

_____

TeamWork

Evaluate

Pros and Cons Evaluate the black box. Does it solve problems? With your group, discuss the points for (pros) and against (cons) installing the box in all teen drivers' cars. List your ideas below.

Pros: _____

_____

Cons: _____

_____

Buddy Up

Understanding Facts and Statistics

1. Facts Please Review the article with your partner, looking for passages where the author uses facts or numbers to support his ideas. Choose three examples that you consider particularly convincing. Arrange them in order of importance on the lines below. Discuss your choices with another pair of students.

_____

_____

_____

2. Driver's Ed With your partner, make a poster that lets new drivers know some of the information introduced in this article. Choose the ideas that you consider most important and arrange them with key supporting facts and statistics on a sheet of paper or poster board. Use large print, clever slogans, and interesting designs to create an eye-catching display. Copy the written content from the poster in the space below.

_____

_____

_____

Standardized Test Practice

Choose the best answer for each multiple-choice question. Fill in the circle in the spaces for questions 1 and 2 on the right.

1. According to this article, teen drivers may best be described as
   A. defensive and selfish.
   B. inexperienced and unaware.
   C. irresponsible and dangerous.
   D. immature and undereducated.

2. The author suggests that the black box
   A. might be useful.
   B. is unpopular with all teenagers.
   C. is likely to become required by law.
   D. can significantly lower teen accident rates.

Write your answer to open-ended question A in the space provided below.

A. According to this article, why might parents or guardians install a black box in their child's car?

Multiple-Choice Questions

1. Ⓐ Ⓑ Ⓒ Ⓓ   2. Ⓐ Ⓑ Ⓒ Ⓓ

Open-Ended Question

A. _____

_____

_____

_____

word power   Vocabulary Check

Write the word that best completes each sentence.

monitor *v.* to check; watch; keep track of

data *n. pl.* information that conclusions can be drawn from; facts and figures

exuberant *adj.* overflowing with high spirits or vigor

mandate *v.* to require; make compulsory

revelation *n.* something suddenly revealed that was not known before

1. Next year our state legislature will _____ more classroom hours for all students in drivers' education.

2. After the graduation ceremony, the _____ seniors threw their caps into the air.

3. The news that my quiet Uncle José was once a war hero came as a _____ to me.

4. The new security system can _____ every room in the building.

5. Checking all of this _____ will keep the scientist busy for weeks.

Reading **Functional Documents**

People often complain about all the rules in modern life, but imagine the world without written information and regulations. Imagine people driving cars without licenses. Imagine if the bank didn't tell you about your balance. Imagine trying to figure out when to catch a plane without a schedule. And what about playing a new board game without the instructions?

Functional documents are just what their name suggests—documents that perform a useful function. They may range from the fat booklet telling you how to fill out your income-tax form to a postcard from the dentist reminding you to schedule a checkup. They may be for the expert or the amateur—instructions on repairing a jet engine or a sign that posts a store's hours. Whatever their purpose, functional documents serve to inform or instruct. Life would be difficult without them.

Mark the text Functional documents are everywhere. Beside each object or location below, write the type of functional document you associate with it.

school office _____   army recruiting center _____

online bookstore _____   new computer _____

bus station _____   cake mix _____

package of cereal _____   post office _____

Why Read Functional Documents?

If you lived on a desert island, you wouldn't need to read functional documents. But in a complex society, it's hard to function without them. In the world of cars, apartment leases, taxes, job interviews, college applications, security clearances, electronic equipment, building codes, and dangerous toys, you need all the help you can get to operate successfully. Functional documents help do just that.

What's the Plan?

Typically functional documents don't include a lot of details. The point is to give readers specific information clearly and quickly. Most functional documents use a logical plan—a **text structure**—to help you find and understand the information you need. Here are some text structures, or patterns of organization, that you'll find in functional documents.

Functional Document	Text Structure
Directions for a process	Sequence, or step-by-step order
Map or seating plan	Space order
Application or form to fill out	Category, or topic, order
Schedule	Time order

What Do I Look For?

Many functional documents share the **organizational features** and **design elements** of this catalog order form.

A **heading** at the top includes important information, such as a company's name and address.

Bold type and **capital letters** draw the reader's eye to different sections of the form.

Tables and other graphics help you know which parts to fill in and where to find specific information.

Boxed information visually separates sections of a document, making it easier to concentrate on one step at a time.

Mark the text **Find It!** Circle the section of this form that you should fill out if you're paying by credit card.

Mail Order Form
Runner's Lane
P.O. Box 1234
Anytown, Anystate 56789

ORDERED BY:

Name:

Address:

City: State: Zip:

Daytime Phone Number:

SHIP TO: (if different from ORDERED BY)

Name:

Address:

City: State: Zip:

Daytime Phone Number:

MAY WE SEND A CATALOG TO A FRIEND?

Name:

Address:

City: State: Zip:

Name:

Address:

City: State: Zip:

PAGE #	ITEM #	ITEM DESCRIPTION	UNIT PRICE	QUANTITY	TOTAL PRICE

PAYMENT METHOD

☐ Check or Money Order
  A $25 fee will be charged for returned checks.

☐ Credit Card:
  Indicate card name.

DAYTIME PHONE NUMBER:
Required for all orders.

EVENING PHONE NUMBER:

CREDIT CARD NUMBER:
☐☐☐☐ ☐☐☐☐ ☐☐☐☐ ☐☐☐☐

EXPIRATION DATE:
☐☐☐☐   X
Month Year   SIGNATURE OF AUTHORIZED BUYER

MERCHANDISE TOTAL:	
SALES TAX: For deliveries to VA (4.5%), to MD (5%)	$
SHIPPING CHARGE:	$
ADDITIONAL SHIPPING CHARGE: If applicable	$
OPTIONAL NEXT DAY AIR: See chart on page 50	$
ORDER TOTAL: Thank you for your order!	$

How Do I Read It?

These **reading strategies** will help you get the most out of functional documents.

Skim: Before you start to read, look over the whole document. This will let you know what information is offered or required.

Scan: Sometimes you need to find specific information from a document. By scanning for key words and headings, you can focus on the sections that are important to you.

Identify Sequence: Many functional documents lead you through a series of steps or actions. You'll follow the process better if you understand the organization behind this sequence.

Review: Did you understand the instructions? Did you fill out all the sections? Can you use that warranty? Go back over the document to make sure that you've gotten the information you needed.

For more information on **reading strategies,** see pages 216–222 in the **Reading Handbook.**

Read the functional documents that follow. Be sure to

• use the **text structure** and **text features** to help you understand the material

• use **reading strategies** to help you get the most from your reading

GET READY TO READ!

Connect

Group Discussion What's your favorite food for dinner? Write your answer on the line.

_____

Why do you like that meal so much? What are some of the ingredients that go into it? How much do you know about preparing that meal? Discuss your thoughts with a small group.

The recipe you are about to read shows all the ingredients and work that go into preparing a main dish for dinner.

Did You Know?

Building Background A good recipe is easy to follow and has delicious results. But here are some important things to think about before you turn on the oven or break the first egg.

- **Pots and Pans?** Do you have all the pots, pans, bowls, knives, and mixers you need? That turkey won't squeeze into a muffin tin.

- **Have Everything?** There's nothing more irritating than discovering you're out of milk (or onions or butter) when you're halfway through cooking. Check that you have all the ingredients beforehand.

- **Enough for Everyone?** Be sure your recipe will make enough servings for everyone.

Reason to Read

Setting a Purpose for Reading Read this recipe to learn how to make Mom's Tuna-Noodle Casserole.

 As you read, use this **Foldable** to track all the steps you need to follow to prepare Mom's Tuna-Noodle Casserole.

1. Fold a sheet of paper in thirds from top to bottom.

2. Without unfolding, fold the paper in half the long way.

3. Unfold the paper and draw lines along the folds. You'll have six boxes on the page.

4. Label the boxes **Before Step 1, Step 1, Step 2, Step 3, Step 4,** and **Step 5.**

5. In the **Before Step 1** box, summarize what you have to do just before starting Step 1. For example, you might start by writing "Set out all the ingredients."

6. Then, as you read, write a short summary of each step in the correct box.

word power

Cooking Terms

Cooking has its own special vocabulary. Even the simplest recipe may have puzzling words. Here are a few terms from the recipe for Mom's Tuna-Noodle Casserole.

- **Casserole** can refer to two things: 1) a deep dish for cooking food in the oven, and 2) the food baked in such a dish.

- **Condensed** soup has had some of the liquid removed. You have to add water or milk before serving it.

- When food is **chopped** it is cut into pieces. **Finely chopped** means that the pieces are very small.

- **Skillet** is just another way of saying frying pan.

- When you **sauté** food, you cook it in a skillet with a little oil, turning it frequently.

- Onions are often sautéed until they are **translucent.** That means you can almost see through them.

What You'll Learn

Key Goals In this lesson, you will learn these key skills, strategies, and concepts.

- **Reading Focus:** Sequence

- **Reading Coach:** Understanding Abbreviations

MOM'S TUNA-NOODLE CASSEROLE

What you need: **A**

- (1) 16 oz. pkg. egg noodles
- (2) 6 oz. cans tuna fish
- (1) 11 oz. can condensed cheddar cheese soup
- 1/2 cup sour cream
- 1/3 cup milk
- 1 cup frozen peas
- 1 large onion, finely chopped
- 1 large green pepper, finely chopped
- 2 ribs celery, finely chopped
- 1–2 cups shredded cheddar cheese, to taste
- 3 tbsps. olive oil or canola oil
- 2 tbsps. butter or margarine

Directions:

1. Preheat your oven to 350 degrees.

2. Put noodles in boiling water and cook according to package directions. When noodles are nearly done, add frozen peas. When the water returns to a boil, remove from heat and drain. Place noodles and peas into a bowl and toss with 1 tablespoon butter or margarine to prevent sticking.

3. Heat oil in a 12-inch heavy skillet over moderately high heat until hot but not smoking. Then sauté onion, pepper, and celery in the oil. Cook until the onions are translucent, about 10 minutes. Add salt and pepper to taste.

4. Mix the tuna, soup, sour cream, milk, and sautéed vegetables in a large bowl. Add the noodles and peas. Toss lightly to combine.

5. Use remaining butter or margarine to grease baking pan or casserole dish. Add noodle mixture. Top with shredded cheddar cheese to taste. Cover with aluminum foil and bake in 350 degree oven for 30 minutes. **B**

Serves 6–8

Reading Coach

◆ **Understanding Abbreviations** Recipes often use **abbreviations**—shorter forms of common words. An abbreviation usually ends with a period. For example, the abbreviation *tsp.* stands for *teaspoon.* Read the "What you need" list on this recipe and circle the abbreviations you find. Then write each abbreviation next to the word below that it stands for. **A**

Mark the text

_____ package

_____ ounce

_____ tablespoons

Reading Focus

◆ **Sequence** The order in which events happen is called **sequence.** In a recipe, the sequence is important. Review the recipe's directions. Then number the following actions in the correct sequence. **B**

☐ top with cheese

☐ boil noodles

☐ sauté vegetables

☐ combine ingredients

Reading Check

Review your **Foldable.** How would you summarize this recipe?

_____

_____

_____

_____

_____

 **Reading Check**

READING WRAPUP

TeamWork

🔑 Sequence

1. Don't Forget! There are important things to do *before* you start Step 1 of this recipe. Share with your group what you wrote in the **Before Step 1** box of your **Foldable**. Then, as a group, decide on the three most important things to do before Step 1. Write them on the lines below.

_____

_____

_____

_____

_____

2. Oh, No—I Forgot!! There are some things you will need that the recipe doesn't remind you of. Step 2 tells you to drain the noodles. But what do you use to drain the noodles? (You can use a strainer.) With your group, think of more tools this recipe doesn't remind you to get. Write two on the lines below. Tell when you would use each. (Hints: Remember that the tuna is in a can. Remember also that you have to chop the vegetables.)

_____

_____

_____

_____

_____

Standardized Test Practice

Choose the best answer for each multiple-choice question. Fill in the circle in the spaces for questions 1 and 2 on the right.

1. Which step should you do before putting the noodles in water?

    A. Heat oil in a 12-inch skillet.

    B. Preheat the oven to 350 degrees.

    C. Bake at 350 degrees for 30 minutes.

    D. Remove noodles from boiling water.

2. Which is a correct definition for the word *casserole?*

    A. a frying pan or skillet

    B. a deep dish to bake in

    C. any dish made with tuna

    D. any dish prepared according to a recipe

Write your answer to open-ended question A in the space provided below.

A.   How would you describe Mom's Tuna-Noodle Casserole in a short e-mail to friends who are coming over for dinner? Write your answer in one sentence.

Multiple-Choice Questions

1. Ⓐ Ⓑ Ⓒ Ⓓ   2. Ⓐ Ⓑ Ⓒ Ⓓ

Open-Ended Question

A. _____

_____

_____

_____

GET READY TO READ!

Connect

Write and Discuss Have you ever come home and found a note someone left for you? Maybe the note told you what to eat for a snack or asked you to feed the cat. Take a moment to recall one of these notes (or make one up). Write it on a piece of paper. Then imagine writing a note to communicate with a lot of people in a business office or at a school. How might a message you write at home be different from office or school messages? What might they all have in common? Discuss these questions with your class. Write one of your ideas on the lines below.

This school memorandum, or memo, shows one way people communicate in writing at a school or office.

Did You Know?

Building Background A **memorandum,** or memo, is a school or workplace message from one person or group to another.

- Memos usually begin with these headings, or lines:
  - —The **Subject** line tells what the memo is about.
  - —The **To** line tells who is receiving the memo.
  - —The **From** line tells who sent the memo.
  - —The **Date** line tells when the memo was written.
- The first paragraph, or opening statement, of a memo usually gives the writer's purpose, or reason for writing.
- The middle paragraphs, or body, give facts and details to support that purpose.
- The conclusion might invite readers to ask questions if they need more information. Memos often conclude by calling for some kind of action.

Reason to Read

Setting a Purpose for Reading Read to learn about two important reminders for students in Greentown High's after-school work program.

word power

Vocabulary Preview

Read the words and definitions below. Try pronouncing each word aloud. As you read, use context clues to help unlock the meaning of the words you don't know.

detention (di ten′ shən) *n.* the state of being held in temporary confinement, as in an early-morning detention in high school

supervise (sōō′ pər vīz′) *v.* to direct or oversee someone or something

etiquette (et′ i kət) *n.* the acceptable way to behave; good manners

violate (vī′ ə lāt′) *v.* to break or disregard a law, policy, or promise

Hot Words Journal

As you read, circle words from the memo that you find interesting or difficult. After reading, record those words and further explore their meanings in your **Hot Words Journal** at the back of this book.

What You'll Learn

Key Goals In this lesson, you will learn these key skills, strategies, and concepts.

- **Reading Focus:** Skim
- **Author's Plan:** Author's Purpose

Reading Focus

← **Skim** When you **skim** a memo, you look it over quickly to get a general idea of what it's about. That way, you can decide whether the message is important to you. Imagine that you're a senior at Greentown High School and you're involved in the after-school work program.

Mark the text Skim the memo. Underline two sentences that might show you that this memo was important for you to read. **A**

Author's Plan

← **Author's Purpose** Reread the memo carefully. Then mark a check before each statement below that describes a problem the dean of students is trying to solve by writing this memo. **B**

❏ After-school work program students are leaving class too early.

❏ After-school work program students are being extremely rude to their teachers.

❏ After-school work program students are getting detentions for bad behavior.

❏ After-school work program students aren't telling supervising teachers ahead of time about absences.

Reading Check

In your own words, list two instructions this memo gives to seniors in the after-school work program.

_____

_____

_____

_____

Greentown High School
1222 School House Lane

MEMORANDUM **A**

Subject   After-school work program

To All Seniors   **From** Elena Ramos, Dean of Students

Cc All Teachers
        Angela Dunbar, Principal   **Date** March 24, 2004

All seniors employed in our after-school work program need to pay close attention to the following important reminders. This includes students who help Ms. King in the library, Mrs. Wojcik in the athletic department, and Mr. Barrett in the grounds-keeping department.

1. You may leave your sixth-period class **no earlier than 2:35.** This will give you time to get to your after-school responsibilities. Students observed in the hallways before that time will be issued hall reports. Two hall reports are grounds for detention.

    (**Note to teachers:** Please assign homework to sixth-period classes before 2:35 so that students with after-school jobs can collect their assignments before they leave.)

2. If for any reason you cannot attend your after-school work shift, please inform your supervising teacher as soon as possible, and no later than noon on the day you'll be missing work. This is a courtesy to the teacher who expects your assistance as well as basic job etiquette. When you fill out your time sheets at the end of each week, be sure to report any missed work days.

Remember that participation in the after-school work program is a privilege. These rules are in place so that the program can run smoothly. Students who violate these policies will lose the opportunity to grow, learn, and earn with Greentown's outstanding program.

Thank you in advance for your cooperation. **B**

Reading Check

TeamWork

Author's Purpose

1. Picture This! Instead of writing this memo, Elena Ramos, Dean of Students, could have created a wall poster on the same subject. With your group, draw sketches of the poster she might have created. In your sketches, show the main problems Ms. Ramos mentions in the memo. On the lines below, describe the pictures you would have on your finished poster.

_____

_____

_____

_____

_____

2. A Visit from the Dean Elena Ramos, Dean of Students, might have decided to visit classrooms instead of writing this memo. With your group, take turns role-playing Ms. Ramos talking to a class on the topic of the memo. What might she say? On the lines below, summarize what you said in your role-play of Ms. Ramos.

_____

_____

_____

_____

_____

Standardized Test Practice

Choose the best answer for each multiple-choice question. Fill in the circle in the spaces for questions 1 and 2 on the right.

1. Which of the following people or groups receive a special note in the memo?

   A. teachers

   B. all students

   C. Angela Dunbar, principal

   D. Elena Ramos, Dean of Students

2. What example does the writer give of "basic job etiquette"?

   A. staying in class until 2:35

   B. assigning homework before 2:35

   C. getting detentions for hall reports

   D. telling the supervising teacher about absences

Write your answer to open-ended question A in the space provided below.

A. What might Ms. Ramos say to a student in the after-school work program if she met the student in the hall at 2:20?

Multiple-Choice Questions

1. Ⓐ Ⓑ Ⓒ Ⓓ   2. Ⓐ Ⓑ Ⓒ Ⓓ

Open-Ended Question

A. _____

_____

_____

GET READY TO READ!

Connect

List Ideas How healthful was the cereal you had for breakfast today? If you're like most people, you probably don't know because you didn't read the Nutrition Facts panel. What do you think that panel said? With a partner, list information you'd expect to find in a nutrition guide. Share your ideas with the class and make a master list on the board. Write two of your ideas on the lines below.

_____

_____

This panel from a food label gives detailed nutrition information about Toasty Flakes cereal.

Did You Know?

Building Background It's the law—all packaged food must have a nutrition panel. These panels may be different, but they share certain features.

- All information for a product is based on an average serving size—for example, 1 cup. You can find the serving size near the top of the panel.

- Nutrients are substances that are "good for you," such as vitamins. A nutritional panel tells you the **percent daily value** (% DV) you get of each nutrient per serving. For example, the government recommends 3,500 milligrams of potassium a day. A serving of Toasty Flakes gives you 7% of that total.

- Sometimes we combine foods—like milk and cereal. In these cases, the panel might give two % DV figures for each nutrient. The first is for the food by itself. The second is for the two foods together.

Reason to Read

Setting a Purpose for Reading Read to learn the nutrition facts about Toasty Flakes cereal.

word power

Nutrition Terms
Many of the words on the nutrition panel may sound familiar, but what do they mean? Below are some of the most important terms.

- **Calories** are a measure of the energy-producing value of food. (The more you eat, the more you must move around to burn the calories off!)

- **Fats** are a necessary part of the human diet, but too much fat can damage health. Too much **saturated fat** can lead to heart disease.

- **Cholesterol** is a substance found in animal products. Too much of it can also cause heart disease.

- **Sodium** is a mineral found in salt.

- **Carbohydrates** are nutrients found in sugars and starchy foods, such as bread, pasta, and potatoes.

- **Protein** is an important source of energy. It helps build muscle, bone, blood, and skin.

- **Vitamins** are important to human health, often in tiny amounts.

What You'll Learn

Key Goals In this lesson, you will learn these key skills, strategies, and concepts.

- **Reading Focus:** Scan

- **Author's Plan:** Text Features

TOASTY FLAKES

Nutrition Facts Ⓐ Ⓑ

Serving size 1 cup (49g)
Servings Per Container About 10

Amount Per Serving	Toasty Flakes	with 1/2 cup skim milk
Calories	160	200
Calories from Fat	17	17
	% Daily Value**	
Total Fat 2g*	**3**%	**3**%
Saturated Fat 0.5g	**3**%	**3**%
Cholesterol 0mg	**0**%	**0**%
Sodium 240mg	**10**%	**12**%
Potassium 250mg	**7**%	**13**%
Total Carbohydrate 34g	**11**%	**13**%
Dietary Fiber 4g	**16**%	**16**%
Sugars 9g		
Other Carbohydrates 21g		
Protein 4g		
Vitamin A	10%	15%
Vitamin C	10%	10%
Calcium	10%	25%
Iron	60%	60%
Vitamin E	10%	10%
Thiamin	25%	30%
Riboflavin	25%	35%
Niacin	25%	25%
Vitamin B6	25%	25%
Folic Acid	75%	75%
Phosphorous	12%	26%
Magnesium	11%	16%
Zinc	25%	30%

*Amount in Cereal. One half cup skim milk contributes an additional 65mg Sodium, 6g Total Carbohydrate (6g sugars), and 4g Protein.

**Percent Daily Values are based on a 2,000 calorie diet. Your daily values may be higher or lower depending on your calorie needs:

	Calories	2,000	2,500
Total Fat	Less than	65g	80g
Sat Fat	Less than	20g	25g
Cholesterol	Less than	300mg	300mg
Sodium	Less than	2,400mg	2,400mg
Potassium		3,500mg	3,500mg
Total Carbohydrate		300g	375g
Dietary Fiber		25g	30g

📖 **Reading Check**

Author's Plan

← **Text Features** This Nutrition Facts panel is arranged in columns and rows. (Columns run up and down; rows run across the chart.) Below, copy the information you find in the row directly beneath *Vitamin E*. Ⓐ

_____

In the answer you've just written, what does the information from the middle column tell you?

_____

Reading Focus

← **Scan** When you **scan**, you glance quickly over a selection to find specific information you're looking for.

Mark the text → Scan the Nutrition Facts panel and circle the following information. Ⓑ

- the serving size
- the number of calories from fat (without milk)
- the percent daily value of iron (without milk)

📖 **Reading Check**

Imagine that a friend wants to find out what percent of the daily value of vitamin A she would get from one serving of Toasty Flakes with milk. What directions would you give her so she could find that information?

_____

_____

_____

READING WRAPUP

Buddy Up

Scan

1. Scan Challenge! Choose any word or number on the Nutrition Facts panel. Tell it to your partner. Give your partner ten seconds to scan and point out that word or number. (There may be more than one correct answer.) Take turns asking questions and scanning. On the lines below, write each word and number you chose. Write a check next to each one your partner found in ten seconds or less. Whoever has the most check marks wins!

_____

_____

_____

_____

2. Nutrition Q & A With your partner, write four or five questions asking about information on the Nutrition Facts panel. *(Example: What's the percent daily value of sodium in a serving without milk?)* Exchange your questions with another pair. Take turns with your partner asking each other the new questions. Scan to find the answers. Write two of your questions and their answers below.

_____

_____

_____

_____

Standardized Test Practice

Choose the best answer for each multiple-choice question. Fill in the circle in the spaces for questions 1 and 2 on the right.

1. How many servings of Toasty Flakes with milk would give you 100% daily value of calcium?

   A. one

   B. two

   C. three

   D. four

2. Which nutritional value doesn't change when you add milk to a serving of Toasty Flakes?

   A. calcium

   B. calories

   C. iron

   D. zinc

Write your answer to open-ended question A in the space provided below.

A. What do the two columns on the right of the panel tell you? What can you learn from comparing them?

Multiple-Choice Questions

1. Ⓐ Ⓑ Ⓒ Ⓓ   2. Ⓐ Ⓑ Ⓒ Ⓓ

Open-Ended Question

A. _____

_____

_____

_____

_____

GET READY TO READ!

Connect

Giving Directions Imagine this: It's the first week of school and a confused freshman stops you in the hall to ask directions. Can you help? With a partner, practice giving directions. Choose places in the school as points to start from and to get to. *(Example: How do I get from the gym to room 223?)* Work out the directions carefully in your mind. Then write them down for your partner. Can your partner understand your directions? If not, revise them. Write your directions on the lines below.

_____

_____

_____

This road map with driving directions helps a driver get from one address to another.

Did You Know?

Building Background One way to get driving directions is by going on the Internet. Just type the key words *driving directions* into a search engine. Then hit *Enter.* You'll get referred to a number of Web sites. The way to get directions on most of these sites is similar.

- Click on *driving directions.*
- Type in where you're starting from and where you want to go.
- Print out the step-by-step instructions and the map.

As you read road maps and driving directions, look for these common symbols.

- 🛡(10) stands for a U.S. highway (here, US-10).
- 🛡(20) stands for an interstate highway (here, I-20).
- (30) stands for a local route or highway.

Reason to Read

Setting a Purpose for Reading Read to learn driving directions from one address to another.

word power

Direction Terms

What words do you use when you give someone driving directions? A number of useful terms apply to roads and travel.

- When the road you are driving on joins another road, it **merges** with the other road.
- A **fork** in the road is a place where the road branches off in two directions.
- When you reach a fork in the road, you can **bear** either right or left.
- An **intersection** is a place where two or more roads cross.

What You'll Learn

Key Goals In this lesson, you will learn these key skills, strategies, and concepts.

- **Reading Focus:** Scan
- **Author's Plan:** Text Features
- **Reading Coach:** Following Directions

Reading Focus

➡ **Scan** To **scan,** you glance over a selection to find the information you need. On this map, you'll need to find directions from a "start" (1820 Vine St.) to an "end" (2200 Ashland Pkwy.). Find and *Mark the text* circle the word *Start* and the star next to the word. Then find and circle the word *End* and the star next to it. **A**

Author's Plan

➡ **Text Features** This map has a **compass rose** in the upper right to show direction. The compass rose is labeled **N** for *Mark the text* north. Write **S** (for south), **E** (for east), and **W** (for west) in the correct places on the compass rose. Use the compass rose to help you find directions as you trace routes on the map. **B**

On the line below, answer this question. Which direction would you go on Elm St. to get from Des Moines St. to Vine St.?

_____

Road Map A

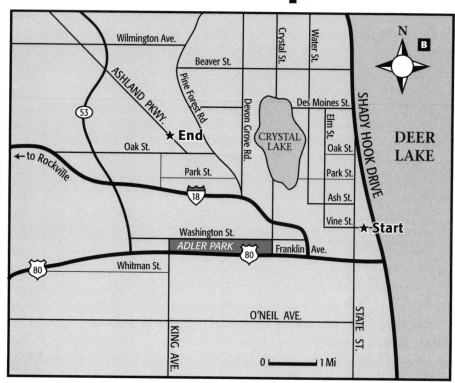

DRIVING DIRECTIONS **C**

FROM: 1820 Vine St.

TO: 2200 Ashland Pkwy.

DIRECTIONS **D**	**DISTANCE**
1. Start out going West on VINE ST toward STATE ST.	.01 mile
2. Turn LEFT onto STATE ST.	.65 mile
3. Turn RIGHT onto FRANKLIN AVE/US-80.	.97 mile
4. Merge onto I-18 W toward ROCKVILLE (portions toll).	2.00 miles
5. Take the DEVON GROVE RD exit.	.07 mile
6. Turn SLIGHT LEFT to take the ramp toward PINE FOREST RD.	.01 mile
7. Merge onto PINE FOREST RD.	1.00 mile
8. Turn LEFT onto OAK ST.	.55 mile
9. Turn RIGHT onto ASHLAND PKWY.	.45 mile

Total Estimated Time:	**Total Distance:**
8 minutes	5.71 miles

Reading Check

Text Features These driving directions provide visual clues. The boldface heading **DRIVING DIRECTIONS** tells the main point of this page. Circle other boldface terms that point out important information. Then write two things besides **DIRECTIONS** that you get from this page. **C**

Reading Coach

Following Directions When you use driving directions, it's helpful to highlight your route on the map. Read the first step

Mark the text of the directions. Then use a light-colored marker to trace that step on the road map. Continue until you have the whole route highlighted. **D**

Reading Check

Think about the driving instructions you've read and the route you traced on the map. Then mark a check next to each statement below that is true.

❑ From Vine St., you turn left onto State St.

❑ You take Pine Forest Road all the way to Wilmington Ave.

❑ Total estimated time is 30 minutes.

❑ Total distance is 5.71 miles.

Going Solo

🔑 Following Directions

1. Going Swimming Imagine that you live at 1820 Vine St., the starting point in these directions. You want to drive to Crystal Lake for a swim. Write the directions below.

_____

_____

_____

_____

_____

2. Last-Minute Change! Imagine that you are about to set out from 1820 Vine St. for 2200 Ashland Pkwy. But you hear about an accident blocking traffic on highway I-18. Look at the map to find another way of getting to your destination. Be sure to take a highway route. Write the steps below.

_____

_____

_____

_____

_____

Standardized Test Practice

Choose the best answer for each multiple-choice question. Fill in the circle in the spaces for questions 1 and 2 on the right.

1. Where would you most likely drive to get to the best views of Deer Lake?

   A. along Shady Hook Drive

   B. north on Pine Forest Rd.

   C. south on Devon Grove Rd.

   D. along Water St.

2. Which of the following roads intersects with I-18?

   A. State St.

   B. Park St.

   C. Vine St.

   D. Route 53

Write your answer to open-ended question A in the space provided below.

A.   Imagine that you are returning from 2200 Ashland Pkwy. to 1820 Vine St. What are the first three steps you would take in your journey?

Multiple-Choice Questions

1. Ⓐ Ⓑ Ⓒ Ⓓ   2. Ⓐ Ⓑ Ⓒ Ⓓ

Open-Ended Question

A. _____

_____

_____

STANDARDIZED TESTS

Reading Standardized Tests

Quiet classrooms, number-two pencils, and timed exams. Do you know what this setting suggests? If you said standardized tests, you're right! Pretty soon you and other students across your state will be tested on what you've learned throughout the year. How confident will you be when you sit down to take the test? Mark your level of confidence on the following scale.

This part of **The Glencoe Reader** will teach you reading strategies that will help you feel confident of your ability to succeed on **standardized tests** in **Reading, English/Language Arts,** and **Writing.**

Least Confident   Most Confident

Why Read Standardized Tests?

Read standardized tests to understand various types of test items so you can answer them! Then you'll be able to show how well you've learned your subjects and mastered the skills covered in your state's academic standards.

When you learn how to read the tests in this part of **The Glencoe Reader,** you'll learn strategies that will help you on other standardized tests.

The military, colleges, and even some jobs will require you to take standardized tests. By learning how to read standardized tests now, you'll be better prepared to take other important tests after high school. And scoring well on these standardized tests will help you to take charge of your future!

What's the Plan?

The plan for standardized tests in reading, language arts, and writing depends on the kinds of skills covered.

- Reading tests may have a number of reading selections. The reading selections are followed by multiple-choice questions and possibly a few open-ended questions that you will answer in your own words.

- Language arts tests may consist of multiple-choice questions related to a variety of skills, including spelling, punctuation, grammar, sentence combining, and paragraph organization.

- Writing tests usually provide you with a writing prompt that invites you to think about a familiar topic. You will write your response on blank paper that comes with the test.

The test booklet itself might have the following parts.

An **introduction** that describes the test. It may explain how much time you'll have and how to mark your answers.

Directions that tell you what steps to follow for each part of the test.

Reading passages that are either fiction or nonfiction. These passages may include a visual such as a map, a chart, or an illustration.

Test items that check how well you understand a reading passage or what you know about grammar, punctuation, and spelling. There might also be writing prompts that let you show your writing ability.

What Do I Look For?

Standardized tests have many of the same **text features.** Take a look at this example of a typical reading test.

Test directions are usually set in darker type so you can see them easily.

The **passage title** gives you a clue about what a reading will cover.

The **reading passage** on many kinds of tests gives information you'll be asked about later.

Test items are numbered. **Answer choices** are labeled with letters of the alphabet.

An **arrow** is a sign for you to go on to the next page. A **stop sign** signals the end of a test section. Don't turn the page!

Section 1 of this test has forty-five questions. Read each passage and choose the best answer for each question. Fill in the circle in the spaces provided for questions 1 through 45 on your answer sheet.

Read the passage and answer the questions that follow.

A Tall Achievement

Most people know Sir Edmund Hillary as the first person to reach the summit of Mount Everest. However, few know that Hillary had a companion on the expedition. Tenzing Norgay, a Nepalese Sherpa, accompanied Hillary on his ascent. In fact, it was Tenzing, not Hillary, who first stepped onto the summit. When they were near the top, Hillary urged Tenzing to go ahead of him. Since it was Tenzing's home country, Hillary believed Tenzing deserved the honor of being the first person to reach the summit.

Twenty years before his heroic feat, Tenzing had been involved with Everest expeditions. He had once come within 1,000 feet of the summit, only to be forced back down the mountain by inclement weather. But Tenzing desperately wanted to reach the summit and refused to give up. Time and time again, he climbed the mountain in hopes of reaching his goal. "For in my heart," Tenzing is quoted as saying, "I needed to go. . . . The pull of Everest was stronger for me than any force on Earth." Finally, at 11:30 A.M. on May 29, 1953, Tenzing Norgay fulfilled his dream, becoming the first person to set foot on the summit of Mount Everest.

1. How did Tenzing Norgay feel about Mount Everest when he said "For in my heart, I needed to go. . . . The pull of Everest was stronger for me than any force on Earth"?
   A. Tenzing felt an obligation to protect Mount Everest from an onslaught of climbers.
   B. Tenzing felt isolated when he was not enjoying the comforts of nature.
   C. Tenzing felt that his previous failure to reach the summit proved he was a coward.
   D. Tenzing felt compelled to reach the summit no matter how difficult the task.

2. The person best qualified to write these articles would be someone who
   A. had researched Mount Everest in books and magazines.
   B. had spoken to Sherpas in Nepal and listened to their stories.
   C. had had articles published in *National Geographic*.
   D. was a cartographer.

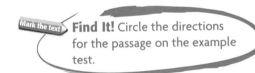

Mark the text **Find It!** Circle the directions for the passage on the example test.

How Do I Read It?

Use these **reading strategies** to successfully read the standardized tests.

Preview: Take a quick look at all directions, headings, test items, and answer choices. Skimming these parts will give you clues about what to look for as you read.

Clarify: Try restating directions, questions, and answer choices in your own words to make sure you understand them.

Scan: Look for key words in the test items that will point you to the details you'll need when answering the questions.

Analyze: Carefully examine each question and answer choice. Look for a clue to the right answer.

For more on reading strategies, see pages 216–222 in the **Reading Handbook.**

Read the sample standardized tests that follow. Be sure you

• use **text features** to help you know what to do

• use and practice **reading strategies** that will help you get the most from reading standardized tests

GET READY TO READ!

Connect

List Ideas Think of your favorite animal. Now imagine seeing this animal in a helpless situation. How would you feel? What action would you take to come to its rescue? List your answers on the appropriate lines below.

Animal: _____

Helpless situation: _____

Your feelings: _____

_____

Action: _____

In this lesson, you will read about legendary wild horses and their second chance at survival. As you read, you will learn various reading strategies that you can use to perform well on standardized reading tests.

Did You Know?

Building Background You will be better prepared to take a standardized reading test if you know something about the details and features of the test.

- The purpose of a standardized reading test is to see how well you understand what you read.
- The reading passages you will see on the test will be similar to other materials you have read in class or on your own—poems, short stories, and magazine articles.
- Most of the questions are multiple choice, but some questions might ask you to write answers in your own words.
- To answer the test questions, you might need to
  - **find** the answer somewhere in the reading passage
  - **collect** information from various parts of the passage
  - **combine** material from the passage with what you already know

Reason to Read

Setting a Purpose for Reading Read this lesson to learn strategies that will help you to do well on a standardized reading test. In the reading passage, you will learn how wild horses escaped extinction.

Test power

Test-Taking Tips

For extra test-taking power on **standardized reading tests,** keep these tips in mind.

- If it's OK to write in the test booklet, underline words, make markings, and jot down notes that will help you understand or identify key information.
- Use the process of elimination on multiple-choice questions. Cross out any answers that you know are wrong. Then choose the best answer from those that are left.
- For open-ended questions, underline key words in the questions. Then scan the passage for those words or details related to them.
- Find out if it's better to make a guess than to leave a blank space. On some tests, there is no penalty for guessing.
- Be sure to get enough sleep the night before the test. You want to be well rested and ready to go!

What You'll Learn

Key Goals In this lesson, you will learn these key skills and strategies.

- 🔑 **Reading Focus:** Predict
- 🔑 **Think It Over:** Main Idea
- 🔑 **Reading Coach:** Defining Unfamiliar Words

Reading Test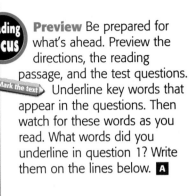

Section 1 of this test has forty-five questions. Read each passage and choose the best answer for each question. Fill in the circle in the spaces provided for questions 1 through 45 on your answer sheet.

Read the passage and answer the questions that follow.

Halfway House for Horses

by Melanie L. Stephens, *Time*, January 1, 1990

Their high-pitched whinnies roll across the plains like a tumbleweed-scattering wind. At dusk one of them rears and paws the air, casting a silhouette that is the very image of freedom. These are mustangs, the legendary wild horses of the American West. Two decades ago, mustangs were headed for extinction. Now, at Mustang Meadows Ranch, a 32,000-acre spread near St. Francis, S. Dak., 1,500 of them have found sanctuary and a managed independence that may help assure their survival. **B**

Reading Focus

Preview Be prepared for what's ahead. Preview the directions, the reading passage, and the test questions. **Mark the text** Underline key words that appear in the questions. Then watch for these words as you read. What words did you underline in question 1? Write them on the lines below. **A**

_____

_____

Think It Over

🗝 **Main Idea** Active readers think about the main idea as **Mark the text** they read. Underline the sentence that tells what this paragraph is about. On the lines below, jot down a key phrase to remind yourself of the main idea of this paragraph. **B**

_____

_____

_____

Keep This in Mind

Mark the text Underline key words as you read each paragraph and jot down a note about the main idea.

Reading
Coach

Defining Unfamiliar Words You can use context clues to figure out the meaning of the highlighted word *dwindled.* **C**

Model: *The author says that "millions of mustangs roamed the prairie" in the 19th century. Then the author says that the number dwindled and explains that "by 1970 only 17,000 were left."*

Use the information in this model to find the word below that means the same as *dwindled.* Circle that word.

increased   remained

decreased   doubled

Draw Conclusions Combine the highlighted details in this paragraph to **draw a conclusion** about BLM's efforts to help the wild horses. Write your conclusion below. **D**

_____

_____

_____

_____

Reading Focus

Predict What do you think Hyde will do in response to what he saw? Write your prediction below. **E**

_____

_____

_____

Descended from horses that escaped from Spanish herds,
10 millions of mustangs roamed the prairie at the start of the 19th century. But as the wildness went out of the West and more and more rangeland was plowed for crops or fenced off for cattle, the number of mustangs dwindled. By 1970 only 17,000 were left, despite the passage of federal laws that banned the use of airplanes and motor vehicles to round them up for slaughter. In 1971 Congress responded to a massive letter-writing campaign by enacting the Wild Free-Roaming Horses and Burros Act, which assigned the federal Bureau of Land Management [BLM] the responsibility for protecting these "living symbols of the historic
20 and pioneer spirit of the West." **C**

Under BLM, the mustangs have recovered: 42,000 horses now run free on the range. But their numbers have greatly surpassed the ability of the land to support them. To ease the overpopulation, BLM in 1976 inaugurated a national Adopt-a-Horse program, under which 90,000 wild horses have been sold to private owners. But the mustangs taken off the range annually include many that are too old, crippled, ugly, or mean to make good pets. Until two years ago, thousands of unadoptable mustangs were crowded into dusty feeding pens in Nebraska,
30 Nevada, and Texas at a cost to taxpayers of $13 million a year. **D**

Enter Dayton Hyde, an Oregon rancher with a reputation for unorthodox management and a deep interest in conservation. "In my travels I kept going by feedlots, seeing these poor creatures cooped up," says Hyde, 64. "I thought, 'That's no way to treat a wild horse.' My dream was to get these horses out of the feedlots and running free again." **E**

In 1988 Hyde founded the nonprofit Institute for Range and the American Mustang [IRAM] in order to create sanctuaries— retirement homes of sorts—where unadoptable wild horses could
40 once again roam freely. He convinced BLM that with foundation and public funds he could establish a self-sustaining sanctuary

within three years. IRAM's first project was a 12,600-acre sanctuary in the Black Hills of South Dakota. . . . The project makes Hyde smile. "The horses are finally getting over their depression," he says. "They got so bored in the feedlots that they didn't know how to run anymore."

Hyde's ambition went beyond his successes at the Black Hills sanctuary. He next sought to establish a larger range that could accommodate thousands of horses. But since IRAM lacked both money and land, Hyde needed the help of a private investor. He turned out to be Alan Day, an owner of cattle ranches in Arizona and Nebraska. Day, says Hyde, "knew how to manage grass and was not afraid of the immensity of my dream." **F** **G**

50

The first mustangs arrived in August 1988. After being cooped up in corrals anywhere from one month to several years, they needed to readjust psychologically to the comparative freedom of the ranch's open pastures. By gradually approaching the wary mustangs in corrals, Day and his wranglers taught them to become comfortable around people. "They have had so much negative training before they get here, they think they are going to suffer if they see a man on horseback," says Day. "We want to show them that we are not the enemy." **H**

60

Reading Coach

← **Defining Unfamiliar Words** Not sure what *immensity* means? Relate it to other words that you know. What word does *immensity* remind you of? What does that word mean? Jot down your answers below. **F**

_____

Now relate the definition you wrote to the word *immensity*. Circle the word or phrase below that means the same as *immensity*.

weakness   lack of money

huge size   benefits

← **Predict** Do you think Hyde and Day will be able to work together successfully? Explain your answer. **G**

_____

_____

_____

Think It Over

← **Main Idea** When you finish reading a passage, it's a good idea to jot down a note about the main idea. What main point does the writer make in this article? Write your answer below. **H**

_____

_____

_____

Reading Focus

Review Look back at the main idea note that you wrote about the passage. Then circle the answer that best matches *Mark the text* what you wrote. **I**

Reading Focus

Scan Question 2 asks you to find specific details in the passage. Underline key words in the question. What words did *Mark the text* you underline? Write them on the lines below. **J**

_____

_____

_____

Now scan the passage for the paragraph containing those key words. Reread the paragraph and any notes you wrote. Circle the *Mark the text* letter of the correct answer.

Try this approach for number 3. *Mark the text* Circle your answer for test item 3.

Choose the best answer for each multiple-choice question.

1. What is the main idea of this passage? **I**

   A. After mustangs were saved from extinction, some were taken to sanctuaries.

   B. Mustangs have been saved from extinction, but most surviving mustangs are old and ugly.

   C. Alan Day's money and land saved the mustang by teaching them new survival techniques.

   D. Wild horses can learn to trust human beings and, as a result, to live a peaceful existence.

2. What was the effect of the federal laws that prohibited the use of motorized vehicles for rounding up mustangs for slaughter? **J**

   A. The mustang population began to flourish.

   B. The mustang population slowly rose.

   C. The mustang population continued to decrease.

   D. The mustang population decreased to 10,000.

3. How did the relationship between humans and mustangs change as a result of Alan Day's methods?

   A. Humans caused the mustang population to decrease.

   B. Mustangs caused the humans working with them to become depressed.

   C. Humans are no longer able to keep mustangs as pets.

   D. Mustangs became more comfortable interacting with humans.

Go On

4. What did Hyde mean when he said that Day was not afraid of the "immensity" of his dream?

    A. Day was not afraid of the amount of work that had to be done.

    B. Day was hopeful that the mustang population would be restored.

    C. Day had achieved many other ambitious goals in his life.

    D. Day would do anything to restore the mustang population.

5. What was the author's main reason for writing this article? **L**

    A. to provide information on the history of mustangs

    B. to explain how sanctuaries have helped prevent the extinction of the mustang

    C. to persuade the reader to contribute to the well-being of mustangs

    D. to entertain the reader with information about the Wild West

6. This article would be **most useful** in **M**

    A. understanding how private investment works.

    B. learning about the daily chores of a ranch hand.

    C. researching the effects of good land management.

    D. understanding how human intervention can protect wild animals.

Think It Over

Synthesize Look back at the margin notes on page 185 for the definition you circled for the word *immensity*. Then combine that meaning with what you know about Hyde's dream. Mark the text ▶ Circle the letter of the best answer. **K**

Reading Focus

Question This question asks you to identify the author's purpose. Ask yourself, Why did the author write this article? Jot down your answer on the lines below. **L**

_____

_____

_____

Mark the text ▶ Circle the answer that most closely matches what you wrote.

Think It Over

Evaluate The word *most* is a clue that each answer choice may be partly correct, but one Mark the text ▶ choice is best. Cross out the answer choices that are only partly correct. Now circle the answer choice that tells how the article would be "most" useful. **M**

Go On

Reading Focus

Clarify Be sure you understand what this test item is asking you to find. Ask yourself, Am I to find a specific detail from the article, or am I looking for something else? Explain your answer below. **N**

_____

_____

_____

Mark the text Now circle the best answer.

Reading Focus

Review The key words in this question are "beauty of the mustang." Think about what makes a mustang beautiful. Then jot down two kinds of details you will look for in the passage. **O**

_____

_____

_____

Reading Check

Step 1 Did you find one reading strategy more helpful than the other strategies? Explain.

_____

_____

Step 2 Which strategies will you use the next time you take a standardized reading test?

_____

_____

7. Dayton Hyde is a reliable source of information about mustangs because **N**

    A. he founded the Institute for Range and the American Mustang.

    B. he has worked with mustangs all his life.

    C. he has personally funded the creation of two self-sustaining sanctuaries.

    D. he has a deep interest in conservation.

Write your answer to open-ended question A in the space provided.

A. How does the author portray the beauty of the mustang? Support your answer with details and information from the passage. **O**

STOP

······················ ### Reading Check ·······················

Going Solo

⚊ Defining Unfamiliar Words

1. Unlock the Meaning Look back at the two Reading Coach notes on pages 184 and 185. What strategies do those notes describe to help you figure out the meaning of words you don't know? On the lines below, explain how these strategies can help you on a reading test when you come to a word you don't know.

_____

_____

_____

_____

2. Try It! Review the two strategies that helped you to define unfamiliar words in this lesson. Use those strategies to define the words from the article that are listed below. Find each word in the line of the article given in parentheses. Reread the sentence in which the word appears. Then use one or both strategies to define the word. Write your definitions on the lines below.

sanctuary (line 7) _____

_____

comparative (line 56) _____

_____

Standardized Test Practice

Choose the best answer for each multiple-choice question. Fill in the circles in the space provided.

1. Hyde's actions showed that he
    A. lacked ambition.
    B. supported feedlots.
    C. had an interest in nature.
    D. knew the history of cattle.

2. Which of the following did NOT happen as a result of the Adopt-a-Horse program?
    A. Hyde founded BLM.
    B. Ninety thousand horses were sold.
    C. Private owners got involved.
    D. Feedlots became overcrowded.

3. What word **best** describes Alan Day?
    A. self-taught
    B. competitive
    C. independent
    D. experienced

4. The article suggests that feedlots
    A. lacked sufficient space.
    B. were in South Dakota.
    C. were inexpensive.
    D. were too big.

Multiple-Choice Questions

1. Ⓐ Ⓑ Ⓒ Ⓓ   2. Ⓐ Ⓑ Ⓒ Ⓓ   3. Ⓐ Ⓑ Ⓒ Ⓓ   4. Ⓐ Ⓑ Ⓒ Ⓓ

GET READY TO READ!

Connect

Questionnaire By now, you've probably taken more standardized language arts tests than you can remember. Still, it's a good idea to review the strategies you use for taking these tests. Some strategies—such as reading answer choices carefully—are good to follow. Others—such as spending all your test time on the most difficult questions—aren't. Read each statement below. If you agree with the statement, write *yes* on the line. If you disagree, write *no*.

_____ **1.** To do well on a standardized language arts test, you need to learn all the rules of grammar.

_____ **2.** When the test gives you a passage to read and some questions to answer about that passage, it's a good idea to look at the items first to guide your reading.

_____ **3.** The night before the test, you should get some good rest.

_____ **4.** No matter what anyone says, it's always a good idea to guess at answers.

As you work through this lesson, keep your answers to this questionnaire in mind. You may want to change some of your answers as you learn more about test-taking strategies.

The sample English/Language Arts test that follows is a typical example of standardized language arts tests you might take in high school, for placement in college courses, or even as part of a job application.

Did You Know?

Building Background In general, standardized language arts tests check what you already know about spelling, grammar, punctuation, vocabulary, sentence combining, and other language skills. For this test, you will read passages or sentences and answer some multiple-choice questions about them.

Reason to Read

Setting a Purpose for Reading Read the English/Language Arts test to understand the test items and their answer choices. Read the lesson to learn strategies for reading a test. Then you'll be prepared to do your best on a real test.

Test Power

Test-Taking Tips

For extra test-taking power, keep these tips in mind.

- Keep your cool. If a question stumps you at first, often a little confidence and careful reading will help you figure out an answer.

- Think up your own answer to a question before you evaluate the answer choices. Then choose the choice that most closely matches your thinking.

- Read every answer choice for an item carefully, because some of the choices may be only partly right. You want to find the choice that's totally right.

- When you fill in the answer sheet, make sure the item number for the answer space matches the item number of the question you're answering.

- Manage your test time well. Don't spend too much time on difficult items.

What You'll Learn

Key Goals In this lesson, you will learn these key skills and strategies.

- **Reading Focus:** Preview

- **Think It Over:** Analyze

- **Reading Coach:** Reading Test Items and Passages Together

English/Language Arts Test A

Section 1 of this test has forty-five multiple-choice questions. Choose the best answer for each question. Fill in the circle in the spaces provided for questions 1 through 45 on your answer sheet.

B On November 19, 1863, Abraham Lincoln gave a brief speech at the dedication of the National Cemetery at Gettysburg. Read this speech and answer questions 1 through 5.

1 C Four score and seven years ago our fathers brought forth on this continent, a new nation, conceived in liberty, and dedicated to the proposition that all men are created equal. Now we are engaged in a great civil war, testing whether that nation or any nation so conceived and so dedicated, can long endure. We are met on a great battlefield of that war. We have come to dedicate a portion of that field, as a final resting place for those who here gave their lives that that nation might live. It is altogether fitting and proper that we should do this.

2 But, in a larger sense, we can not dedicate—we can not consecrate—we can not hallow—this ground. The brave men, living and dead, who struggled here, have consecrated it, far above our poor power to add or detract. The world will little note, nor long remember what we say here, but it can never forget what they did here. It is for us the living, rather, to be dedicated here to the unfinished work which they who fought here have thus far so nobly advanced. It is rather for us to be here dedicated to the great task remaining before us—that from these honored dead we take increased devotion to that cause for which they gave the last full measure of devotion—that we here highly resolve that these dead shall not have died in vain—that this nation, under God, shall have a new birth of freedom—and that government of the people, by the people, for the people, shall not perish from the earth.

Reading Focus

Clarify To get an idea of what you will be doing on the test, look for directions that apply to *all* of the test items. Mark the text Circle those directions and then read them carefully. A

How many items are there on this section of the test?

_____

What type of items are they?

_____

Reading Focus

Preview Skim the introduction and the passage to get an idea of what the passage is about. Then scan test items 1 through 5 for key words. Mark the text Underline the key words so you'll know what to look for as you read the passage. What key word or words did you underline in item 3? B

_____

Main Idea The **main idea** of a paragraph is the most important point of that paragraph. As Mark the text you read the passage, underline key phrases and write a label next to each paragraph that will help you remember what the main idea is. What label will you write next to paragraph 1? C

_____

_____

← **Analyze** When you **analyze** a test item, you look at its parts to understand the whole thing. Here, analyze the answer choices to see which ones can be answered through research. **D**

Model: *When I do research, I find facts and records that tell what happened. So the correct answer choice will be about a topic that I can find facts and records for. I probably couldn't find evidence to answer A, B, or D. They seem to be matters of opinion. I probably could find out what people thought about Lincoln's speech.*

Mark the text Now circle the letter of the best answer.

← **Reading Test Items and Passages Together** One good way to find support for a claim is to turn the claim into a question. Then find the part of the passage that answers your question. Write the claim as a question here. **E**

_____

_____

_____

Mark the text Circle the letter of the answer choice that best answers your question.

1. Which of the following questions about the Gettysburg Address could **best** be answered through more research? **D**

   A. Was the Gettysburg Address Lincoln's best speech?

   B. Who was the bravest soldier to fight during the Battle of Gettysburg?

   C. What did people think about the Gettysburg Address just after Lincoln delivered it?

   D. Was Lincoln correct when he said it was "fitting" to dedicate a portion of the battlefield as a graveyard?

2. Which of these statements from the speech **best** supports Lincoln's claim that "we can not dedicate—we can not consecrate—we can not hallow—this ground"? **E**

   A. ". . . government of the people, by the people, for the people, shall not perish from the earth."

   B. "The brave men, living and dead, who struggled here, have consecrated it, far above our poor power to add or detract."

   C. "Now we are engaged in a great civil war, testing whether that nation or any nation so conceived and so dedicated, can long endure."

   D. "We have come to dedicate a portion of that field, as a final resting place for those who here gave their lives that that nation might live."

3. To which audience does Abraham Lincoln address his speech? **F**

   A. the men who fought the Battle of Gettysburg

   B. the people gathered at the cemetery

   C. all the people in the world

   D. the U.S. Congress

4. In the context of the first sentence, <u>proposition</u> means **G**

   A. fact.

   B. danger.

   C. principle.

   D. disagreement.

Read the following excerpt from the speech and answer question 5.

> The world will little note, nor long remember what we say here, but it can never forget what they did here.

5. What is the **best** paraphrase of the excerpt? **H**

   A. This memorial service will soon be forgotten, but the actions of those who fought here will be remembered forever.

   B. The men who fought here did not die in vain, because their bravery guaranteed a Union victory in the Civil War.

   C. There are people in the world who do not even know that the Civil War is taking place in the United States, but someday they will know about the war.

   D. In a few years, no one will remember the Gettysburg Address.

Think It Over

Draw Conclusions The answer to this item is not directly in the passage. Think about Lincoln's tone and his purpose for writing this speech. Then read each answer choice and ask yourself, Whom did Lincoln hope to reach with his speech? Jot down your answer below **F**

_____

Mark the text Circle the letter of the answer that most closely matches what you wrote.

Reading Focus **Scan** Find and circle the word *proposition* in the first sentence. Then read the sentence, substituting each answer choice in place of **Mark the text** *proposition.* Circle the answer choice that makes the most sense. **G**

Reading Coach

◆— **Reading Test Items and Passages Together** Make sure you understand what test item 5 is asking. What part of the passage are you to paraphrase? **H**

_____

Think about how you would paraphrase, or restate, that text. Then circle the letter for the **Mark the text** answer choice that comes closest to your own paraphrase.

Reading Focus

← **Preview** These directions tell you that items 6 and 7 will be about a new passage. Preview this part of the test by skimming the items and underlining their key words. Jot down what you'll look for in the passage to answer each item. **I**

Mark the text

item 6:

_____

_____

_____

item 7:

_____

_____

Mark the text As you read the passage, make notes that will help you answer the items.

Reading Coach

← **Reading Test Items and Passages Together** Review your key words and labels. Which paragraph probably has the answer to this item? **J**

_____

Scan the paragraph for a reason similar to one of the answer choices. Circle the best answer.

Mark the text

Read the following passage and answer questions 6 and 7. I

> The novels of British author Jane Austen are admired for their keen representation of human strengths and weaknesses, their piercing and humorous descriptions of everyday life, and their elegant prose style.
>
> Austen's first novel, published in 1811, was *Sense and Sensibility.* It follows the lives of two sisters with different personalities. Austen's second novel, *Pride and Prejudice,* is her most famous. Published in 1813, the novel presents a feisty heroine. In 1814 Austen published *Mansfield Park,* whose heroine is mistreated by her relatives, although she manages to maintain her integrity throughout. In *Emma,* published in 1816, the heroine's matchmaking plans come close to ruining her chances for happiness. Two more novels were published after Austen's death in 1817: *Northanger Abbey,* a satire of the Gothic tales of romance and terror, and *Persuasion,* a book about a couple whose love survives challenges.
>
> Perhaps the best testimonial to Austen's work is that almost two hundred years after her novels were written, people can still relate to their characters and plots.

6. According to the passage, one of the reasons people enjoy reading Austen's novels is her **J**

   A. realistic settings.

   B. frightening plots.

   C. humorous observations.

   D. descriptions of early America.

7. In the passage on page 194, the writer's primary purpose is to _____ the reader. **K**

    A. inform

    B. instruct

    C. entertain

    D. persuade

Read the following passage and answer questions 8 and 9. L

> As environmental concerns become more and more dire, it is encouraging to see organizations that are trying to reduce environmental waste. Every year the steel industry in North America is responsible for the recycling of cans, discarded appliances, auto parts, and other steel products. Millions of tons of scrap steel are recycled for future use. Steel used in the production of auto bodies, appliances, and steel framing is made of a minimum of 25 percent recycled steel. Products like railroad ties and bridge supports are made up of almost 100 percent recycled steel. All new steel products contain at least some recycled steel, so purchasing steel is purchasing a recycled product.

8. Which conclusion can you draw from the information in the passage? **M**

    A. Steel is used to make recycling machines.

    B. An abundance of steel can be found in nature.

    C. It is important to reduce environmental waste.

    D. Purchasing steel supports poorly paid steelworkers.

9. According to this writer, the steel industry in North America recycles steel because of

    A. the railroad industry.

    B. the production of auto bodies.

    C. the Environmental Protection Agency.

    D. the need to reduce steel waste in the environment.

Analyze In this item, the key word "primary" means you should look for the writer's main purpose. Think about the writer's tone, the kind of information given about Jane Austen, and the meaning of this passage. **Mark the text** Circle the letter of the answer choice that best fits your impression of the writer's main purpose for writing. **K**

Reading Focus **Preview** Remember to preview items 8 and 9 so you'll know what to look for as you read the passage. What will you look for to answer item 9? **L**

_____

_____

Draw Conclusions For item 8, you'll put together several pieces of information to make a general statement about something. Think about what you already know and about the facts in the **Mark the text** passage. Circle the letter of the answer choice that is best supported by the information in the passage. **M**

Now use the same process to **Mark the text** answer item 9. Circle the letter of the best answer choice.

Reading Focus

← **Preview** Here's a new set of instructions and a new passage. Which items apply to the passage on this page?

Mark the text ▸ Underline key words in those items to remind yourself what to look for when you read the passage.

Think It Over

Infer One of the key words in item 10 is "theme." *Theme* is another way of saying "message."

Mark the text ▸ Look back over the passage, circling details that help you decide what the writer's message is. Below, write a one-sentence description of the theme. **O**

Mark the text ▸ Now circle the answer choice that most closely matches what you wrote.

Read the following passage and answer questions 10 through 12.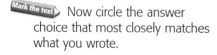

> "Dad! Dad!" Jana called out excitedly as she burst through the front door, almost out of breath. She had run all the way home from school.
>
> "What is it, honey?" Jana's father asked as he rushed into the living room.
>
> "Guess what?" Jana said, grinning. "I got a 95 percent on my math test! I only missed one of the questions about logarithms."
>
> "That's terrific!" her father replied.
>
> "All my hard work paid off," Jana said as she handed her father the test. "I'm glad I studied as hard as I did."
>
> Her father smiled as he looked over the test. "I'm quite impressed," Jana's father said, handing the paper back to Jana.
>
> "May I go to Adam's house before dinner?" Jana asked.
>
> "I don't see why not," her father answered. "What are you and Adam doing that's so important?"
>
> "He asked me to help him with his math homework. Can you believe it? Mr. Mechanical Genius needs my help."

10. Which sentence **best** describes the theme of this passage? **O**

   A. Hard work will pay off in the end.

   B. Logarithms are difficult to understand.

   C. Students need to study only when they have tests.

   D. People should only study before dinner so they can get to bed early.

11. The author is **most likely** trying to convey

    A. the benefits of striving toward a goal.

    B. the father's happiness for his daughter.

    C. Jana's decision to help Adam with his homework.

    D. the need for communication between generations.

12. The author characterizes the father as **Q**

    A. mild-mannered and impassive.

    B. alarmed and dismayed.

    C. controlling and guarded.

    D. concerned and supportive.

Read the following passage and answer questions 13 and 14.

> Aquaculture—the production of fish and other seafood under controlled conditions—is the fastest growing segment of American agriculture. Researchers reason that aquaculture can reduce the strain placed on wild fish populations by commercial fishing. As the amount of fish produced by fish farms increases, the amount of wild-catch fish consumed should decrease. This should help nearly depleted wild populations to replenish themselves.

13. Which of these statements from the passage is a fact? **R**

    A. Aquaculture—the production of fish and other seafood under controlled conditions—is the fastest growing segment of American agriculture.

    B. Aquaculture can reduce the strain placed on wild fish populations by commercial fishing.

    C. As the amount of fish produced by fish farms increases, the amount of wild-catch fish consumed should decrease.

    D. This should help nearly depleted wild populations to replenish themselves.

Reading Focus

Question Ask yourself, What does the author want me to learn from this passage? Jot down your answer. **P**

_____

_____

_____

Mark the text Circle the answer choice that most closely matches what you wrote.

Reading Focus

Question For this item, ask yourself, What do I learn about the father from his words and actions? Underline details in the *Mark the text* passage that give clues about the father's personality. Then circle the answer that best matches these details. **Q**

Analyze When you carefully analyze the test item, you'll see that only one answer choice is a fact—a statement *Mark the text* that can be proved. Circle words such as *could, would, should, might,* and *can* in the answer choices. These words are clues that the statements are opinions or guesses about what might happen. Now reread the answer choices and find the one that could be proved. *Mark the text* Circle the answer that states a fact. **R**

14. Which of the following statements does NOT support the assertion that the growth of aquaculture "should help nearly depleted wild populations to replenish themselves"? **S**

   A. Only in relatively recent times has aquaculture become a major industry in the United States.

   B. The growth in demand for seafood is far greater than the growth in aquaculture production.

   C. As the amount of fish produced by fish farms increases, the amount of wild-catch fish consumed should decrease.

   D. Researchers reason that aquaculture can reduce the strain placed on wild fish populations by commercial fishing.

Read the passage and answer question 15. **T**

> "I think I'd really have my hands full trying to bake two cakes by myself," said Tyrone. "Would anyone like to lend a hand? I think it'll be fun."

15. Which of the following literary techniques is used in this passage? **U**

   A. personification

   B. alliteration

   C. simile

   D. idiom

16. Which of the following literary techniques is used in the sentence below?

> Warren was weary on Wednesday.

   A. onomatopoeia

   B. alliteration

   C. rhyme

   D. simile

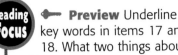

Read this poem and answer questions 17 and 18.

BOY AT THE WINDOW

Seeing the snowman standing all alone
In dusk and cold is more than he can bear.
The small boy weeps to hear the wind prepare
A night of gnashings and enormous moan.
His tearful sigh can hardly reach to where
The pale-faced figure with bitumen eyes
Returns him such a god-forsaken stare
As outcast Adam gave to Paradise.

The man of snow is, nonetheless, content,
Having no wish to go inside and die.
Still, he is moved to see the youngster cry.
Though frozen water is his element,
He melts enough to drop from one soft eye
A trickle of the purest rain, a tear
For the child at the bright pane surrounded by
Such warmth, such light, such love, and so much fear.

(Richard Wilbur)

---

17. The mood of this poem can **best** be described as

   A. frigid and energetic.

   B. upbeat and optimistic.

   C. sorrowful and compassionate.

   D. lighthearted and understanding.

18. The point of view used in this poem is

   A. first person.

   B. third-person limited.

   C. third-person subjective.

   D. third-person omniscient.

Reading Focus
➔ **Preview** Underline key words in items 17 and 18. What two things about this poem will you try to identify?

_____

_____

Think It Over

➔ **Analyze** Notice that each answer choice in this item is a pair of words. *Both* words have to describe the poem for the answer choice to be correct. ▸**Mark the text** Cross out words that don't describe the mood of the poem, circle words that do describe the mood of the poem, and put a question mark next to words you're not sure about. Circle the letter of the answer choice that has two words circled.

Reading Focus
Recall You may not remember all four points of view listed here. Define those you do remember and write one definition below.

_____

_____

_____

_____

Use your definitions to help you decide which point of view is ▸**Mark the text** correct. Circle the best answer.

Preview How is this passage different from the other passages you've seen so far? Write your answer here.

_____

_____

Mark the text Circle the sentence numbers that items 19 and 20 refer to. Underline errors in these sentences as you read the passage.

Scan Look over the passage to see if you underlined any errors in sentences 1 and 3. Circle the letter of the answer **Mark the text** choice in items 19 and 20 that shows the errors, if any, that you noted. **Z**

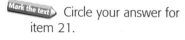

Reading Test Items and Passages Together For test items like number 21, you need to recall the rules for grammar, punctuation, and spelling. Read the boxed sentence carefully and decide whether it has one of the errors that appears in the answer choices. What error, if any, did you find in the sentence? **AA**

_____

Mark the text Circle your answer for item 21.

Read the following passage and answer questions 19 and 20. **Y**

> (1) The greenhouse effect is the name, of the effect that Earth's lower atmosphere has on temperatures at the surface of Earth. (2) Atmospheric gases, such as water vapor, carbon dioxide, methane, and ozone, keep temperatures at the surface of Earth warm. (3) Without these gases, the average Global temperature would be below the freezing point of water.

19. What revision, if any, is needed in sentence 1? **Z**

   A. Change _greenhouse_ to <u>green-house</u>.

   B. Add a comma after _effect_.

   C. Remove the comma after _name_.

   D. No revision is needed.

20. What revision, if any, is needed in sentence 3?

   A. Change _Without_ to <u>without</u>.

   B. Change _average Global_ to <u>Average Global</u>.

   C. Change _Global_ to <u>global</u>.

   D. No revision is needed.

Read the following sentence and answer question 21.

> In the barren desert that lays along the border of Arizona and Nevada, a dam would be built that could control the Colorado River.

21. What revision, if any, is needed? **AA**

   A. Change _lays_ to <u>lies</u>.

   B. Change _desert_ to <u>dessert</u>.

   C. Change _along_ to <u>among</u>.

   D. No revision is needed.

Read the following sentence and answer question 22.

> A newspaper usually will replace these instant reports with a researched news story: a deliberate, measured consideration of the issues and events.

22. What revision, if any, is needed?

    A. Change *will* to <u>will be</u>.

    B. Change *measured* to <u>measuring</u>.

    C. Change *issues* to <u>issued</u>.

    D. No revision is needed.

Read the following passage and answer questions 23 through 25. CC

> (1) Many scientists contributed to our present understanding of DNA and genetics. (2) One important scientist was Francis Crick. (3) Crick was a physicist from England. (4) Francis Crick worked to identify the shape of the DNA molecule.
>
> (5) In 1951 Francis Crick befriended James Watson, a biochemist from America. (6) Crick and Watson spent two years working together to identify the shape of the DNA molecule. (7) As a result of their research, they came to the conclusion that DNA was shaped like a double helix. (8) In 1962 they were awarded the Nobel Prize for their double-helix theory of DNA structure.
>
> (9) It is somewhat odd that these two scientists worked so well together. (10) Neither one was a biologist by training. (11) When they worked together, they made one of the most important biological discoveries of all time. **DD**

Think It Over

⬅ **Analyze** As you reread the boxed sentence, underline anything you know or think is an error. If you're not sure, analyze the changes suggested in answer choices A, B, and C. **BB**

Circle your answer for item 22.

Reading Focus

⬅ **Preview** Skim items 23–25 on page 202 before you read the passage. In the passage, circle the sentence numbers that items 23–25 refer to. In which sentences will you look for a possible error? **CC**

_____

Which sentence will you be adding a transition to?

_____

Think It Over

⬅ **Analyze** You know from previewing that one item asks about adding a word or phrase to the beginning of sentence 11. Analyze sentences 10 and 11. What word or phrase could you add to the beginning of sentence 11 to make it flow logically from sentence 10? Write the word or phrase below. **DD**

Evaluate Reread sentences 2 and 3. Then read the answer choices, pausing slightly for each comma. Which choices sound awkward or change the meaning of the original sentences? **EE**

Mark the text Circle the answer that sounds most natural and means the same as the original sentences.

Reading Coach

🔑 **Reading Test Items and Passages Together** Look back over sentences 6 and 7 on page 201 for errors that you might have marked. **FF**

Mark the text Circle the letter of the answer choice that shows the errors, if any, that you underlined. If you're unsure about your underlining, try substituting the answer choices in the sentences. If none of the revisions seem right, circle answer choice D.

Reading Focus **Review** Look back at the word or phrase you wrote in Think It Over note DD on page 201. Circle the letter of the *Mark the text* answer choice that most closely matches your word or phrase. **GG**

23. Which of the following **best** combines sentences 2 and 3? **EE**

   A. Francis Crick was one important scientist, a physicist from England.

   B. One important scientist was Francis Crick, a physicist from England.

   C. One Francis Crick, an important scientist, was a physicist from England.

   D. One physicist from England, an important scientist, was Francis Crick.

24. What revision, if any, is needed in sentences 6 and 7? **FF**

   A. Change *working* to worked.

   B. Remove the period after *molecule*.

   C. Remove the comma after *research*.

   D. No revision is needed.

25. Which transition would **best** begin sentence 11? **GG**

   A. Yet

   B. Thus

   C. Furthermore

   D. For example,

Buddy Up

🔑 Reading Test Items and Passages Together

1. Talk It Out With a partner, compare your underlining in the passage on page 195. Then discuss these questions: Did your underlining lead you to the correct answer D for item 9? If yes, how? If no, what changes to your underlining would help you pick the correct answer? Summarize your discussion below.

_____

_____

_____

_____

2. To Read the Passage or Not to Read It With a partner, look back at item 14 on page 198. How helpful would reviewing the passage be in answering item 14? Discuss this question with your partner. Then summarize your conclusions.

_____

_____

_____

_____

Standardized Test Practice

Choose the best answer for each multiple-choice question. Fill in the circles in the space provided.

1. Which of the following would be the **best** title for the passage on page 195?
   A. Recycling in North America
   B. How to Buy Recycled Steel
   C. One Industry's Contribution to the Environment
   D. The Use of Recycled Steel in Auto Body Production

2. Which of the following literary techniques is used in the sentence below?

   Salvador's criticism stung me like a wasp.

   A. onomatopoeia
   B. metaphor
   C. rhyme
   D. simile

3. Which of the following **best** combines the sentences below?

   Tanya took up cycling. She wanted to get fit.

   A. Tanya took up cycling and wanted to get fit.
   B. Tanya took up cycling because she wanted to get fit.
   C. Tanya, who took up cycling, wanted to get fit.
   D. Tanya took up cycling, but she wanted to get fit.

4. What revision, if any, is needed in the sentence below?

   There are two magnetic poles, a North Pole, and a South Pole, on Earth.

   A. Change *Earth* to earth.
   B. Change *poles* to Poles.
   C. Remove the comma after *North Pole.*
   D. No revision is needed.

Multiple-Choice Questions

1. Ⓐ Ⓑ Ⓒ Ⓓ   2. Ⓐ Ⓑ Ⓒ Ⓓ   3. Ⓐ Ⓑ Ⓒ Ⓓ   4. Ⓐ Ⓑ Ⓒ Ⓓ

GET READY TO READ!

Connect

K-W-L What do you know about standardized writing tests? What would you like to find out about these tests? Answer these questions by filling in the first and second columns of the K-W-L (**K**now, **W**ant to Know, Have **L**earned) chart. When you finish the lesson, come back to this chart and fill in the third column.

K	W	L

This lesson may provide answers for what you want to know about standardized writing tests. A writing test assesses your writing skills. The test consists of one writing **prompt**—a sentence or two that starts you thinking about a familiar topic. The prompt often focuses on persuasive or expository writing. Here's an example of a persuasive writing prompt: *Inventions have helped to advance our society. What do you think is the most important invention of all time?* A prompt like this one gets you thinking about a topic so you can write about it.

This section of **The Glencoe Reader** has two sample writing prompts. The lesson will provide practice with **reading strategies** you can use when you read and respond to a writing prompt.

Did You Know?

Building Background There are many types of writing prompts. In this lesson, you will learn to read these two types.

- The first prompt, **type 1,** presents an issue and then explains how you should write about that issue.
- The second prompt, **type 2,** presents a situation and then gives directions for writing about it.

Reason to Read

Setting a Purpose for Reading Read this lesson to see two types of prompts and to learn strategies for reading the prompts carefully. Then you'll be ready to write good responses on an actual writing test.

WRITING PROMPTS

Test-Taking Tips

Your score on a writing test depends on how well you think about, plan, and write your answer to a writing prompt. You may find these tips helpful.

- Be sure to read the prompt carefully so you know what topic to write about and what type of details to include.
- If it's okay to write in the test booklet, underline key words, and jot down notes that will answer questions like these.
  - What does the prompt tell me to think about?
  - What do I know about this topic?
  - What type of paper am I supposed to write? Should I explain how to do something? Share a personal experience? Take a stand on an issue? Persuade someone?
  - What directions are included for writing a strong response?
  - Where should I write my draft? My final paper?

What You'll Learn

Key Goals In this lesson, you will learn these key skills and strategies.

- **Reading Focus:** Monitor Comprehension
- **Think It Over:** Synthesize
- **Reading Coach:** Reading for Key Words

WRITING PROMPT: TYPE 1 A

Writing Situation

Students in the United States are falling behind those in other countries. Many educators and politicians believe that the school year should be lengthened to eleven months. Many students say that they need to be off during the summer to earn money working summer jobs and to reenergize after nine months of school. Decide how you feel about going to school for eleven months of the year.

Directions for Writing

Write a letter to the editor of your local newspaper in which you either support the movement to lengthen the school year or oppose such a change. Clearly state your position. Try to convince readers of the paper to agree with you by providing well-developed supporting arguments. B C

Reading Coach

Reading for Key Words Skim the prompt and underline key words. What words will you underline in the highlighted sentence to remind yourself of your writing topic? Write them on the lines below. A

_____

_____

_____

Reading Focus

Monitor Comprehension Ask yourself questions to check your understanding. On the lines below, jot down one question you will ask yourself. B

_____

_____

Synthesize On the lines below, state your position on this issue and give two reasons supporting your position. C

_____

_____

_____

_____

_____

_____

_____

Preview Quickly look over the headings and skim the whole prompt. Circle the part **Mark the text** of the prompt that acquaints you with the subject you are to write about. **D**

Reading Coach

⚷ Reading for Key Words Carefully read the prompt and **Mark the text** underline key words to remind yourself what to write. **E**

Model: In the Writing Situation, I'll underline "ways," "new students," "make the most of," and "high school years" to remind myself of the topic. In the Directions for Writing, I'll underline "good," "not-so-good things during," and "high school" so I remember what to think about. In the last sentence, I'll underline "essay explaining how." This is the type of paper I need to write.

Reading Focus ⚷ Monitor Comprehension Check that you understand the prompt. Ask yourself questions like these: What type of paper am I supposed to write? What is the topic? Jot down your answers below. **F**

_____

_____

_____

_____

WRITING PROMPT: TYPE 2 **D**

WRITING SITUATION: E
Your principal has asked for suggestions about ways that new students can make the most of their high school years.

DIRECTIONS FOR WRITING:
Think about both the good things and the not-so-good things during your high school experience.

Now write an essay explaining how incoming high school students can make their high school experience enjoyable and rewarding. **F**

Buddy Up

🔑 Reading for Key Words

1. Look into the Keys With a partner, discuss the key words both of you underlined in Writing Prompt: Type 1. Should the key words you underlined match those underlined by your partner? Why? What kinds of words are "key" in a writing prompt? Summarize your discussion on the lines below.

_____

_____

_____

_____

_____

2. Key into a Prompt On the lines below, write your own prompt modeled after Writing Prompt: Type 2. Then exchange writing prompts with a partner and underline key words in your partner's prompt. When you are finished, discuss which key words you underlined and how you would use them to write a response.

_____

_____

_____

_____

_____

Standardized Test Practice

Choose the best answer for each multiple-choice question. Fill in the circles in the space provided.

1. Which of the following is NOT true about Writing Prompt: Type 1?

    A. It tells the format in which to write your response.

    B. It tells you which side of the issue to support.

    C. It presents an issue to write about.

    D. It is a persuasive writing prompt.

2. Writing Prompt: Type 2 asks you to

    A. write an expository essay.

    B. choose a topic to write about.

    C. list your complaints about school rules.

    D. interview incoming high school students.

3. Which of the following should you keep in mind when underlining key words in a prompt?

    A. Underline all the long words in the prompt.

    B. Underline words only in the Writing Situation.

    C. Underline words only in the Directions for Writing.

    D. Underline the words that remind you what to write about.

4. Which of the following should you do when taking a writing test?

    A. Plan the paper as you write it.

    B. Save time by not writing a draft of the paper.

    C. Underline key words as you read the prompt carefully.

    D. Ignore the Writing Situation and go directly to the Directions for Writing.

Multiple-Choice Questions

1. Ⓐ Ⓑ Ⓒ Ⓓ   2. Ⓐ Ⓑ Ⓒ Ⓓ   3. Ⓐ Ⓑ Ⓒ Ⓓ   4. Ⓐ Ⓑ Ⓒ Ⓓ

REFERENCE

Reading Handbook

Ever notice that words are everywhere? They're on food labels and gum wrappers, in movie credits and CD booklets, in mail and e-mail, in textbooks and comic books. And reading those words is unavoidable. Have you ever tried *not* reading the words you see on a billboard? Can't do it, can you?

This handbook focuses on skills and strategies that can help you understand what you read. The strategies you use to understand individual words are pretty much the same, no matter what you're reading. But the strategies you use to understand whole texts depend on the kind of text you're reading. In other words, you don't read a news article the way you read a novel. You read a news article mainly for information; you read a novel mainly for fun. To get the most out of your reading, you need to choose the right reading strategy to fit the reason you're reading.

Use this handbook to help you learn

- how to identify new words and build your vocabulary
- how to read fluently
- how to adjust the way you read to fit your reason for reading
- how to become an engaged reader
- how to use specific reading strategies to better understand what you read
- how to use critical thinking strategies to think more deeply about what you read

You'll also learn about

- text structures
- reading for research
- reading consumer, workplace, and public documents

Identifying Words and Building Vocabulary

What do you do when you come across a word you don't know? Do you skip over the word and keep reading? If you're reading for fun or entertainment, you might. And that's just fine. But if you're reading for information, an unfamiliar word may get in the way of your understanding. When that happens, try the following strategies to figure out how to say the word and what it means. These strategies will help you better understand what you read. They will also help you increase the vocabulary you use in everyday speaking and reading.

Reading Unfamiliar Words

Sounding the word out One way to figure out how to say a new word is to sound it out, syllable by syllable. Look carefully at the word's beginning, middle, and ending. Inside the new word, do you see a word you already know how to pronounce? What vowels are in the syllables? Use the following tips when sounding out new words.

Ask Yourself

- What letters make up the beginning sound or beginning syllable of the word?

  Example: In the word *coagulate*, *co-* rhymes with *so*.

- What sounds do the letters in the middle part of the word make?

  Example: In the word *coagulate*, the syllable *ag* has the same sound as the *ag* in *bag*, and the syllable *u* is pronounced like the letter *u*.

- What letters make up the ending sound or syllable?

  Example: In the word *coagulate*, *late* is a familiar word you already know how to pronounce.

- Now try pronouncing the whole word: *co ag u late*.

Using word parts Sounding out an unfamiliar word syllable by syllable is one way to learn how to say the word. Looking closely at the parts of the word is another way. By studying word parts—the root or base word, prefixes, and suffixes—you may discover more than just how to pronounce a word. You may also find clues to the word's meaning.

- **Roots and base words** The main part of a word is called its **root.** When the root is a complete word, it may be called the **base word.** Many roots in English come from an old form of English called Anglo-Saxon. You probably know many of these roots already. For example, *endearing* and *remarkable* have the familiar words *dear* and *mark* as their roots. Other roots come from Greek and Latin. You may not be as familiar with them. For example, the word *spectator* contains the Latin root *spec*, which means "to look at."

  When you come across a new word, check whether you recognize its root or base word. It can help you pronounce the word and figure out the word's meaning.

- **Prefixes** A prefix is a word part that can be added to the beginning of a root or base word. For example, the prefix *semi-* means "half" or "partial," so *semicircle* means "half a circle." Prefixes can change, or even reverse, the meaning of a word. For example, *un-* means "not," so *unhappy* means "not happy."

- **Suffixes** A suffix is a word part that can be added to the end of a root or base word to change the word's meaning. Adding a suffix to a word can also change that word from one part of speech to another. For example, the word *joy* (which is a noun) becomes an adjective when the suffix *-ful* (meaning "full of") is added. *Joyful* means "full of joy."

Determining a Word's Meaning

Using syntax Like all languages, the English language has rules and patterns for the way words are arranged in sentences. The way a sentence is organized is called the **syntax** of the sentence. If English is your first language, you have known this pattern since you started talking in sentences. If you're learning English now, you may find the syntax is different from the patterns you know in your first language.

In a simple sentence in English, someone or something (the **subject**) does something (the **predicate** or **verb**) to or with another person or thing (the **object**).

The **dog chased** the **cat.**

Sometimes **adjectives, adverbs,** and **phrases** are added to spice up the sentence.

The scruffy brown dog **angrily** chased **the adorable little** cat **around the corner.**

CHECK iT OUT

Knowing about syntax can help you figure out the meaning of an unfamiliar word. Just look at how syntax can help you figure out the following nonsense sentence.

The blizzy kwarkles sminched the flerky fleans.

Your experience with English syntax tells you that the action word, or verb, in this sentence is *sminched.* Who did the *sminching*? The *kwarkles.* What kind of kwarkles were they? *Blizzy.* Whom did they *sminch*? The *fleans.* What kind of fleans were they? *Flerky.* Even though you don't know the meaning of the words in the nonsense sentence, you can make some sense of the entire sentence by studying its syntax.

Using context clues You can often figure out the meaning of an unfamiliar word by looking at its context (the words and sentences that surround it).

Do iT!

To learn new words as you read, follow these steps for using context clues.

1. Look before and after the unfamiliar word for

    —a definition or a synonym (another word that means the same as the unfamiliar word)

    *Some outdoor plants need to be **insulated,** or <u>shielded</u>, against cold weather.*

    —a general topic associated with the word

    *The <u>painter</u> brushed **primer** on the walls before the <u>first coat of paint</u>.*

    —a clue to what the word is similar to or different from

    <u>Like a spinning top</u>, the dancer **pirouetted** gracefully.

    —an action or a description that has something to do with the word

    *The cook used a **spatula** to <u>flip</u> the pancakes.*

2. Connect what you already know with what the author has written.

3. Predict a possible meaning.

4. Use the meaning in the sentence.

5. Try again if your guess does not make sense.

Using reference materials Dictionaries and other reference sources can help you learn new words. It takes a little time to look up a word in a reference book, but it's worth the effort. Check out these reference sources:

- A **dictionary** gives the pronunciation and the meaning or meanings of words. Some dictionaries also give other forms of words, their parts of speech, and synonyms. You might also find the historical background of a word, such as its Greek, Latin, or Anglo-Saxon origins.

- A **glossary** is a word list that appears at the end of a book or other written work and includes only words that are in that work. Like dictionaries, glossaries have the pronunciation and definitions of words. However, the definitions in a glossary give just enough information to help you understand the words as they are used in that work.

- A **thesaurus** lists groups of words that have the same, or almost the same, meaning. Words with similar meanings are called **synonyms.** Seeing the synonyms of words can help you build your vocabulary.

Understanding denotation and connotation Words have two types of meaning. Each word has a **denotation,** which is the literal meaning, the meaning you find in dictionaries. Many words also have a **connotation,** which is a meaning or feeling that people connect with the word.

For example, you may say that flowers have a *fragrance* but that garbage has a *stench.* Both words mean "smell," but *fragrance* has a pleasant connotation, while *stench* has a very unpleasant one. As you read, it's important to think about the connotation of a word to completely understand what a writer is saying.

Recognizing Word Meanings Across Subjects

Have you ever learned a new word in one class and then noticed it in your reading for other subjects? The word probably won't mean exactly the same thing in each class. But you can use what you know about the word's meaning to help you understand what it means in a different subject area.

CHECK iT OUT!

Look at the following example from three subjects:

Social studies: *One major **product** manufactured in the South is cotton cloth.*

Math: *After you multiply those two numbers, explain how you arrived at the **product.***

Science: *One **product** of photosynthesis is oxygen.*

You may know that a product is something manufactured by a company. In math, a product is a number that you get from multiplying two numbers. In science, it's the result of a chemical reaction. In all three subject areas, a product is the result of something.

Reading Fluently

Reading fluently is reading easily. When you read fluently, your brain recognizes each word so you can read aloud without skipping or tripping over words. If you're a fluent reader, you can concentrate on the ideas in your reading because you don't have to worry about what each word means or how to say it.

Fluency in reading does not come automatically. As with any new skill, it takes practice. The rewards are great, though. As you read more quickly and with better understanding, reading will become more fun, and assignments and tests will feel less challenging and easier to complete.

Do iT!

Follow these tips for reading fluency.

- **Read often!** The more, the better. Reading often will help you develop a good **sight vocabulary**—the ability to quickly recognize words.

- **Practice reading aloud.** Believe it or not, reading aloud does help you become a better silent reader.

—Begin by reading aloud a short, interesting passage that is easy for you.

—Reread the same passage aloud at least three times or until your reading sounds smooth. Make your reading sound like you are speaking to a friend.

—Then move on to a longer passage or a slightly more difficult one.

Reading for a Reason

Why are you reading that paperback mystery? What do you hope to get from your science textbook? And are you going to read either of these books in the same way that you read a restaurant menu? The point is, you read for different reasons. The mystery may be for entertainment or escape, the science text for knowledge, and the menu for choosing a sandwich. The reason you're reading something helps you decide on the reading strategies you use with a text. In other words, how you read will depend on why you're reading.

Knowing Your Reason for Reading

In school and in life, you'll have many reasons for reading, and those reasons will lead you to a wide range of materials. For example,

- **To learn and understand new information,** you might read news magazines, textbooks, news on the Internet, books about your favorite pastime, encyclopedia articles, primary and secondary sources for a school report, instructions on how to use a calling card, or directions for a standardized test.

- **To find specific information,** you might look at the sports section for the score of last night's game, a notice on where to register for a field trip, weather reports, bank statements, or television listings.

- **To be entertained,** you might read your favorite magazine, e-mails or letters from friends, the Sunday comics, or even novels, short stories, plays, or poems!

Adjusting How Fast You Read

How quickly or how carefully you should read a text depends on your purpose for reading it. Because there are many reasons and ways to read, think about your purpose and choose a strategy that works best. Try out these strategies:

- **Scanning** means quickly running your eyes over the material, looking for **key words or phrases** that point to the information you're looking for. Scan when you need to find a particular piece or type of information. For example, you might scan a newspaper for movie show times or an encyclopedia article for facts to include in a research report.

- **Skimming** means quickly reading a piece of writing to **find its main idea** or to **get a general overview** of it. For example, you might skim the sports section of the daily newspaper to find out how your favorite teams are doing. Or you might skim a chapter in your science book to prepare for a test.

- **Careful reading** involves **reading slowly and paying attention** with a purpose in mind. Read carefully when you're learning new concepts, following complicated directions, or preparing to explain information to someone else. You definitely should read carefully when you're studying a textbook to prepare for class. But you might also use this strategy when you're reading a mystery story and don't want to miss any details. Below are some tips you can use to help you read more carefully.

  —**Take breaks** when you need them. There's no point in reading when you're sleepy.

  —**Take notes** as you read. Write in your book if it's OK or use a notebook or sticky notes on the pages. Your notes may be just words or phrases that will jog your memory when you need to review. If you use a notebook, write page numbers from the book in the margin of your notes. That way you can quickly find the original material later if you need it.

  —**Make graphic organizers** to help you organize the information from your reading. These can help you sort out ideas, clear up difficult passages, and remember important points. For example, **webs** can show a main idea and supporting details. A **flowchart** can help you keep track of events in a sequence. A **Venn diagram,** made up of overlapping circles, can help you organize how two characters, ideas, or events are alike and different.

  —**Review material** before stopping. Even a short review will help you remember what you've read. Try rereading difficult passages. They will be much easier to understand the second time.

Becoming Engaged

No, it's not what you're thinking. In reading, *engagement* means something different from planning to get married. It means relating to what you're reading in a way that makes it meaningful to you. It means finding links between the text you're reading and your own life. As you begin to read something, be ready to become engaged with the text. Then as you read, react to the text and relate it to your own experience. Your reading will be much more interesting, and you'll find it easier to understand and remember what you read.

Here are two useful strategies for engaging with the text.

Connect

You will become more involved with your reading and remember events, characters, and ideas better if you relate what you're reading to your own life. Connecting is finding the links between what you read and your own experience.

ASK YOURSELF

Have I been to places similar to the **setting** described by this writer?

What **experiences** have I had that compare or contrast with what I am reading?

What **opinions** do I already have about this topic?

What **characters** from life or literature remind me of the characters or narrator in the selection?

Respond

Enjoy what you read and make it your own by responding to what's going on in the text. Think about and express what you like or don't like, what you find boring or interesting. What surprises you, entertains you, scares you, makes you angry, makes you sad, or makes you laugh out loud? The relationship between you and what you're reading is personal, so react in a personal way.

Understanding What You Read

Reading without understanding is like trying to drive a car on an empty gas tank. You can go through all the motions, but you won't get anywhere! Fortunately, there are techniques you can use to help you concentrate on and understand what you read. Skilled readers adopt a number of strategies before, during, and after reading to make sure they understand what they read.

Previewing

If you were making a preview for a movie, you would want to let your audience know what the movie is like. When you preview a piece of writing, you're treating yourself like that movie audience. You're trying to get an idea about that piece of writing. If you know what to expect before reading, you will have an easier time understanding ideas and relationships. Follow these steps to preview your reading assignments.

Do iT!

1. **Look** at the title and any illustrations that are included.

2. **Read** headings, subheadings, and anything in bold letters.

3. **Skim** over the passage to see how it is organized. Is it divided into many parts? Is it a long poem or short story? Don't forget to look at the graphics—pictures, maps, or diagrams.

4. **Set a purpose** for your reading. Are you reading to learn something new? Are you reading to find specific information?

Using What You Know

Believe it or not, you already know quite a bit about what you're going to read. You don't know the plot or the information, of course, but keep in mind that you bring knowledge and unique personal experience to a selection. Drawing on your own background is called **activating prior knowledge,** and it can help you create meaning in what you read. Ask yourself, What do I already know about this topic? What do I know about related topics?

Predicting

You don't need a crystal ball to make **predictions** when you read. The predictions don't even have to be accurate! What's important is that you get involved in your reading from the moment you turn to page one. Take educated guesses before and during your reading about what might happen in the story.

TRY THiS

1. Use your prior knowledge and the information you gathered in your preview to predict what you will learn or what might happen in a selection. Will the hero ever get home? Did the butler do it?

2. As you read on, you may find that your prediction was way off base. Don't worry. Just adjust your prediction and go on reading.

3. Afterwards, check to see how accurate your predictions were. You don't have to keep score. By getting yourself involved in a narrative, you always end up a winner.

Visualizing

Creating pictures in your mind as you read—called visualizing—is a powerful aid to understanding. As you read, set up a movie theater in your imagination. Imagine what a character looks like. Picture the setting—city streets, the desert, or the surface of the Moon. When reading nonfiction, you can picture the steps in a process or the evidence that an author wants you to consider. If you can visualize what you read, selections will be more vivid, and you'll recall them better later on.

Identifying Sequence

When you discover the logical order of events or ideas, you are identifying sequence. Are you reading a story that takes place in chronological, or time, order? Do you need to understand step-by-step directions? Are you reading a persuasive speech with the reasons listed in order of importance? Look for clues and signal words that will help you find the way information is organized. You'll understand and remember the information better when you know the organization the author has used.

Determining the Main Idea

When you look for the main idea of a selection, you look for the most important idea. The examples, reasons, or details that further explain the main idea are called supporting details. Some main ideas are clearly stated within a passage—often in the first sentence of a paragraph, or sometimes in the last sentence of a passage. Other times, an author doesn't directly state the main idea but provides details that help readers figure out what the main idea is.

ASK YOURSELF

- What is each sentence about?
- Is there one sentence that tells about the whole passage or that is more important than the others?
- What main idea do the supporting details point out?

Questioning

Keep up a conversation with yourself as you read by **asking questions** about the text. Feel free to question anything! Ask about the importance of the information you're reading. Ask how one event relates to another or why a character acts a certain way. Ask yourself if you understand what you just read. As you answer your own questions, you're making sure that you understand what's going on.

Clarifying

Clear up, or **clarify,** confusing or difficult passages as you read. When you realize you don't understand something, try these techniques to help you clarify the ideas.

- Reread the confusing parts slowly and carefully.
- Diagram relationships between ideas.
- Look up unfamiliar words.
- Simply "talk out" the part to yourself.

Then read the passage once more. The second time through is often much easier and more informative.

Reviewing

You probably **review** in school every day in one class or another. You review what you learned the day before so the ideas stick in your mind. Reviewing when you read does the same thing. Take time now and then to pause and review what you've read. Think about the main ideas and reorganize them for yourself so you can recall them later. Filling in study aids such as graphic organizers, notes, or outlines can help you to review.

Monitoring Your Comprehension

Who's checking up on you when you read? You are! There's no teacher standing by to ask questions or to make sure that you're paying attention. As a reader, you are both the teacher and the student. It's up to you to make sure you accomplish a reader's most important task: understanding the material. As you read, check your understanding by using the following strategies.

- **Summarize** Sum up what you read by pausing from time to time and telling yourself the main ideas of what you've just read. When you summarize, include only the main ideas of a selection and only the useful supporting details. Answer the questions *Who? What? Where? When? Why?* and *How?* Summarizing tests your comprehension by encouraging you to clarify key points in your own words.

- **Paraphrase** Sometimes you read something that you "sort of" understand, but not quite. Use paraphrasing as a test to see whether you really got the point. **Paraphrasing** is retelling something in your own words. So shut the book and try putting what you've just read into your own words. If you can't explain it clearly, you should probably have another look at the text.

Thinking About Your Reading

You've engaged with the text and used helpful reading strategies to understand what you've read. But is that all there is to it? Not always. Sometimes it's important to think more deeply about what you've read so you can get the most out of what the author says. These critical thinking skills will help you go beyond what the words say and get at the important messages of your reading.

Interpreting

When you listen to your best friend talk, you don't just hear the words he or she says. You also watch your friend, listen to the tone of voice, and use what you already know about that person to put meaning to the words. In doing so, you are making meaning from what your friend says by using what you understand. You are interpreting what your friend says.

Readers do the same thing when they interpret as they read. **Interpreting** is more than just understanding the facts or story line you read. It's asking yourself, What's the writer *really* saying here? and then using what you know about the world to help answer that question. When you interpret as you read, you come to a much better understanding of the work—and possibly also of yourself.

Inferring

You may not realize it, but you infer, or make inferences, every day. Here's an example: You run to the bus stop a little later than usual. There's no one there. "I've missed the bus," you say to yourself. You may be wrong, but that's the way our minds work. We look at the evidence (you're late; no one's there) and come to a conclusion (you've missed the bus).

When you read, you go through exactly the same process because writers don't always directly state what they want you to understand. By providing clues and interesting details, they suggest certain information. Whenever you combine those clues with your own background and knowledge, you are making an inference. An **inference** involves using your thinking and experience to come up with an idea based on what an author implies or suggests. In reading, you **infer** when you use context clues and your own knowledge to figure out the author's meaning.

Drawing Conclusions

Skillful readers are always **drawing conclusions,** or figuring out much more than an author says directly. The process is a little like a detective solving a mystery. You combine information and evidence that the author provides to come up with a statement about the topic, about a character, or about anything else in the work. Drawing conclusions helps you find connections between ideas and events and helps you have a better understanding of what you're reading.

Analyzing

Analyzing, or looking at separate parts of something to understand the entire piece, is a way to think critically about written work.

- In analyzing **fiction,** for example, you might look at the characters' values, events in the plot, and the author's style to figure out the story's theme.
- In analyzing persuasive **nonfiction,** you might look at the writer's reasons to see if they actually support the main point of the argument.
- In analyzing **informational text,** you might look at how the ideas are organized to see what's most important.

Distinguishing Fact from Opinion

Distinguishing between fact and opinion is one of the most important reading skills you can learn. A **fact** is a statement that can be proved with supporting information. An **opinion,** on the other hand, is what a writer believes, on the basis of his or her personal viewpoint. Writers can support their opinions with facts, but an opinion is something that cannot be proved.

FOR EXAMPLE

Look at the following examples of fact and opinion.

Fact: *New York State produces fruits and other agricultural products.*

Opinion: *New York is a wonderful place for a vacation.*

You could prove that fruits and other agricultural products are grown in New York. It's a fact. However, not everyone might agree that New York State is a great vacation site. That's someone's opinion.

As you examine information, always ask yourself, Is this a fact or an opinion? Don't think that opinions are always bad. Very often they are just what you want. You read editorials and essays for their authors' opinions. Reviews of books, movies, plays, and CDs can help you decide whether to spend your time and money on something. It's when opinions are based on faulty reasoning or prejudice or when they are stated as facts that they become troublesome.

Evaluating

When you form an opinion or make a judgment about something you're reading, you are **evaluating.** If you're reading informational texts or something on the Internet, it's important to evaluate how qualified the author is to be writing about the topic and how reliable the information is that's presented. Ask yourself whether the author seems biased, whether the information is one-sided, and whether the argument presented is logical.

If you're reading fiction, evaluate the author's style or ask yourself questions such as whether a character is interesting or dull, whether events in the plot are believable or unrealistic, and whether the author's message makes sense. Learning to evaluate what you're reading helps make you a smart and sensible reader.

Synthesizing

When you **synthesize,** you combine ideas (maybe even from different sources) to come up with something new. It may be a new understanding of an important idea or a new way of combining and presenting information. Many readers enjoy taking ideas from their reading and combining them with what they already know to come to new understandings. For example, you might read a manual on coaching soccer, combine that information with your own experiences playing soccer, and come up with a winning plan for coaching your sister's team this spring.

Understanding Text Structure

What do you think of when you hear the word *structure?* Probably something that you can see, like a house or a bridge. But writing has structure too. After all, good writers don't just throw sentences and paragraphs together in any order. Writers organize each piece of their writing in a specific way for a specific purpose. That pattern of organization is called text structure. When you know the text structure of a selection, you'll find it easier to locate and recall an author's ideas. Here are four ways that writers organize text, along with some signal words and phrases containing clues to help you identify their methods.

Comparison and Contrast

Comparison-and-contrast structure shows the similarities and differences between people, things, and ideas. Maybe you've overheard someone at school say something like "She's way more popular than I am, but I've got cooler friends." This student is using comparison-and-contrast structure. When writers use comparison-and-contrast structure, often they want to show you how things that seem alike are different or how things that seem different are alike.

- **Signal words and phrases:** *similarly, on the one hand, on the other hand, in contrast to, but, however*

Example: *That day had been the best and worst of her life.* **On the one hand,** *the tornado had destroyed her home.* **On the other hand,** *she and her family were safe. Her face was full of cuts and bruises,* **but** *she smiled at the little girl on her lap.*

Cause and Effect

Just about everything that happens in life is the cause or the effect of some other event or action. Sometimes what happens is pretty minor: You don't look when you're pouring milk (cause); you spill milk on the table (effect). Sometimes it's a little more serious: You don't look at your math book before the big test (cause); you mess up on the test (effect).

Writers use cause-and-effect structure to explore the reasons for something happening and to examine the results of previous events. Put a little more simply, this structure helps answer the question that everybody is always asking: *Why?* A scientist might explain why the rain falls. A sports writer might explain why a team is doing badly. A historian might tell us why an empire rose and fell. Cause-and-effect structure is all about explaining things.

- **Signal words and phrases:** *so, because, as a result, therefore, for the following reasons*

Example: *The blizzard raged for twelve hours.* **Because of** *the heavy snow, the streets were clogged within an hour of being plowed.* **As a result,** *the city was at a standstill. Of course, we had no school that day,* **so** *we went sledding!*

Problem and Solution

How did scientists overcome the difficulty of getting a person to the Moon? How can our team win the pennant this year? How will I brush my teeth when I've forgotten my toothpaste? These questions may be very different in importance, but they have one thing in common: Each identifies a problem and asks how to solve it. Problems and solutions are part of what makes life interesting.

With so many problems to solve, it's no wonder that writers often examine how conflicts or obstacles are overcome. By organizing their texts around that important question-word *how,* authors state the problem and suggest a solution. Sometimes they suggest many solutions. Of course, it's for you to decide if they're right.

- **Signal words and phrases:** *how, help, problem, obstruction, difficulty, need, attempt, have to, must*

Example: *A major* **difficulty** *in learning to drive a car with a standard shift is starting on hills. Students* **need** *to practice starting slowly and smoothly on a level surface before they graduate to slopes. Observing an experienced driver perform the maneuver will also* **help.**

Sequence

Consider these requests: Tell us what happened at the picnic. Describe your favorite CD cover. Identify the causes of the Civil War. Three very different instructions, aren't they? Well, yes and no. They are certainly about different subjects. But they all involve sequence, the order in which thoughts are arranged. Take a look at three common forms of sequencing.

- **Chronological order** refers to the order in which events take place. First you wake up; next you have breakfast; then you go to school. Those events don't make much sense in any other order. Whether you are explaining how to wash the car, giving directions to a friend's house, or telling your favorite joke, the world would be a confusing place if people didn't organize their ideas in chronological order. Look for signal words such as *first, next, then, later,* and *finally.*

- **Spatial order** tells you the order in which to look at objects. For example, take a look at this description of an ice cream sundae: *At the bottom of the dish are two scoops of vanilla. The scoops are covered with fudge and topped with whipped cream and a cherry.* Your eyes follow the sundae from the bottom to the top. Spatial order is important in descriptive writing because it helps you as a reader to see an image the way the author does. Signal words include *above, below, behind,* and *next to.*

- **Order of importance** is going from most important to least important or the other way around. For example, a typical news article has a most-to-least-important structure. Readers who don't have the time to read the entire article can at least learn the main idea by reading the first few paragraphs. Signal words include *principal, central, important,* and *fundamental.*

Reading for Research

An important part of doing research is knowing how to get information from a wide variety of sources. The following skills will help you when you have a research assignment for a class or when you want information about a topic outside of school.

Reading Text Features

Researching a topic is not only about asking questions. It's about finding answers. Textbooks, references, magazines, and other sources provide a variety of text features to help you find those answers quickly and efficiently.

CHECK iT OUT

- **Tables of contents** Look at the table of contents first to see whether a resource offers information you need.

- **Indexes** An index is an alphabetical listing of significant topics covered in a book. It is found in the back of a book.

- **Headings and subheadings** Headings often tell you what information is going to follow in the text you're reading. Subheadings allow you to narrow your search for information even further.

- **Graphic features** Photos, diagrams, maps, charts, graphs, and other graphic features can communicate large amounts of information at a glance.

Interpreting Graphic Aids

When you're researching a topic, be sure to read and interpret the graphic aids you find. **Graphic aids** explain information visually. When reading graphic aids, read the title first to see if you're likely to find information you want.

- **Reading a map** Maps are flat representations of land. A **compass rose** shows you directions—north, south, east, and west. A **legend** explains the map's symbols, and a **scale** shows you how the size of the map relates to the actual distances.

- **Reading a graph** A graph shows you how two or more things relate. Graphs can use circles, dots, bars, or lines. For example, on the front page of a newspaper you might see a weather graph that predicts how the temperatures for the next five days will rise and fall.

- **Reading a table** A table groups numbers or facts and puts them into categories so you can compare what is in each category. The categories are usually organized in rows or columns. Find the row that has the category you're looking for. Then read across to the column that has the information you need.

Organizing Information

When researching a topic, you can't stop after you've read your sources of information. You also have to make sense of that information, organize it, and put it all together in ways that will help you explain it to someone else. Here are some ways of doing just that.

- **Record** information from your research and keep track of your resources on note cards.

- **Summarize** information before you write it on a note card. That way you'll have the main ideas in your own words.

- **Outline ideas** so you can see how subtopics and supporting information will fit under the main ideas.

- **Make a table or graph** to compare items or categories of information.

Reading Consumer, Workplace, and Public Documents

Every day you come into contact with a wide variety of reading materials that affect your life in one way or another—from teaching you something new to showing you which exit to take off the highway or helping you choose laundry detergent. Here are some tips for dealing successfully with consumer, workplace, and public documents.

Following Technical Directions

Whether you are assembling a model airplane, installing a software program on your computer, or using a cookbook, you need to know how to follow written directions.

- Skim all of the directions to get an idea of how long and complicated the task might be. As you skim, check for diagrams, lists of parts, and glossaries of technical terms.

- Start with step 1. Don't skip steps to save time. If steps aren't clearly labeled, look for transition words such as *first, next,* and *finally.*

- If there are diagrams or pictures, use them to help you interpret the written instructions.

- If you have trouble understanding a step, look at the next step. The next step may help clarify the step you're on.

Interpreting Product Information

So, you've got money in your pocket and you want to shop. You want to be an informed shopper, so read about the products you're buying. Here are some tips to help you read to know what you're buying.

- **Look at the wording of product descriptions.** Manufacturers describe their products in a way that will appeal to you, the customer. Keep this in mind when you read product descriptions. Don't believe or be impressed by everything you read. Keep asking yourself, What real information is here? For example, a food product called "cheese-like" or "cheese flavored" may not contain real cheese.

- **Check special labels.** What are the contents or **ingredients** of a product? How do you **care** for it? What **warnings** should you be aware of? Answers to these questions appear on special tags or labels, often in small print.

- **Scan product warranties for limitations.** A product warranty typically guarantees two things: that the product is in good condition and that the manufacturer will repair or replace the product if the product isn't in good condition. Read carefully to see whether the warranty is limited or whether it lasts as long as you own the product.

Using Workplace Documents

Maybe you want to apply for a part-time job. Or maybe you have a job and are wondering what office e-mail requires a response. Here are some tips to help you interpret the documents you might see in the world of business.

- **Job application forms** In the near future, you will be old enough to have a work permit, and you may decide to apply for a part-time job. When filling out an application form, keep the following directions in mind.

  1. **Skim** the entire application to get a general idea of what information the employer is looking for.

  2. **Scan** section headings to identify which sections you fill out. Some sections may be optional. Other sections may be for the employer to fill out.

  3. **Read** carefully all the instructions before filling in any blanks.

- **Business memos** It is not too early to start learning the skills you'll need to read and interpret business memos. Business memos are used within a company as a way for employees to communicate with one another. On paper or as e-mail, a good memo will have the following information: the receiver's name, the sender's name, a subject title, and date. Memos that begin with *FYI* ("For Your Information") are telling you that you don't need to respond or perform any specific task. Memos containing questions usually do require your response.

Hot Words Journal

Use the following pages to create your personal Hot Words Journal—a sampling of the interesting or difficult words you circle as you read the selections in this book.

1. In each reading selection, choose words to include in your **Hot Words Journal.** Highlight or underline the sentence in which each word occurs.

2. On the following lines, list each word you've chosen under its selection title. Include the page number where the word occurs and a short definition.

3. Use a dictionary to check the word's meaning.

Hot Words Activities

Select a word from your Hot Words Journal and complete one of these activities or another vocabulary activity that your teacher suggests. Use a separate sheet of paper. Be sure to write down the activity prompts or questions as well as your responses.

Concept of Definition
Write the word.
What is it? (category)
What is it like? (properties)
What are some examples? (illustrations)

Possible Sentence
Choose a word and confirm its definition in a dictionary. Then write a sentence using the word either correctly or incorrectly. Ask a partner to read your sentence and guess whether or not the sentence is "possible." Discuss your partner's response.

What It Is, What It Isn't
(This activity works best with nouns and verbs)

Write the word and its definition.
What are some examples?
What are not some examples?
What are the main characteristics of this word?
What are not characteristics of this word?

Word Web
Choose a word and confirm its definition in a dictionary. Then write the word in the center circle of a word web. List other related words in bubbles around the center circle. Use a dictionary or a thesaurus to help you.

Context Clues
Choose a word and write a sentence that includes the word and a context clue to help convey the word's meaning. Be sure to underline your word. Ask a partner to use the context clue in your sentence to define the underlined word. Some examples of context clues are synonyms, antonyms, examples, related ideas, and definitions.

Sentence Invention
Choose a word and copy the selection sentence where it occurred in this book. Then write another sentence of your own using the word. Underline your chosen word in both sentences.

My Hot Words

Araby

imperturbable	p. 5	not easily excited or disturbed; calm

A Cup of Tea

The Demon Lover

A Mild Attack of Locusts

from The Canterbury Tales: The Pardoner's Tale

Death Be Not Proud

My Hot Words

Ozymandias

_____ _____ _____
_____ _____ _____
_____ _____ _____

from MacBeth: Act I, Scenes 1–2

_____ _____ _____
_____ _____ _____
_____ _____ _____

from Beowulf: The Coming of Beowulf

_____ _____ _____
_____ _____ _____
_____ _____ _____

A Modest Proposal

_____ _____ _____
_____ _____ _____
_____ _____ _____

from The Diary of Samuel Pepys

_____ _____ _____
_____ _____ _____
_____ _____ _____

Be Ye Men of Valor

_____ _____ _____
_____ _____ _____
_____ _____ _____

My Hot Words

Britain's Eden

_____ _____ _____

_____ _____ _____

_____ _____ _____

Teen at wheel makes driving doubly deadly

_____ _____ _____

_____ _____ _____

_____ _____ _____

Technical Document: Recipe

_____ _____ _____

_____ _____ _____

Workplace Document: Memo

_____ _____ _____

_____ _____ _____

Consumer Document: Nutrition Guide

_____ _____ _____

_____ _____ _____

Map: Road Map with Driving Directions

_____ _____ _____

_____ _____ _____

Acknowledgments

Fiction, Poetry, Drama, and Legends

Fiction, Poetry, Drama, and Epics

"Araby" from *Dubliners* by James Joyce. The corrected text © 1967 by the Estate of James Joyce. Reprinted by permission.

"A Cup of Tea" from *The Stort Stories of Katherine Mansfield* by Katherine Mansfield. Copyright 1923 by Alfred A. Knopf and renewed 1951 by John Middleton Murry. Reprinted by permission of the publisher.

"The Demon Lover" from *Collected Stories* by Elizabeth Bowen. Copyright 1946 and renewed 1974 by Elizabeth Bowen. Reprinted by permission of Alfred A. Knopf, Inc.

"A Mild Attack of Locusts" from *The Habit of Loving* by Doris Lessing. Copyright © 1957 by Doris Lessing. Reprinted by kind permission of Jonathan Clowes, Ltd., London, on behalf of Doris Lessing. "A Mild Attack of Locusts" from *The Habit of Loving* by Doris Lessing. Copyright © 1957 by Doris Lessing. Copyright renewed. Reprinted by permission of HarperCollins Publishers, Inc.

From *The Canterbury Tales,* by Geoffrey Chaucer, translated by Nevill Coghill. Reproduced with permission of Curtis Brown Ltd., London, on behalf of the Estate of Nevill Coghill. Copyright Nevill Coghill.

Abridged from *Beowulf,* translated by Burton Raffel. Translation copyright © 1963 by Burton Raffel, Afterword © 1963 by New American Library. Used by permission of Dutton Signet, a division of Penguin Books USA Inc.

Nonfiction and Informational Text

"Britain's Eden" from *inTime* vol. 3, copyright 2003. Reprinted by permission.

"Teen at wheel makes driving doubly deadly" from *USA TODAY,* July 5, 2002. Reprinted by permission.

Standardized Tests

"Halfway House for Horses" by Melanie L. Stephens. Copyright © 1990 Time, Inc. Reprinted by permission.

"Boy at the Window" from *Things of This World,* copyright 1952 and renewed 1980 by Richard Wilbur. Reprinted by permission of Harcourt, Inc.